Mac® OS 9 For Dummies

D1077700

The Top Six Things You Should Never Do

1. You should never keep only one copy of your work. Instead, make at least two backups and keep one of them in a safe place. Period.

2. You should never bump, drop, shake, wobble, dribble, drop kick, or play catch with a hard disk while it's running. Don't forget that your Mac (unless it's ancient) has a hard disk inside it, too.

3. You should never get up from your Mac without saving your work. Instead, just before your butt leaves the chair, your fingers should be pressing ⌘+S. Make it a habit.

4. You should never shut off your Mac by pulling the plug or flipping the power switch. Instead, always use the Shut Down command in the Special menu or press the Power Key and then click the Shut Down button.

5. You should never pay list price for any hardware or software. What lists for $499 at Pierre's Chrome and Glass Computer Boutique may cost only $275 at Bubba's Mail-Order Warehouse and Chili Emporium.

6. You should never pay attention to anyone who says that Windows is just like the Mac. Yeah, right. And Yugo is the Eastern-European cousin of BMW.

Finder Keyboard Shortcuts

You should know the following shortcuts because the less time you spend working, the more time you have to waste.

Command	Keyboard Shortcut
Close All	⌘+Option+W
Close Window	⌘+W
Copy	⌘+C
Cut	⌘+X
Duplicate	⌘+D
Eject Disk	⌘+E
Find (Sherlock 2)	⌘+F
Find Again	⌘+G
Get Info	⌘+I
Make Alias	⌘+M
New Folder	⌘+N
Open	⌘+O
Paste	⌘+V
Print	⌘+P
Put Away	⌘+Y
Select All	⌘+A
Undo	⌘+Z

Do I need an antivirus program?

"Do you need an antivirus program?" The answer is, "You do if you're at risk." How do you know if you're at risk? You're at risk if you

- ✔ Download files from the Internet
- ✔ Receive e-mail with attachments
- ✔ Are on a network and share files with others
- ✔ Use floppy disks that have been inserted in anyone else's Mac

Those are the ways viruses spread, so if any or all of the preceding apply to you, you'd be well served to run an antivirus program, such as Dr. Solomon's Virex or Symantec's Norton Anti-Virus for Macintosh.

For Dummies ... *for Beginners*

Mac® OS 9 For Dummies®

Cheat Sheet

Adjusting an Application's Preferred Size

1. Make sure that the application is not open.

2. In the Finder, select the application's icon.

3. Choose File➪Get Info or use the keyboard shortcut ⌘+I.

4. At the bottom of the Info window, double-click the Preferred Size text box.

5. With the number in the Preferred Size text box highlighted, do one of the following:

   If you want to give the application more RAM (to improve performance, enable it to open larger documents, or prevent out-of-memory errors), type a higher number in the Preferred Size text box.

   If you want to give the application less RAM (to make room to run more applications at once), type a lower number in the Preferred Size text box. You shouldn't go below the application's Minimum Size.

6. Close the Info window by clicking its close box (on the left side of the title bar) or by pressing the keyboard shortcut ⌘+W.

Keyboard Shortcuts in Open and Save Dialog Boxes

- Eject Disk: ⌘+Shift+1
- Desktop: ⌘+D
- Cancel: ⌘+period or Escape
- Open/Save: Return or Enter
- Move up one folder: ⌘+up arrow
- Move down into the highlighted folder: ⌘+down arrow (also Return or Enter)
- Switch disks: ⌘+left arrow or ⌘+right arrow

Repeat after me: The Open and Save dialog boxes are just another view of the Finder.

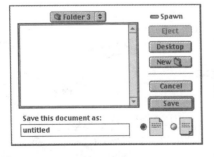

Hungry Minds™

For Dummies™: Bestselling Book Series for Beginners

Mac® OS 9 FOR DUMMIES®

by Bob LeVitus

Foreword by Steven Bobker

Hungry Minds™

Best-Selling Books • Digital Downloads • e-Books • Answer Networks • e-Newsletters • Branded Web Sites • e-Learning

New York, NY ◆ Cleveland, OH ◆ Indianapolis, IN

Mac® OS 9 For Dummies®

Published by
Hungry Minds, Inc.
909 Third Avenue
New York, NY 10022
www.hungryminds.com
www.dummies.com (Dummies Press Web site)

Library of Congress Catalog Card No.: 99-66422

ISBN: 0-7645-0652-8

Printed in the United States of America

10 9 8 7 6

1B/QW/QT/QS/IN

Distributed in the United States by Hungry Minds, Inc.

Distributed by CDG Books Canada Inc. for Canada; by Transworld Publishers Limited in the United Kingdom; by IDG Norge Books for Norway; by IDG Sweden Books for Sweden; by IDG Books Australia Publishing Corporation Pty. Ltd. for Australia and New Zealand; by TransQuest Publishers Pte Ltd. for Singapore, Malaysia, Thailand, Indonesia, and Hong Kong; by Gotop Information Inc. for Taiwan; by ICG Muse, Inc. for Japan; by Intersoft for South Africa; by Eyrolles for France; by International Thomson Publishing for Germany, Austria and Switzerland; by Distribuidora Cuspide for Argentina; by LR International for Brazil; by Galileo Libros for Chile; by Ediciones ZETA S.C.R. Ltda. for Peru; by WS Computer Publishing Corporation, Inc., for the Philippines; by Contemporanea de Ediciones for Venezuela; by Express Computer Distributors for the Caribbean and West Indies; by Micronesia Media Distributor, Inc. for Micronesia; by Chips Computadoras S.A. de C.V. for Mexico; by Editorial Norma de Panama S.A. for Panama; by American Bookshops for Finland.

For general information on Hungry Minds' products and services please contact our Customer Care Department within the U.S. at 800-762-2974, outside the U.S. at 317-572-3993 or fax 317-572-4002.

For sales inquiries and reseller information, including discounts, premium and bulk quantity sales, and foreign-language translations, please contact our Customer Care Department at 800-434-3422, fax 317-572-4002, or write to Hungry Minds, Inc., Attn: Customer Care Department, 10475 Crosspoint Boulevard, Indianapolis, IN 46256.

For information on licensing foreign or domestic rights, please contact our Sub-Rights Customer Care Department at 650-653-7098.

For authorization to photocopy items for corporate, personal, or educational use, please contact Copyright Clearance Center, 222 Rosewood Drive, Danvers, MA 01923, or fax 978-750-4470.

For information on using Hungry Minds' products and services in the classroom or for ordering examination copies, please contact our Educational Sales Department at 800-434-2086 or fax 317-572-4005.

Please contact our Public Relations Department at 212-884-5163 for press review copies or 212-884-5000 for author interviews and other publicity information or fax 212-884-5400.

Hungry Minds™ is a trademark of Hungry Minds, Inc.

About the Author

Bob LeVitus (pronounced Love-eye-tis) was the editor-in-chief of the wildly popular MACazine until its untimely demise in 1988. Since 1989, he has been a contributing editor/columnist for *MacUser* magazine, writing the "Help Folder," "Beating the System," "Personal Best," and "Game Room" columns at various times in his illustrious career. In his spare time, LeVitus has written 33 popular computer books, including *Macworld Office 98 Bible* and *Mac OS 8.5 For Dummies*.

Always a popular speaker at Macintosh user groups and trade shows, LeVitus has spoken at more than 200 international seminars, has presented keynote addresses in several countries, and serves on the Macworld Expo Advisory Board. He was also the host of Mac Today, a half-hour television show syndicated in over 100 markets, which aired in late 1992.

LeVitus has forgotten more about the Macintosh than most people know. He won the Macworld Expo MacJeopardy World Championship an unbelievable four times before retiring his crown. But most of all, LeVitus is known for his clear, understandable writing, his humorous style, and his ability to translate techie jargon into usable and fun advice for the rest of us.

He lives in Austin, Texas, with his wife, two children, and a small pack of Welsh Springers and Vizslas.

Dedication

For Jodie, Andy, Robyn, Dad, Cousin Nancy, and all my other friends and relatives with new Macs. Now you can stop calling me at all hours.

And for my family — Lisa, Allison, and Jacob. Thanks for being there.

Author's Acknowledgments

Special thanks to my friends at Apple, who were there for me every step of the way: Tim "The Shortstop" Holmes, Nathalie Welch, Keri Walker, and everyone on the Mac OS 9 development team; the Apple evangelists; and the Apple fellows. Thank you all. I couldn't have done it without your help.

Thanks also to superagent Carole "Damn-It-Stop-Calling-Me-Swifty" McClendon of Waterside Productions, for deal-making beyond the call of duty. You're a wonder!

Super-geeky thanks to Shelly "Networking Is Fun" Brisbin for her help with this edition. Her hard work and thoroughness made this project go a lot more quickly and smoothly.

Big-time thanks to the gang at IDG Books: Mike Roney, Mike Kelly, Diane Steele, Mary Bednarek, and the big guy himself, John Kilcullen. Nobody does it better.

Extra special thanks to my editor, Susan "The Whipcracker" Pink, who has been better than great.

Thanks to my family for putting up with my all-too-lengthy absences during this book's gestation.

And finally, thanks to you for buying it.

Publisher's Acknowledgments

We're proud of this book; please register your comments through our Online Registration Form located at www.dummies.com.

Some of the people who helped bring this book to market include the following:

Acquisitions, Editorial, and Media Development

Project Editor: Susan Pink
    (Previous Edition: Tim Gallan)

Acquisitions Editor: Michael Roney

Technical Editor: Christopher Breen

Production

Project Coordinator: Regina Snyder

Layout and Graphics: Karl Brandt, Beth Brooks, Brian Drumm, Oliver Jackson, Barry Offringa, Jill Piscitelli, Doug Rollison, Brent Savage, Janet Seib, Brian Torwelle, Maggie Ubertini, Erin Zeltner

Proofreaders: Laura Albert, Laura L. Bowman, Rebecca Senninger, Charles Spencer

Indexer: Sharon Hilgenberg

Special Help
    Constance Carlisle, Suzanne Thomas

General and Administrative

Hungry Minds Technology Publishing Group: Richard Swadley, Vice President and Executive Group Publisher; Bob Ipsen, Vice President and Group Publisher; Joseph Wikert, Vice President and Publisher; Barry Pruett, Vice President and Publisher; Mary Bednarek, Editorial Director; Mary C. Corder, Editorial Director; Andy Cummings, Editorial Director

Hungry Minds Manufacturing: Ivor Parker, Vice President, Manufacturing

Hungry Minds Marketing: John Helmus, Assistant Vice President, Director of Marketing

Hungry Minds Production for Branded Press: Debbie Stailey, Production Director

Hungry Minds Sales: Michael Violano, Vice President, International Sales and Sub Rights

Contents at a Glance

Cartoons at a Glance

By Rich Tennant

page 215

page 135

page 5

page 365

page 349

Cartoon Information:
Fax: 978-546-7747
E-Mail: richtennant@the5thwave.com
World Wide Web: www.the5thwave.com

Table of Contents

Foreword

Some people say that Apple's Mac OS 9 is just a pretty face on old software. Some people say Bob LeVitus is just a pretty face. This book conclusively proves both sets of people wrong.

Mac OS 9 adds cosmetic improvements to the best interface in personal computing, but it's what it adds under the skin that really makes it worth your time and money. There's a whole bunch of new functionality and speed. A lot more of the code is optimized for Power Macs. And as usual, Apple only sketches out the new features and power in their documentation. Fortunately, there's no one better at analyzing and explaining the works of Apple than Bob LeVitus.

Bob's name is a working definition for Not Dull. No matter where you run into Bob — in conversation, around the poker table, or in his writings about the Mac — you are not going to be bored. You will pay attention, not that he'll give you much of a choice. And that's good. His opinions tend to be provocative and well thought out, his poker playing skilled enough to empty your wallet if you're not both good and lucky, and his knowledge of the Mac and ability to communicate it to readers unparalleled.

You need this book because Apple manuals are Apple manuals; you won't get a lot of explanation or help from them. To get at the new power, you could hire a consultant, but that's expensive and not at all necessary: Just read this book. It's a wonderful guide to all of Mac OS 9.

Like its System 7.x cousins, *Mac OS 9 For Dummies* might be better called The Best Mac System Software Book Ever. Bobby has gone past his usually really good writing level here, and taken a dry subject (who really gets excited about an operating system? A game, sure; and maybe even that exceptional productivity application, but the system software?) and created a book that makes you want to learn and use this important advance in Mac software.

He's also achieved the difficult trick of writing a book that works for first-time users as well as power users who have been using Macs since January 1984. That's no mean accomplishment. I've been writing for and editing Mac magazines since 1985 firsthand and understand (and stand in awe of) the magnitude of Bobby's achievement here.

This book is not free; Apple manuals come with the product. Why buy this book? Why not stick with the oh-so-pretty Apple manuals? Surely, they have everything you're going to find here? Well, no, that's not so. The Apple manuals are pretty. But readable? I don't think so. They're so dry that they should be declared a fire hazard. They're very full of themselves and at the same time so carefully worded that it seems certain their final editing was at the hands of Apple's legal staff.

They tell you the good parts, not the bad parts. And they'd choke before allowing that there are power tips that can really make you productive. Their "avoid all risks; take no shortcuts because it might not be perfectly 100% safe" approach means that the Apple manuals are incomplete.

You can't accuse *Mac OS 9 For Dummies* of being incomplete. It goes beyond the too-dry manuals and the too-brief magazine articles and tells you everything about Mac OS 9. After you digest it you have the choice of doing things the Apple manual way, or really using and enjoying your Mac.

Here's an example of manual dry versus Bob LeVitus: backing up. Apple tells you to do it. Period. Bobby tells you why you must back up frequently, the absolute best hardware and software tools, the tools to use if you can't afford the best tools, and the absolute need for multiple back up sets.

With a wonderful and refreshing attitude for a person who didn't grow up (or even ever live) in New York, Bobby gets vital information like his instructions on backing up right in your face. He's never been shy, and if something is important, he makes sure you get it.

The greatest strength of *Mac OS 9 For Dummies* is the breadth and depth of its content. Mac OS 9 opens a lot of new ground for Mac users and this book covers it all. You're not going to find a better helper as you move into Mac OS 9.

The second greatest strength of *Mac OS 9 For Dummies* is its solid dose of in-your-face attitude. This is a readable helper that cares. All too many computer books today are either chores to read or in a couple of cases, simply unreadable because they seem to think dry seriousness is a "business-like" virtue. They're wrong. Readability counts big-time, and *Mac OS 9 For Dummies* can be as hard to put down as the latest potboiler. You not only learn from it, but you enjoy the process.

Mac OS 9 For Dummies jumps right to the top of the class in Mac system software books. Any book that surpasses it is going to have to be awfully good. And it wouldn't surprise me if Bob LeVitus is the author.

Steven Bobker

Introduction

· ·

You made the right choice twice: Mac OS 9 and this book.

Take a deep breath and get ready to have some fun. That's right. This is a computer book and it's going to be fun. What a concept! Whether you're brand-spanking new to the Mac or a grizzled old Mac-vet, I guarantee that discovering the ins and outs of Mac OS 9 will be easy and fun. They couldn't say it on the cover if it weren't true!

About This Book

This book started with the international bestseller *Macintosh System 7.5 For Dummies,* an award-winning book so good it was offered by now-deceased Mac cloner Power Computing instead of a system software manual. Now I'm back with *Mac OS 9 For Dummies,* which combines all the old, familiar features of my previous book with updated information about the latest, greatest offering from Apple.

Why a *...For Dummies* book about Mac OS 9? Mac OS 9 is a big, complicated personal computer operating system. *Mac OS 9 For Dummies* is a not-so-big, not-very-complicated book that shows you what Mac OS 9 is all about without boring you, confusing you, or otherwise making you uncomfortable.

In fact, you'll be so darned comfortable that I wanted to call this book *Mac OS 9 without the Discomfort,* but the publishers wouldn't let me. Apparently we *...For Dummies* authors have to follow some rules, and using the word *Dummies* in the title is one of them.

And speaking of dummies, remember that it's just a word. I don't think you're dumb. Quite the opposite. I also wanted to call this book *Mac OS 9 For People Smart Enough to Know They Need Help,* but you can just imagine what IDG Books thought of that. (If you're reading this in a bookstore, approach the cashier with your wallet in your hand, buy the book, and I'll think you're even smarter!)

This book is chock-full of information and advice and explains everything you need to know about Mac OS 9 in language you'll understand. It's also supplemented with tips, tricks, techniques, and steps, served up in generous quantities.

Conventions Used in This Book

Here are a few conventions I use in this book:

- ✔ When I refer to an item in a menu, I use something like File⇨Open, which means "Pull down the File menu and choose the Open command."

- ✔ For keyboard shortcuts, something like ⌘+A means hold down the ⌘ key (the one with the little pretzel on it) and press the letter A on the keyboard. ⌘+Shift+A means hold down the ⌘ and Shift keys while pressing the A key.

- ✔ Web addresses are shown in a special typeface, `like this`.

What You're Not to Read

We start off real slow. The first few chapters are where we get to know each other and where I describe the basic everyday things you need to understand to operate your Mac or Mac-compatible effectively.

The first part, in fact, is so basic it will probably bore you old-timers to tears. But hey, not-so-old-timers need a solid foundation. Long-time Mac users can feel free to skip through stuff they know to get to the better stuff faster.

A word of warning: If you skip something important, such as why you absolutely must back up your hard drive (see Appendix B), don't come crying to me when you lose all your valuable data in a horrendous disk crash. In other words, it's probably not a bad idea to read the whole book, even if you think you already know it all.

Another thing: Perform the hands-on steps while sitting at your Mac. They're much less effective if you read them anywhere else.

Foolish Assumptions

I assume that you, gentle reader, know nothing about using a Mac. So I do my best to explain each new concept in full and loving detail. Maybe that's foolish, but . . . oh well. Oh, and I also assume that you can read.

How This Book Is Organized

Mac OS 9 For Dummies is divided into five logical parts, numbered parts one through five. It's better if you read them in order, but if you already know a lot or think you know a lot, feel free to skip around and read the parts that interest you.

Part I: Basic Training

The first part is very, very basic training. From the mouse to the desktop, from the menus to the tricky-for-beginners Open and Save dialog boxes, it's all here. Everything you need to know to operate Mac OS 9 safely and sanely. Old-timers can skim through it; you newbies should read every word. Twice.

Part II: Making Your Mac Purr

In Part II, I discuss hands-on stuff, with chapters on organizing, printing, sharing (files, that is), and memory management. By the time you finish this part, your system will be finely tuned and running like a champ.

Part III: U 2 Can B A Guru

Now we're cooking. Part III is about how things work and how to make them work better.

Tips, tricks, techniques, control panels, scripts, and much more, plus the most useful chapter in the whole book, Chapter 16, which details each and every gosh darn file in your System Folder and why you need it or don't. If your Mac runs like a champ after Part II, wait'll you see it after Part III.

Part IV: The Part of Tens

Last but not least, it's The Part of Tens, which is mostly a Letterman rip-off, though it does include heaping helpings of tips, optional software, great Mac Web sites, and hardware ideas.

Part V: Appendixes

Appendix A lends a hand with installing Mac OS 9. Appendix B browbeats you into routinely backing up the files on your hard drive. Appendix C notes the minor differences between Mac OS 9.0 releases (such as 9.0.1 and 9.0.4) and Mac OS 9.1.

Icons Used in This Book

Put on your propeller beanie hat and pocket protector. This is truly nerdy stuff. It's certainly not required reading, but it must be interesting or informative or I wouldn't have wasted the space.

This is where you'll find the juiciest morsels: shortcuts, tips, and undocumented secrets. Try them all; impress your friends.

Read these notes very, very, very carefully. Did I say *very*? Warning icons flag important information. The author and publisher will not be responsible if your Mac explodes or spews flaming parts because you ignored a Warning icon. Just kidding. Macs don't explode or spew (with the exception of a few choice PowerBook 5300s). But I got your attention, didn't I? It's a good idea to read Warning notes carefully.

Me, ranting or raving about something. Imagine foam coming from my mouth. Rants are required to be irreverent, irrelevant, or both. I also try to keep them short, more for your sake than mine.

Where to Go from Here

I'm thrilled at how this book came out — I think it's the best thing I've ever written. But I didn't write it for me. I wrote it for you and would love to hear how it worked for you. So please drop me a line or register your comments through the Online Registration Form located at www.dummies.com.

Did it work for you? What did you like? What didn't you like? What questions were unanswered? Did you want to know more about something? Could you have stood to have found out less about something? Tell me! I've received more than 100 suggestions about previous editions, most of which are incorporated here. So keep up the good work.

You can send snail mail care of Hungry Minds (they'll see that I receive it), or send e-mail to me directly at boblevitus@boblevitus.com. I appreciate your feedback and try to respond to all e-mail within a few days.

P.S. What are you waiting for? Go enjoy the book!

Part I
Basic Training

The 5th Wave   By Rich Tennant

TEACHERS LOUNGE

"Well, the first day wasn't bad—I lost the 'Finder', copied a file into the 'Trash', and sat on my mouse."

In this part . . .

Mac OS 9 sports tons of new goodies and features. I'll get to the hot new goodies soon enough, but you have to crawl before you walk.

In this part, you discover the most basic of basics, such as how to turn your Mac on. Next, I acquaint you with the Mac OS 9 desktop: icons, windows, menus, disks, and trash — the whole shmear.

So get comfortable, roll up your sleeves, fire up your Mac if you like, and settle down with Part I, a delightful little ditty I like to think of as "The Hassle-Free Way to Get Started with Mac OS 9."

Chapter 1

Mac OS 9 101
(Prerequisites: None)

· ·

· ·

Choosing Mac OS 9 was a good move — it's more than just a System software upgrade. Mac OS 9 includes dozens of new or improved features that make using your Macintosh easier and dozens more that help you do more work in less time. In other words, OS 9 will make you more productive, give you fewer headaches, reduce your cholesterol level, and make you fall in love with your Mac all over again.

In this chapter, I start at the very beginning and talk about Mac OS 9 mostly in abstract terms. Don't bother to turn your Mac on because this chapter has no hands-on material. What you find, however, is a bunch of important stuff that will save the beginner from a lot of headaches.

If you already know what System software is and does, how to avoid disasters, what a startup disk is, and how the startup process works, I suggest you read those sections anyway — to refresh your memory — and skim the rest.

Everyone else: Please read every word in this chapter.

What Is System Software?

Along with the code in its read-only memory (ROM), System software (often called the operating system or Mac OS) is what makes a Mac a Mac. Without it, your Mac is a pile of silicon and circuits, no smarter than a toaster. It has a brain (ROM), it has memory (RAM), and it has ten fingers and toes (other stuff), but it doesn't know what to do with itself. Think of System software as an education and Mac OS 9 as an Ivy League education. (A PC clone with Windows dropped outta high school in the tenth grade and flips burgers for a living.)

With Mac OS 9, your Mac becomes an elegant, powerful tool that's the envy of the rest of the computer industry. (Or so we Macintosh lovers like to think!)

Most of the world's personal computers use Windows. Poor schmucks. You're among the lucky few with a computer whose operating system is intuitive, easy to use, and, dare I say, fun. Windows — even Windows 98 — is a cheap imitation of the Macintosh System software. Try it sometime. Go ahead. You probably won't suffer any permanent damage. In fact, you'll really begin to appreciate how good you have it. Feel free to hug your Mac. Or give it a peck on the floppy drive opening (if you have one — some Macs don't any more!) — just try not to get your tongue caught.

What Does System Software Do?

"What does System software do," you ask? Good question. It controls the basic — and most important — operations of your computer. In the case of Mac OS 9 and your Mac, System software manages memory; controls how windows, icons, and menus work; keeps track of files; and does lots of other housekeeping chores. Other forms of software, such as a word processor, rely on System software to create and maintain the environment in which application software does its work.

When you create a memo, for example, the word processor provides the tools for you to type and format the information. System software provides the mechanism for drawing and moving the window in which you write the memo; it keeps track of the file when you save it; it helps the word processor create drop-down menus and dialog boxes and communicate with other programs; and it does much, much more.

Now you have a little background in System software. Before you do anything else with your Mac, take a gander at the next section.

A Safety Net for the Absolute Beginner — or Any User

If you're a first-time Macintosh user, please, please read this section of the book carefully. It could save your life. Well, I'm being overly dramatic. I meant to say that it could save your Mac. I deal with the stuff that the manual that came with your Mac doesn't cover or doesn't cover in nearly enough detail. If you're an experienced Mac user, read this section anyway. Chances are, you need a few reminders:

✔ **If you don't know how to turn your Mac on, get help.** Don't feel bad. Apple, in its infinite wisdom, has manufactured Macs with power-on switches on every conceivable surface: the front, side, back, and the keyboard. Some Macs (most older PowerBooks) even hide the power-on button behind a little plastic door.

Like personal fouls in the NBA, authors are allowed only so many weasel-outs per book. I hate to use one so early, but in this case, I think it's worth it for both of us. I promise this is the first and only time I'll say "Look in the manual." Maybe.

✔ **Always use the Shut Down (Special menu) command.** Or press the Power key once and then click the Shut Down button to turn off your Mac. Turning off the power without shutting your Mac down properly is one of the worst things you can do to your poor Mac. It can screw up your hard disk real bad, or scramble the contents of your most important files, or both.

Of course, most of us have broken this rule several times without anything horrible happening. Don't be lulled into a false sense of security. Do it one time too many and your most important file will be toast.

The only times you should turn off your Mac without shutting down properly is if your screen is frozen or you crash and can't do anything else. This doesn't happen often, but when it does, turning your Mac off and then back on is the only solution.

Mac OS 9 actually scolds you if you don't shut down properly. If you break this rule, the next time your Mac is turned on, it will politely inform you that your Mac was shut down improperly and is trying to repair the damage, if any, as shown in Figure 1-1.

If you find the little "This Mac was shut down improperly" reminder annoying, you can turn it off in the General Controls control panel. I actually like it and leave the warning enabled. You should, too.

✔ **Don't unplug your Mac when it's turned on.** See my blurb in the preceding bullet.

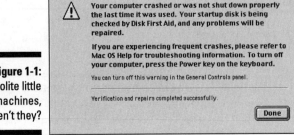

Figure 1-1:
Polite little
machines,
aren't they?

The warning box reads:

> Your computer crashed or was not shut down properly the last time it was used. Your startup disk is being checked by Disk First Aid, and any problems will be repaired.
>
> If you are experiencing frequent crashes, please refer to Mac OS Help for troubleshooting information. To turn off your computer, press the Power key on the keyboard.
>
> You can turn off this warning in the General Controls panel.
>
> Verification and repairs completed successfully.
>
> [Done]

✔ **Don't use your Mac when lightning is near.** Lightning strike = dead Mac. 'Nuff said. Oh, and don't place much faith in inexpensive surge protectors. A good jolt of lightning will fry the surge protector right along with your computer. There are surge protectors that can withstand most lightning strikes, but they're not the cheapies you buy at your local computer emporium. Unplugging your Mac from the wall during electrical storms is safer and less expensive. (Don't forget to unplug your modem as well — lightning can fry it, too.)

✔ **Don't jostle, bump, shake, kick, throw, dribble, or punt your Mac, especially while it's running.** Unless your Mac is ancient, it contains within it a hard disk drive that spins at 5,400+ rpm. A jolt to a hard disk while it's reading or writing a file can cause the head to crash into the disk, which can render many or all the files on it totally and irreversibly unrecoverable.

✔ **Turn off your Mac before plugging in or unplugging any cables.** This advice may be overkill, because even Apple seems to say that you can safely plug cables into the serial ports — the modem or printer ports — while your Mac is turned on. But other cables, specifically SCSI cables and ADB cables, should never under any circumstances be plugged in or unplugged without first shutting down your Mac.

The one exception is if your Mac has USB or FireWire ports, such as the iMac (USB), the blue-and-white Power Mac (USB and FireWire), and the newest PowerBook (also USB and FireWire), which you can plug in and unplug safely even while the Mac is powered up.

Okay, that about does it for bad stuff that can happen. If something bad has already happened to you, see Chapter 18.

What You Should See after Turning On the Power

After a small bit of whirring, buzzing, and flashing (System software is loading), you should see a cheerful little happy Mac in the middle of your screen, like the one in Figure 1-2.

Figure 1-2:
The Mac
startup icon.

Soon thereafter comes a soothing blue Mac OS logo, with the message "Welcome to Mac OS 9," followed by "Starting Up" and the infamous march of the icons across the bottom of the screen. Makes you feel kind of warm and fuzzy, doesn't it? These things indicate that Mac OS 9 is loading properly.

This might be a good time to take a moment to think good thoughts about the person who convinced you that you wanted a Mac. That person was right.

Anyway, in a few more seconds, the familiar Macintosh desktop materializes before your eyes. If you haven't customized, configured, or tinkered with your desktop, it should look something like Figure 1-3. Don't worry if you don't see a desktop printer icon on your desktop (mine is named HP LaserJet 4ML); I cover desktop printers in Chapter 9. And don't worry if you don't see a little control strip hanging out near the bottom of your screen; I cover the ingenious control strip in Chapter 14.

In the unlikely event that you didn't see the smiling Mac, soothing messages, and the familiar desktop, read the next section — "What's Happening Here? (The Startup Process Revealed)" — carefully. If this section doesn't set things right, skip to Chapter 18.

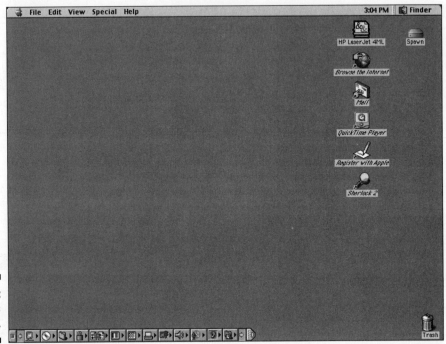

Figure 1-3:
The Mac
desktop.

What's Happening Here? (The Startup Process Revealed)

When you turn on your Macintosh, you set in motion a sophisticated and complex series of events that culminates in the loading of Mac OS 9 and the appearance of the familiar Mac desktop. Fortunately, the mechanics of the process are unimportant. In brief, your Mac tests all your hardware — slots, ports, disks, memory (RAM), and so on. If everything passes, you hear a pleasing chord and see the happy Mac, the Mac OS logo, "Welcome to Mac OS 9," and "Loading" on your monitor as your Mac loads the System software it needs from disk to RAM.

You're not a failure

If any of your hardware fails when it is tested, you'll see a black screen with the dreaded sad Mac icon (see Figure 1-4) and hear a far less pleasing musical chord known by Mac aficionados as the Chimes of Doom. The fact that something went wrong is no reflection on your prowess as a Macintosh user.

Something inside your Mac is broken, and it probably needs to go in for repairs (usually to an Apple dealer). If it's under warranty, dial 1-800-SOS-APPL and they'll tell you what to do.

Figure 1-4:
The Sad
Mac icon.

Before you do anything, though, skip ahead to Chapter 18. It's entirely possible that one of the suggestions there can get you back on track without your having to spend even a moment on hold.

A pop quiz on mousing

For those of you who need to hone your mousing skills, here's a little quiz:

1. How do you select an icon on the desktop?

   A. Stare at it intently for five seconds.

   B. Point to it with your finger, slap the side of your monitor, and say "That one, stupid!"

   C. Move the mouse pointer on top of the icon and click once.

2. When do you need to double-click?

   A. Whenever you find yourself saying, "There's no place like home."

   B. When you're using both hands to control the mouse.

   C. When you want to open a file or folder.

3. How do you select multiple items or blocks of text?

   A. Get several people to stare intently at the items you want to select.

   B. Attach multiple mice to your Mac.

   C. Slide the mouse on your desk, moving the on-screen pointer to the location where you want to begin selecting. Press and hold down the mouse button. Drag the pointer across the items or text that you want to select. Then let go of the mouse button.

4. How do you move a selected item?

   A. Call U-Haul.

   B. Pick up and tilt your monitor until the item slides to the proper location.

   C. Click the item and hold down the mouse button. With the mouse button still held down, drag the pointer to the new location and let go of the mouse button.

If you haven't figured it out by now, the correct answer to each of these questions is C. If any other answer sounded remotely plausible, sit down with your Mac and just play with it for a while. If you have kids at your disposal, watch them play with your Mac. They'll show you how to use it in no time.

Question Mark and the Mysterians

Although it's unlikely that you'll see a sad Mac, all users eventually encounter the flashing question mark (shown in Figure 1-5) or the flashing folder (not shown) in place of the usual happy Mac at some time in their lives. Don't worry. These icons mean that your Mac can't find a startup disk: a floppy disk, hard disk, or CD-ROM containing valid System software.

Figure 1-5:
Your Mac is
having an
identity
crisis.

When you turn on your Mac, the first thing it does (after the aforementioned hardware tests) is check the floppy disk drive for a startup disk (something with Mac OS 9 on it). If it doesn't find one there, it scans the SCSI or IDE bus. At this point, your Mac usually finds your hard disk, which contains a System folder, and the startup process continues on its merry way with the happy Mac and all the rest.

Think of the flashing question mark as your Mac's way of saying, "Please provide me with a disk that contains some System software."

If Apple can figure out a way to put a flashing question mark on the screen, why the heck can't the software engineers find a way to put the words "Please insert a startup disk" on the screen as well? The curtness of the flashing question mark is one of my pet peeves about the Macintosh. I know, you're clever and smart (you're reading *Mac OS 9 For Dummies,* aren't you?), so you know that a flashing question mark means that you should insert a startup disk. But what about everyone else?

The ultimate startup disks

Chances are, you have a copy of the ultimate startup floppy or CD-ROM right there on your computer table. The floppy is usually called Disk Tools, and it's one of the disks that come with many older versions of Mac OS. If you get a flashing question mark, pop Disk Tools into your floppy drive and your Mac will boot, just like magic.

Or, if your Mac has no floppy drive or your Mac or System Software update didn't include disks, use the included bootable CD-ROM disc. To boot from a

CD-ROM, you need to hold down the C key during startup on most Mac models. If that doesn't work, try holding down these four keys in the infamous four-finger salute: Delete+Option+⌘+Shift.

A good way to remember this keyboard combination — which is generally used to start up from a disk other than your internal hard drive, including a bootable CD-ROM — is to think of the mnemonic device DOCS, that is, Delete+Option+⌘ (Command)+Shift.

Disk Tools or a bootable System software CD make the ultimate startup disks because, in addition to System and Finder (the two files that must be present on a startup disk), they also have copies of Disk First Aid, Apple HD SC Setup, and/or Drive Setup, three programs that you may need if you see a flashing question mark. Disk First Aid can repair hidden damage to your hard disk; HD SC Setup or Drive Setup can install new hard disk drivers. Both Disk First Aid and Apple HD SC Setup/Drive Setup are described more completely in Chapter 18.

Now what?

So your Mac boots from the Disk Tools disk or System Software CD-ROM, but you still have this little problem. You would prefer that your Mac boot from your (much faster) hard disk than that piddly little Disk Tools floppy or System software CD-ROM. Not to worry. All you need to do is reinstall Mac OS 9 (see Appendix A).

The legend of the boot

Boot this. Boot that. "I booted my Mac and . . ." "Did it boot?" It seems nearly impossible to talk about computers for long without hearing the word.

But why *boot*? Why not *shoe* or *shirt* or even *shazam*?

It all began in the very olden days, maybe the 1970s or a little earlier, when starting up a computer required you to toggle little manual switches on the front panel, which began an internal process that loaded the operating system. The process became known as *boot-strapping* because if you toggled the right switches, the computer would "pull itself up by its bootstraps." It didn't take long for the phrase to transmogrify into *booting* and *boot*.

Over the years, booting has come to mean turning on almost any computer or even a peripheral device such as a printer. Some people also use it to refer to launching an application: "I booted Excel."

So the next time one of your gearhead friends says the b-word, ask whether he or she knows where the term comes from. Then dazzle them with the depth and breadth of your knowledge.

Those of you who are going to upgrade from an earlier version of Mac OS to Mac OS 9 may want to read Appendix A right about now. The rest of you, the ones whose Macs have already booted from a hard drive with Mac OS 9 installed, can breathe a sigh of relief, read these last few paragraphs, and move on to another chapter.

How do you know which version of the Mac OS your computer has? Simple. Just choose Apple menu⇨About This Computer, the very first choice in the list. A window pops up in the middle of your screen, as shown in Figure 1-6. In the upper-right corner of this window, you find the version number of your System software. As you can see, the About This Computer window not only tells you the version number of the Mac OS you're using but also details your RAM usage. (You can find out more about RAM usage and memory in Chapter 11.)

Figure 1-6:
I'm using
Mac OS 9.
Look, it says
so right
there in the
upper right.

One Last Thing Before We Move On . . .

If the stuff on your hard disk means anything to you, you must back it up. Not maybe. You must. Which is why I recommend that you read Appendix B right now instead of later. Appendix B is a safety net for everyone. Before you do any significant work on your Mac (or even if your most important file is your last saved game of Myth II: Soulblighter), you need to realize how important it is to back up.

Dr. Macintosh sez, "There are only two kinds of Mac users: those who have never lost data and those who will." Which kind will you be?

I beg you: Please read Appendix B now before something horrible happens to your valuable data.

Chapter 2

Meet the Desktop

• •

• •

This is where I get down to the nitty-gritty; this is the chapter about the Macintosh desktop. Your desktop is the center of your Macintosh universe. Just about everything you do on your Mac begins and ends with the desktop. The desktop is where you manage files, store documents, launch programs, adjust the way your Mac works, and do much more. If you ever expect to master your Mac, the first step is to master the desktop.

Those of you who have been using Mac OS for a while might find some of the information in this chapter repetitive; many features described are unchanged from earlier versions of the Mac OS. Still, you'd be foolish to skip it completely. If you do, I assure you you'll miss sarcasm, clever wordplay, shortcuts, awesome techniques, a bad pun or two, and lots of good advice on making the desktop an easier place to be. If that's not enough to convince you, I also provide a bunch of stuff Apple didn't bother to tell you. (As if you read the manual anyway.)

Tantalized? Let's rock.

I Think I-con, I Think I-con

Icons, those funny little pictures on your desktop and in your windows, represent containers, and these containers hold things that you work with on your Mac, such as programs, documents, System software items, and discarded files (the Trash icon). All icons appear on your screen as little pictures with their names attached.

Okay. One type of icon — the Alias — is technically not a container at all. Aliases are pointers. But because I want to keep things simple for now, I tell you about aliases real soon (like in Chapter 4).

The first icon you should become familiar with is the icon for your hard disk, shown in Figure 2-1. It's in the upper-right corner of your desktop and is named Macintosh HD, unless you've renamed it. In upcoming screen shots, you'll notice I renamed mine Spawn.

If you want to give any icon a different picture, you can find out how in Chapter 3.

Figure 2-1:
A plain-
vanilla
hard disk
icon.

The look you want to know better

Icons come in all shapes and sizes. After you've been around the Macintosh for a while, you get a sixth sense about what an icon contains just by looking at it. For example, application (that is, program) icons are often diamond shaped. Unless, of course, they're rectangular or square or oddly shaped (see Figure 2-2).

Figure 2-2:
Application
icons come
in many
different
shapes.

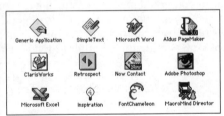

Okay, so application icons are all over the place. Document icons, on the other hand, are almost always reminiscent of a piece of paper, as shown in Figure 2-3.

See? You're already acquiring that sixth sense. Application icons are all over the place; document icons look like paper. Kind of.

Now let's talk about the four types of icons: application, document, folder, and System software. (There are actually five kinds of icons. Aliases are an icon type in their own right. But I'm trying to keep things simple; I discuss these most excellent icons soon enough. Like in Chapter 4.)

Figure 2-3:
Typical
document
icons.

Applications are programs, the software that you use to accomplish tasks on your Mac. Your word processor is an application. So are America Online and Adobe Photoshop. Myth II and SimCity 3000 are applications. (They're also great games.)

Documents are files created by applications. Letter to Mom, which you created in AppleWorks (formerly known as ClarisWorks), is a document. So are Bob's Calendar and Expense Report.

Folders are the Mac's organizational containers. You put icons, usually application or document icons, into folders. You can also put folders inside other folders. Folders look like, well, folders. Some folder icons have pictures; most don't. (See Figure 2-4.)

Figure 2-4:
Typical
folder icons.

System software is the stuff in your System Folder — the System, the Finder, control panels, extensions, and almost everything else. The files that make up your System software have many purposes, most of which will become second nature to you. For now, I'll just talk about the icons, though.

System software icons usually have a distinctive look as well. For example, the System and Finder have distinctive, Mac-flavored icons. (See Figure 2-5.) Control panel icons usually have a slider bar at the bottom or on one side. Extension icons usually look like jigsaw puzzle parts. But the rest of your System software icons may look like just about anything.

I have lots more to say about all these kinds of icons, and I do so in upcoming chapters. But that's enough about what icons look like. I'm sure you're anxious to do something with icons.

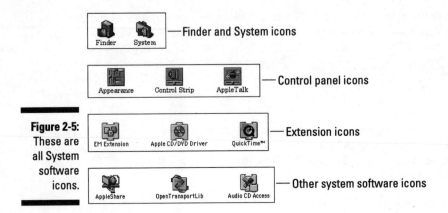

Finder and System icons

Control panel icons

Figure 2-5:
These are
all System
software
icons.

Extension icons

Other system software icons

Open sesame

You can open any icon in three ways. (Okay, there are five ways, but as I said, I'm saving aliases for later.) Anyway, here are the ways:

✔ Click the icon once to select it, point to the File menu (it's the one that says File), and press the word File. A *press* is half a click. Don't release the mouse button yet. A menu drops down. Move the pointer downward until the word Open is highlighted (see Figure 2-6). Then release the mouse button.

(I probably could have saved a whole paragraph by simply saying "Choose File⇨Open." But you may have been pulling down a menu for the first time. I wanted to be safe.) The icon opens.

By the way, in case you hadn't noticed, I just showed you how to choose an item from a menu. Don't go hog-wild. There's a lot more to know about menus, which you can find out about in Chapters 4 and 5.

✔ Double-click the icon by clicking it directly twice in rapid succession. If it doesn't open, you double-clicked too slowly.

✔ Select the icon and then use the keyboard shortcut ⌘+O. That means you press the ⌘ key, the one with the pretzel and the apple on most keyboards, and then press the O key while continuing to hold down the ⌘ key.

✔ Click the icon while holding down the Control key and use the contextual menu's Open command.

Holding down the Control key and clicking almost anywhere on the screen brings up a special menu called a contextual menu. It's called that because its contents (that is, its *context*) change depending on what you Control-click. In other words, the menu items you see when you Control-click a folder are different than the menu items you see when you Control-click the desktop, which are different than the menu items you see when you Control-click the Trash icon. Got it?

Figure 2-6:
Selecting
the Open
command.

If you look at Figure 2-6, you can see that the keyboard shortcut appears on the menu after the word Open. Pretzel-O. Any menu item with one of these pretzel-letter combinations after its name can be executed with that keyboard shortcut. Just press the pretzel (⌘) key and the letter shown in the menu — N for New Folder, F for Find, and so on — and the appropriate command is executed.

It's never too soon to learn good habits, so I'll mention here that experienced Macintosh users use the keyboard shortcuts as often as possible. Keyboard shortcuts let you do things without opening the menu, which means that you don't have to reach for the mouse, which means that you do more in less time. It's a good idea to memorize shortcuts for menu items you use frequently.

Although the letters next to the ⌘ (I've finished calling it a pretzel now) in the Finder's menus are capital letters, you don't have to press the Shift key to use the keyboard shortcut. ⌘+P means that you hold down the ⌘ key and press P. Some programs have keyboard combinations that require the use of ⌘+Shift, but these programs let you know by calling the key combination something like ⌘+Shift+S or ⌘+Shift+O. Or they indicate the shift part with a little up-facing arrow. You don't have to worry about the capitalization of the letter.

The name game

Icon, icon, bo-bicon, banana fanna fo-ficon. Bet that you can change the name of any old icon. Here are two ways:

- Click the icon's name directly. Don't forget to release the mouse button.
- Click the icon and then press the Return or Enter key on your keyboard once.

Either way, the icon's name is selected, the icon is surrounded with a box, and the icon awaits your typing. (See Figure 2-7.)

Figure 2-7:
You can change an icon's name by simply typing a new one when the name is highlighted as shown; just start typing.

In addition to selecting the name, the cursor changes from a pointer to a text-editing I-beam. An I-beam cursor is the Mac's way of telling you that you can type now. At this point, if you click the I-beam cursor anywhere in the name box, you can *edit* the icon's original name. If you don't click and just begin typing, the icon's original name is replaced by what you type.

If you've never changed an icon's name, give it a try. And don't forget: If you click the icon itself, the icon is selected and you won't be able to change its name. (Selecting the icon itself enables you to move, copy, print, or open it, but I'm getting ahead of myself.) If you do select the icon, press Return or Enter to edit the name of the icon.

Other various and sundry icons

Before I get off the subject of icons completely, and because this is the chapter where you meet your desktop, I'd be remiss if I didn't mention one other important icon. . . .

The Trash icon

The Trash is a special container where you put the icons you no longer want on your hard or removable media storage device, such as Zip, SuperDisk, or floppy. Got four copies of SimpleText on your hard disk? Drag three of them to the Trash. Old letters that you don't want to keep? Drag them to the Trash as well. To put an icon in the Trash, drag it on top of the Trash icon. When the tip (cool people call it the *hot spot*) of the pointer is directly over the Trash icon, the icon inverts (as shown in Figure 2-8).

Figure 2-8:
Dragging a
file into the
Trash.

When the Trash inverts (that is, turns black), release the mouse button and, voilà, whatever you dragged to the Trash is trashed. But it's not gone forever until . . .

. . . you choose Special⇨Empty Trash. You know how the garbage in the can in your kitchen sits there until the sanitation engineers come by and pick it up each Thursday? The Mac OS Trash works the same. When you put something in the Trash, it sits there until you choose the Special⇨Empty Trash command.

You can empty the trash also by holding down the Control key when you click the Trash. From the menu shown in Figure 2-9, select the Empty Trash command.

Figure 2-9:
Emptying
the Trash
the
contextual
menu way.

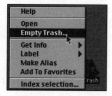

Think twice before you invoke Empty Trash. After the Trash has been emptied, the files it contained are (usually) gone forever (see the next Technical Stuff note). (Of course, you read Appendix B and you've backed up your hard disk several times, right? So even though the files are gone forever from your hard disk, you can get them back if you like, right?)

As with all icons, you can open the Trash (you can find earlier in this chapter at least three ways to open an icon) to see what's in there. You can tell there's something in the Trash because the Trash icon bulges when it's full (as shown in Figure 2-10).

Figure 2-10:
Empty trash
can on the
left. Full and
bulging
trash can on
the right.

Utility programs that let you retrieve a trashed file after you empty the Trash are available. Norton Utilities and Tech Tool Pro are the two most popular. They don't have a 100-percent success rate, so you should still consider the Empty Trash command fatal to files.

If you drag an icon that's locked to the Trash, you'll see a message telling you to hold down the Option key when you choose Special⇨Empty Trash to delete locked items. (To unlock locked icons, select the icon and then choose File⇨Get Info or its keyboard shortcut, ⌘+I, and then click the little box marked *locked*.)

Close encounters of the icon kind

If you've used System 7.5, Mac OS 7.6, or any version of Mac OS 8 for very long, you've most likely encountered a few other icons. You probably have an icon on your desktop for a desktop printer. Check out Figure 2-11.

Most (but not all) printers allow you to create a desktop printer icon. Each desktop printer icon represents one printer available to your Mac or one set of printer-specific settings (scale, tile, crop, and so on). You may have more than one desktop printer icon. If you don't have even one, don't fret. You can make one in Chapter 9.

If you performed a full install of Mac OS 9, you'll see three or four other icons on your desktop, including Browse the Internet, Mail, and Register with Apple. (Refer to Figure 2-11.)

This is a good time to mention that if you need help with any part of Mac OS 9, choose Help Center from the Help menu and you'll get assistance instantly. (See Figure 2-12.) Another way to get help in the Finder is to use the keyboard shortcut ⌘-?. Finally, you can Control-click almost anywhere on-screen and choose Help from the contextual menu.

What the heck's the Finder, anyway?

You may have noticed that I use the words *Finder* and *desktop* interchangeably. As you probably know, the Finder is one of the files in your System Folder. The Finder is the super-program. Among other things, it creates the desktop metaphor — the icons, windows, and menus that make up the Macintosh desktop. Unlike with ordinary programs, you can never quit the Finder. Like Katz's Deli, the Finder never closes. And unlike with ordinary programs, you don't have to open the Finder to use it. The Finder is always open; it opens automatically when you turn on your Mac.

Okay, a few games and several shareware utilities will indeed allow you to Quit the Finder. But under ordinary circumstances, it's always running.

Because the Finder is, among other things, responsible for creating the desktop and its menus, many people, myself included, use the words *Finder* and *desktop* interchangeably. You can, too.

The only time it gets confusing is when you are talking about the Finder icon in your System Folder. Just say "the Finder icon" instead of "the Finder" and you'll sound like a pro. It can also be confusing when you're talking about the background you see on your screen (mine is Mac OS wallpaper), which is also called the desktop.

Figure 2-11: Mac OS 9's four default desktop icons with my desktop printer above them.

I cover the amazing Mac OS 9 Internet capabilities as well as more about the Browse the Internet and Mail icons in Chapter 17.

If you have any other icons on your desktop, ignore them for now. They probably won't hurt anything.

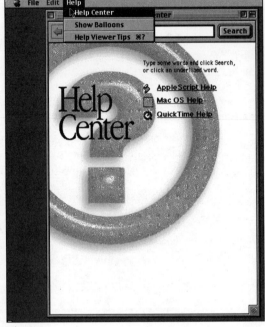

Figure 2-12:
You can
learn a lot
about
Mac OS 9
by exploring
the Help
Center. So
what are
you waiting
for?

Windows (Not the Microsoft Kind)

Windows are such a fundamental part of the Macintosh experience that Microsoft blatantly ripped off the name for their operating system add-on.

If you're relatively new to the Mac, you might want to read this section while sitting at your computer, trying the techniques as you read them. I've always found it easier to remember something I read if I actually do it. If you've been abusing your Mac for a while, you've probably figured out how windows work by now, but you may not have tried some stuff in here.

Doin' windows

Windows are a ubiquitous part of Macintosh computing. Windows on the desktop show you the contents of disk and folder icons; windows in applications usually show you the contents of your documents.

I've already showed you three different ways to open an icon, so you know how to open a window. When you open a window, its icon turns fuzzy gray (see Figure 2-13), which is your Mac's way of letting you know that the icon's window is open. Clever, eh?

Figure 2-13:
A fuzzy gray,
open icon.

Zooming right along

Note how the Spawn window in Figure 2-14 says *9 Items* near the top, but only one item seems to be showing. That's easily remedied. To make a window larger, click the zoom box, one of the two boxes in the upper-right corner of most windows (labeled in Figure 2-15). This action causes the window to grow and should reveal the rest of its contents.

I say *should* because if a window contains more icons than the window can display, it grows as large as it can and still leaves room for your disk and Trash icons on the right side of the screen when you click the zoom box.

Click the zoom box again to return the window to its original size.

Figure 2-14:
This window
says that it
contains
nine items,
but you see
only one.
What gives?

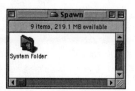

That shady window feeling

The *title bar* is the striped bar at the top of the active window. It contains the window's name, as well as the close box, the windowshade box, and the zoom box. If you want to collapse the window so just its title bar shows, double-click the title bar or click the windowshade box (both are labeled in Figure 2-15).

Click the windowshade box again to return the window to its original size.

You can turn the windowshade's double-click feature on and off in the Appearance control panel, which is covered in Chapter 14.

Close box   Windowshade box

Title bar   Zoom box

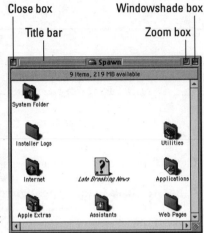

Figure 2-15:
When you
click the
zoom box in
the upper-
right corner
of the
window, the
window
expands to
show all the
items it
contains.

Cutting windows down to size

Another way to see more of what's in a window is by using the sizer in the lower-right corner. Drag the sizer downward and to the right to make the window larger, as shown in Figure 2-16. You may use the sizer to make a window whatever size you like.

Figure 2-16:
Drag the
sizer up or
down to
change the
size of the
window.

Sizer

Notice the faint white lines when you drag? They're there to show you the size the window will be when you release the mouse button. Go ahead and give the sizer a try; it's fun, it's easy, and it's free.

A scroll new world

Yet another way to see more of what is in a window is to scroll. You scroll using scroll bars, which appear on the bottom and right sides of any window that contains more icons than those that you can see in the window. (See Figure 2-17.)

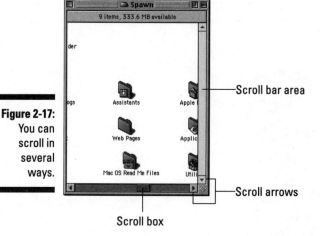

Figure 2-17:
You can
scroll in
several
ways.

Scroll bar area

Scroll arrows

Scroll box

You can scroll in four ways:

- ✔ **Way #1:** Click a scroll box and drag. The window scrolls an amount that corresponds to how far you drag the scroll box.

- ✔ **Way #2:** Click a scroll arrow. The window scrolls a little.

- ✔ **Way #3:** Click in the gray scroll bar area. The window scrolls one page worth. If the scroll bar is white, there are no items to scroll to — everything that the window contains is visible.

- ✔ **Way #4:** Use the keyboard. Select an icon in the window first and then use the arrow keys to move up, down, left, or right. Using an arrow key selects the next icon in that direction and automatically scrolls the window, if necessary.

You can also press the Tab key on the keyboard to select the next icon alphabetically. So if I click SimpleText and then press the Tab key, the System Folder (the icon that comes next alphabetically) is selected. If the System Folder wasn't showing when I selected SimpleText, the Spawn window would scroll automatically to reveal the System Folder after I pressed the Tab key.

For what it's worth, the Page Up and Page Down keys on extended keyboards function the same as clicking the gray scroll bar area (the vertical scroll bar only) in the Finder and many applications. But these keys don't work in some programs, so don't get too dependent on them.

Transportable windows

To move a window, click anywhere in the title bar and drag the window to its new location. Figure 2-18 shows an example of moving a window by dragging its title bar.

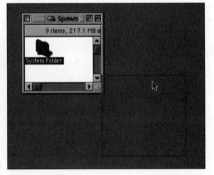

Figure 2-18: Click and drag the title bar to move a window to a new location.

The window moves to its new position as soon as you release the mouse button.

You can also move a window by clicking any side of it. Figure 2-19 shows where to click the edge of a window to move it, and what happens when you do.

Figure 2-19: Dragging the edge of a window moves it across the desktop.

Just below the title bar is the window's status line, which tells you the number of items the window contains (9) and the amount of space available on this hard disk (216.6MB).

Ladies and gentlemen, activate your windows

To work with a window, the window must be *active*. Only one window at a time may be the active window. To make a window active, click it anywhere — in the middle, on the title bar, or on a scroll bar. It doesn't matter where.

The active window is always the frontmost window, and inactive windows always appear behind the active window. The active window's title bar has black lines; its size, zoom, and close boxes are clearly defined, as are its scroll bars. Inactive windows show the window's name but none of those other distinctive window features. See Figure 2-20 for an example of active and inactive windows.

Figure 2-20: An active window in front of an inactive window.

Shutting yo' windows

Now that I've gone on and on about windows, I suppose I ought to tell you how to close them. Here we go again with the ways. You can close an active window in four ways:

- ✔ **Way #1:** Click the close box in the upper-left corner of the title bar. (See Figure 2-15.)

- ✔ **Way #2:** Choose File⇨Close Window. (See Figure 2-21.)

- ✔ **Way #3:** Use the keyboard shortcut ⌘+W. Note that this keyboard shortcut is listed next to the Close Window command in Figure 2-21.

- ✔ **Way #4:** Use the contextual menu shortcut, as shown in Figure 2-22. Just hold down the Control key when you click any window to get the contextual menu.

File

New Folder	⌘N
Open	⌘O
Print	⌘P
Move To Trash	⌘⌫
Close Window	⌘W
Get Info	▶
Label	▶
Duplicate	⌘D
Make Alias	⌘M
Add To Favorites	
Put Away	⌘Y
Encrypt	
Find...	⌘F
Search Internet...	⌘H
Show Original	⌘R
Page Setup...	
Print Window...	

Figure 2-21:
You can use this command to close an active window.

Figure 2-22:
Hold down the Control key while clicking a window to pop up the contextual menu.

If you're like me, by the end of the day your desktop is scattered with open windows — sometimes a dozen or more. Wouldn't it be nice if you could close them all at once with a single "close all windows" command? But you don't see a Close All command in the menus, do you?

Well, there is one, but Apple, in its infinite wisdom, has hidden it from mere mortals. To make this useful command come out and play, merely hold down the Option key as you close the active window using Way #1, Way #2, or Way #3. In other words, hold down the Option key when you click the active window's close box, hold down the Option key when you choose File⇨Close Window, or hold down the Option key and the ⌘ key while you press the W key (⌘+Option+W).

Apple didn't hide the Close All command very well. As Figure 2-23 illustrates, if you press the Option key before pulling down the File menu, Close Window is magically transformed into Close All.

Figure 2-23:
Hold down
the Option
key while
pulling
down the
File menu
and you'll
see the
Close All
command
instead of
the Close
Window
command.

Congrats: You now do windows

You can do windows with the best of them. And I have good news for you:
In 99 percent of all applications (programs) that you will ever encounter,
windows work the same as they do in the Finder. Just about every application
has active and inactive windows with title bars, close boxes, zoom boxes,
scroll bars, scroll arrows, and scroll boxes.

For the most part, windows are windows. As you use different programs,
you'll probably notice that some of them (Microsoft Word, for example) take
liberties with windows by adding features such as page counters and style
indicators to the scroll bar area. Don't worry. You know how to do windows.
That stuff is just window dressing (pun intended).

Chapter 3

Disk Could Be the Start of Something Big

In This Chapter

▶ Initializing and erasing your disks

▶ Using PC disks

▶ Ejecting disks

▶ A treatise on folder management

▶ Icons and the desktop

*I*n this chapter you find out about the disk basics: how to format them, how to format them so our less-fortunate Windows-using brethren (and sisteren) can use them, how to eject them, how to organize them, and much more. So let's get started.

For the lowdown on what floppy disks are and where they came from, you ought to see David Pogue's *Macs For Dummies* (published by IDG Books Worldwide, Inc.). I limit my discussion to stuff you do with disks when they're on the desktop.

You should think of the disk icons that appear on your desktop as if they were folders. When you double-click them, their windows open. You can drag stuff in and out of a disk's window, and you can manipulate the disk's window in all the usual ways.

Initialization and Erasure

Brand-new disks usually need to be *initialized* — prepared to receive Macintosh files — before they can be used. I say *usually* because you can buy new disks that are preformatted and already initialized. It takes only a few minutes to initialize a disk, so don't pay a whole lot more for preformatted disks unless you really believe that time is money.

When you pop in an uninitialized disk, your Mac walks you through all the steps necessary to initialize it.

Surprise! PC Disks Work as Well!

One of the most excellent features of Mac OS 9 (if you have friends unfortunate enough not to own Macs and want to share files with them) is that it reads both Mac and DOS floppy disks without any user intervention. DOS disks are formatted for use with personal computers running DOS or Windows. If a friend has a Windows computer, you can read his or her disks by just sticking them in your floppy drive. Your unfortunate friend, on the other hand, can't do diddlysquat with your Mac-formatted disks — yet another reason why Macs are better.

The preceding applies also to other types of disks, including Zip, Jaz, Orb, and SyQuest.

When you insert a disk formatted for DOS, you see a distinctive PC disk icon like the one in Figure 3-1.

Figure 3-1:
A PC-
formatted
disk on your
Mac
desktop.

You may run into two other disk formats. ProDOS is the Apple II format, rarely used anymore, and Macintosh HFS Interchange Format is a weirdo format that nobody I know uses for anything.

Getting Disks Out of Your Mac

You now know almost everything there is to know about disks except one important thing: how to eject a disk. Piece of cake, actually.

And, of course, there are many ways:

- ✔ **Way #1:** Click the disk's icon to select it. Then choose Special⇨Eject or use the keyboard shortcut ⌘+E.

✔ **Way #2:** Drag the disk's icon to the Trash.

  This drives me nuts. Anything else you drag into the Trash dies (or at least it does when you select Empty Trash). Why does dragging a disk to the Trash eject it?

  ✔ **Way #3:** Select the disk and then choose File⇨Put Away (or use its ⌘-key shortcut, ⌘+Y).

  ✔ **Way #4:** Click the disk while holding down the Control key; then use the contextual menu's Eject command.

  ✔ **Way #5:** Use the keyboard shortcut ⌘+Shift+1. Notice how even though the disk has been ejected and is probably in your right hand, its icon still appears on the desktop, albeit with an unusual ghostly gray pattern. (See Figure 3-2.)

Figure 3-2:
See the
difference?

————Disk ejected with⌘+Shift+1

————Mounted disk with its window open

The ghostly gray indicates that the disk is not currently mounted (inserted). Note that a dismounted disk's icon is not the same as that of a disk with its window open. The icon of a mounted disk with its window open is shown in Figure 3-2 also.

Why would you want the icon for an ejected disk on your desktop? So you can copy files from one floppy disk to another even though you have only one floppy disk drive. A whole section on copying files is coming up in a few pages.

If you use the Eject command, drag a disk's icon to the Trash, or use the Put Away command, the disk's ghost icon is not left on the desktop. If you use Way #1 or Way #2 to eject your disk, you can get rid of its ghost image by dragging the ghost icon to the Trash or selecting it and choosing File⇨ Put Away. Unless you plan to copy files from one floppy to another, you don't want floppy disk icons on your desktop after you eject the disks. Ways #3 and #4 are the most commonly used methods of ejecting a disk.

If you insist on leaving ghost icons of long-ago-ejected disks on your desktop, it's only a matter of time before your Mac presents you with the dreaded "Please insert the disk" dialog box, which is shown in Figure 3-3.

Notice that there is no OK or Cancel button in the dialog box in Figure 3-3. There's no way out but to insert the disk your Mac is asking for.

Figure 3-3:
When you
have
ghosted
icons on
your desk-
top, your
Mac may
ask for the
disks back.

Okay, I lied. There is a way out. Press ⌘+period. This keyboard shortcut can-cels the dialog box and lets you drag the ghost disk icon to the Trash. ⌘+period is a good shortcut to remember. In most dialog boxes, ⌘+period is the same as clicking the Cancel button.

The dreaded "Please insert the disk" dialog box usually appears if you try to open the icon for an unmounted disk or try to open any of the files in the unmounted disk's window.

Get in the habit of dragging disks to the Trash or using the Put Away or Eject commands to get disks off your desktop. These techniques eject the disk and get rid of its pesky ghost icon. Unless you plan to copy files from one floppy to another, which you don't do all that often, avoid the ⌘+Shift+1 method of ejecting disks.

Now that you know disks, it's time to get serious and read about something useful, such as how to work with folders and how to move and copy icons from folder to folder and from disk to disk.

Know When to Hold 'er, Know When to Folder

If your hard disk is a filing cabinet, folders are its folders. Duh. You use fold-ers to organize your icons.

Making folders

To create a new folder, first decide which window you want the new folder to appear in. Make that window active by clicking it. Now either choose File⇨

New Folder or use the shortcut ⌘+N. A new, untitled folder appears in the active window with its name box already highlighted and ready for you to type a new name for it. (See Figure 3-4.)

Figure 3-4:
A brand-
new,
untitled
folder.

Name your folders with relevant names. Folders entitled sfdghb or Stuff — worst of all, names like Untitled — won't make it any easier to find something six months from now.

Using 'em

Folders are icons; icons are containers. Folder icons (like disk icons) can contain just about any other icon.

You use folders to organize your stuff. There's no limit to how many folders you can have, so don't be afraid to create new ones and put stuff in them.

At the very least, you should have a System Folder. (If you don't, read Chapter 1.) Until you get a lot of stuff, may I suggest that you start out with Application and Document folders, at the very least? You can even have the Mac create these two folders automatically by using the General Controls control panel. (More about that in Chapter 14.)

Later, when you get more files, you can subdivide the Documents folder into meaningful subfolders like those shown in Figure 3-5.

As your subfolders get fuller, create subfolders within them. The idea is to have enough folders so that no one folder has hundreds of items in it, while avoiding folders with only one or two items in them. Strive for balance. And try not to go deeper than four or five levels. If you find yourself creating sub-folders that you have to open eight folders to get to, consider reorganizing the stuff in levels five through eight so that your folder hierarchy is no more than five levels deep. Trust me, you can save a lot of time if you don't stash stuff too deep.

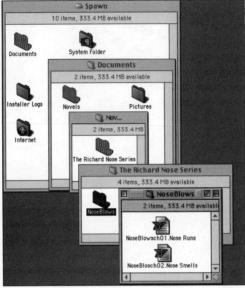

Figure 3-5:
The
Documents
folder
contains
numerous
subfolders,
each of
which
contains
sub-
subfolders.

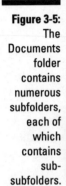

Moving and copying folders

You can move icons around within windows to your heart's content. Just click and drag within the window.

Now I'll run through how you move an item into a folder. For example, take a look at how you move One Folder into Another Folder. As you might expect from me, the King of Ways, there are three ways to do it:

✔ **Way #1:** As shown in Figure 3-6, drag the icon for One Folder onto the icon for Another Folder and release when Another Folder is highlighted. This technique works regardless of whether Another Folder's window is open. If its window is open, you can use the second way.

✔ **Way #2:** Drag the icon for One Folder into the open window for Another Folder (or disk), as shown in Figure 3-7.

✔ **Way #3:** Drag the icon that appears in the title bar of an open folder's window to another folder.

Notice the little gray border that appears around Another Folder's window in Figure 3-7. This is your Mac's way of telling you that if you release the mouse button right this second, the One Folder icon will be moved into Another Folder. If you move the pointer out of the Another Folder window, the gray border disappears.

You can use these two techniques to move any icon — folder, document, System software, or program icon — into folders or disks.

Figure 3-6:
Placing one
folder into
another.

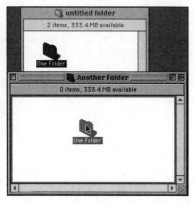

Figure 3-7:
You can also
move a
folder by
dragging its
icon into the
open
window of
another
folder.

You should know that if you try to move an item from one disk to another disk, it will be copied, not moved. Always. Without exception. If you want to move a file or folder from one disk to another, you have to trash the original manually after the copying is complete.

But what if you don't want to move something from one place to another on your hard disk? What if instead you want to copy it, leaving the icon in its original location and an identical copy in the destination window?

You may be thinking, why would I want to do that? Trust me, someday you will. Suppose you have a file called Long Letter to Mom in a folder called 1987 Correspondence. You figure Mom has forgotten it by now, so you want to send the letter again. But before you do, you want to change the date and delete the reference to Clarence, her pit bull, who passed away last year. So you want a copy of Long Letter to Mom in your Current Correspondence folder.

There are three ways to copy, but the first two are the same as you saw in the One Folder and Another Folder example, with one small difference: You must hold down the Option key during the dragging portion of the move. In the Finder, Option-dragging an icon to any folder icon or window copies it instead of moving it. So you Option-drag the Long Letter to Mom icon onto either a folder icon or an open window to deposit a copy.

When you copy something by dragging and dropping, the mouse pointer changes so that it includes a little plus sign (+) next to the arrow. Neat.

Now you have two copies of the file Long Letter to Mom — one in the 1987 Correspondence folder and another in the Current Correspondence folder. Open the one in the Current Correspondence folder and make your changes. Don't forget to save. (There's more about saving in Chapter 7.)

If I were you, I would change the name of the Long Letter to Mom file in the Current Correspondence folder because having more than one file on your hard disk with the same name is not a good idea, even if the files are in different folders. Trust me, having 10 files called Expense Report or 15 files named Randall's Invoice can be confusing, no matter how well organized your folder structure is. Add something distinguishing to file and folder names so that they're Expense Report 10/99 or Randall's Invoice 10/30/99. You'll be glad you did.

The third way to copy a file is to use the Duplicate command in either the File or the contextual menu. For more, check out Chapter 4.

Moving and copying disks

Moving an icon from one disk to another works the same as moving an icon from one folder to another. Because you're moving the icons from one disk to another disk, the copy part is automatic; you don't need the Option key.

When you move a file from one disk to another, you're automatically making a copy of it. The original is left untouched and unmoved. If you want to move a file from one disk to another, copy it. You can then delete the original by dragging it to the Trash.

Copying the entire contents of a floppy disk to your hard disk works a little differently. To do this task, select the floppy disk's icon and drag it onto your hard disk's icon, onto your hard disk's open window, or onto any other folder icon or open folder window.

When the copy is completed, a folder bearing the same name as the floppy disk appears on your hard disk. The folder on your hard disk now contains each and every file that was on the floppy disk of the same name.

Be careful copying disks containing System Folders to your hard disk. You never want to use the preceding technique to copy any type of disk — floppy, CD, Zip, and so on — to your hard disk if that disk has a System Folder. One hard and fast rule of the Mac is that you should never have more than one System Folder on your hard disk.

If a disk contains a System Folder and you want to copy everything else to your hard disk, do the following: Create a new folder on your hard disk. Then select every icon in the disk's window except its System Folder and drag all the selected icons onto the new folder's icon or window.

To select more than one icon, click once and drag. You see an outline of a box around the icons as you drag, and icons within or touching the box become highlighted. (See Figure 3-8.)

Figure 3-8:
To select
more than
one item,
click and
drag with
the mouse.

Another way to select multiple icons is to click one and then hold down the Shift key as you click others. As long as you hold down the Shift key, each new icon you click is added to the selection. To deselect an icon, click it a second time while still holding the Shift key down.

Be careful with multiple selections, especially when you drag icons to the Trash. It's easy to accidentally select more than one icon, so it's possible to put an icon in the Trash by accident if you're not paying close attention.

Meet the Desktop

The terms *Finder* and *desktop* are used interchangeably to refer to the total Macintosh environment you see — icons, windows, menus, and all that other cool stuff. Well, just to make things confusing, the background you see on your screen, the gray or patterned backdrop behind your hard disk icon and open windows, is also called the desktop.

You can move any icon you want to the desktop. The desktop isn't a window, but it acts like one. The desktop is a great place for things you use a lot, such as folders, applications, or particular documents.

Desktop beautification

I would be remiss if I didn't at least mention that you can change the background pattern of your desktop. If you're sick of the Mac OS desktop pattern, you can do either of the following:

- Choose Apple menu⇨Control Panels⇨ Appearance.

- Hold down the Control key, click anywhere on the desktop, and choose the Change Desktop Background menu item.

Either one will lead you to the Appearance control panel, where you can choose from dozens of desktop patterns and pictures.

I am particularly fond of the Desktop Pictures feature. I use the 3-D UFO picture Apple supplied as my everyday background, as shown in the accompanying figure.

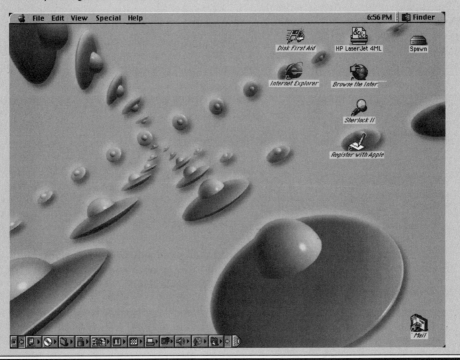

 It's even better to use aliases of things you use often so that you can keep the originals tucked away in one of your perfectly organized folders. (I talk about aliases in Chapter 4.)

In Figure 3-9, you see two icons on my desktop that you haven't seen before: Disk First Aid (application icon) and Internet Explorer (alias icon).

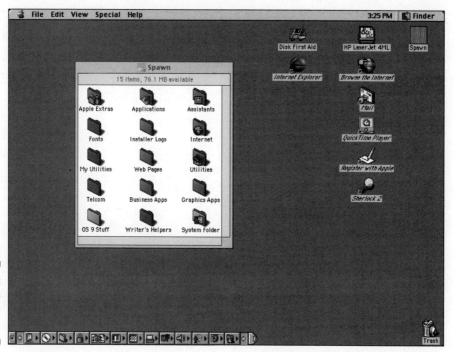

Figure 3-9:
My desktop
with some
stuff on it.

Disk icons always appear on the desktop, as does the Trash icon. The desktop printer, Browse the Internet, Mail, Get QuickTime Player, Register with Apple, and Sherlock 2 icons are created when you install Mac OS 9.

I moved my other icons from inside Spawn to the desktop so that they would be easier to use.

Items on the desktop behave the same as icons in a window. You move them and copy them in the same way you would an icon in a window. The only difference is that desktop items are not in a window; they're on the desktop, which makes them more convenient to use.

Got it? The desktop is convenient. It's fast. Put stuff there.

But not too much. If you keep putting stuff on the desktop, eventually it gets very cluttered. That's the time to put infrequently used icons back in the folder or disk window they came from. Fortunately, your Mac makes this task easy, even if you've forgotten which folder they were in. Select the icon or icons that you want to move back to where they came from, and then choose File⇨Put Away or use the shortcut ⌘+Y. Each icon is magically transported back into the folder or disk icon from which it came and no longer appears on the desktop. Neat, eh?

Chapter 4

Delectable Menus, Volume I

· ·

In This Chapter

▶ All about menus

▶ The File menu

▶ The Edit menu

· ·

*L*ike icons and windows, menus are a quintessential part of the Macintosh experience. In this chapter, you look at the File and Edit menus.

I try to provide an appropriate level of detail based on the menu item's importance. Trust me here. In earlier editions of this book, I said that Mac OS 7.*x*'s Label menu was dumb; apparently Apple agrees because that menu is gone from Mac OS 8 and later. (The old Label menu's functions are available in Mac OS 9 from either the File menu or contextual menus.)

Anyway, I start with a few menu basics and then move on to the first two menus on your screen: File and Edit. In Chapter 5, you get the lowdown on the View, Special, Help, Application, and more about context-sensitive menus (mentioned briefly in Chapter 3). Because the Apple menu is so long and so important, it gets its own chapter, Chapter 6.

Menu Basics

Mac menus are often referred to as *pull-down menus*. That's because, to use them, you click their names to make the menus appear, and then pull (drag) down to select an item. Piece of cake, eh?

Ever since Mac OS 8, the menus now stay down after you click their names. They stay down until you either select an item or click outside the menu's boundaries. They also close if you click and hold on a menu for too long — about 15 seconds — without doing anything. Nice touch, eh?

Command performance

Many menu items have ⌘-key shortcuts after their names. These key combinations indicate that you can activate the menu items without using the mouse by pressing the ⌘ key and then pressing another key without releasing the ⌘ key. It pays to memorize the shortcuts you use often.

It's elliptical

Another feature of Mac menus is the ellipsis after a menu item's name. Ellipses, in case your English teacher forgot to mention them, are the three little dots (...) that appear after certain menu items' names. According to the Bible (actually, *The Chicago Manual of Style,* but for writers, it may as well be the Bible), "Any omission of a word or phrase, line, or paragraph . . . must be indicated by ellipsis points (dots). . . ."

Apple is true to this definition. Ellipsis points in a menu item mean that choosing the item will display a dialog box in which you can make further choices. Choosing a menu item with an ellipsis never actually makes anything happen other than opening a dialog box, where you make further choices and then click a button to make things happen.

Dialog box featurettes

Dialog boxes may contain a number of standard Macintosh features such as radio buttons, pop-up menus, text entry boxes, and check boxes. You see these features again and again in dialog boxes, control panels, and elsewhere. So take a moment to look at each of these featurettes while I demonstrate how they're used.

Radio, radio (buttons)

Radio buttons are called radio buttons because, like the buttons on your car radio (assuming you have a very old car), only one can be pushed at a time. Radio buttons always appear in groups of two or more; when you push one, all the others are automatically unpushed. I think eggheads call this setup *mutually exclusive.* Take a look at Figure 4-1 for an example of radio buttons.

Figure 4-1:
A group
of radio
buttons.

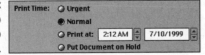

In Figure 4-1, Normal is currently selected. If you click the radio button for Urgent, Print at, or Put Document on Hold, Normal is deactivated.

Menus redux pop-up style

Pop-up menus are called pop-up menus because that's what they do: They pop up after you click them. You can always tell a pop-up menu because it appears in a slightly rounded rectangle and has a double-arrow on its right. Figure 4-2 shows a pop-up menu before you click it and the same menu after you click it and hold down the mouse button.

Figure 4-2:
Pre-pop-up
and post-
pop-up.

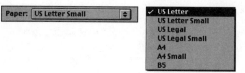

Okay, so now you've looked at two features, radio buttons and pop-up menus, and they both do the same thing: They enable you to make a single selection from a group of options. Sometimes a radio button is associated with a text entry box, which happens to be the feature I cover next.

Championship boxing text entry style

Text entry boxes (sometimes called *fields*) enable you to enter text (including numbers) from the keyboard. When a text entry box appears with a radio button, the text entry box or boxes matter only if the associated radio button is pressed. Take a look at Figure 4-3. You can enter text in the two text entry boxes next to the From radio button, but if you click the All radio button, your text disappears. Conversely, if you click in one of the text entry boxes and type, the From radio button automatically becomes selected.

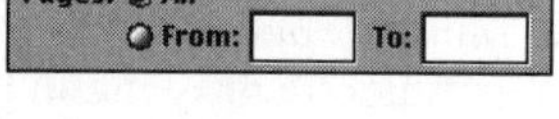

Figure 4-3:
Type letters
or numbers
in text entry
boxes.

Pages: ● All
○ From: [   ] To: [   ]

Had Apple chosen to use a pop-up menu instead of radio buttons in the Figure 4-3 example, the menu would have taken up more valuable screen real estate. So that's the reason for two featurettes that do the same thing.

And now you know how to use both.

Checkmate

The last featurette you see frequently is the check box. Check boxes are used to choose items that are not mutually exclusive. In a group of check boxes, you can turn each one on or off individually. Check boxes are on when they contain a check mark and off when they're empty. Figure 4-4 shows five check boxes, three of which are on.

Figure 4-4:
In this
example,
three out
of five
boxes are
checked.

> **Image & Text:**
> ☑ Substitute Fonts
> ☑ Smooth Text
> ☑ Smooth Graphics
> ☐ Precision Bitmap Alignment
> ☐ Unlimited Downloadable Fonts

Unlike radio buttons, which force you to choose one and only one item, check boxes are independent. Each one can be either on or off.

Here's a nifty and undocumented shortcut: You can usually activate check boxes and radio buttons by clicking their names (instead of the buttons or boxes). Didn't know that, did you?

File Management and More: Meet the File Menu

The File menu (shown in Figure 4-5) contains commands that enable you to manipulate your files and folders.

Menu items that can be used to act upon the item or items selected (the Documents folder in Figure 4-5) in the active window (or on the desktop) appear in black and are currently available. Menu items not available at the current time are displayed in gray. You cannot select a gray menu item.

In this example, only four items are disabled — Print, Put Away, Encrypt, and Show Original. The Print and Encrypt commands appear dimmed because you can print or encrypt only documents, not folders, and the selected item in the active window is a folder (Documents). The Put Away command is dimmed because you can put away only items that reside outside windows on the desktop itself. The Show Original command is dimmed because it works only if the selected item is an alias. (I cover aliases a little later in this chapter.) The rest of the commands appear in black and are valid selections at this time.

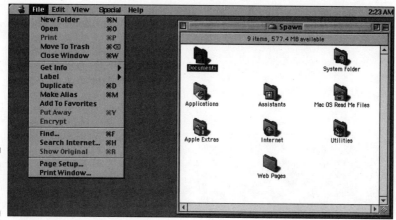

Figure 4-5:
The File
menu.

New Folder (⌘+N)

File⇨New Folder creates a new, untitled folder in the active window. If no
window is active, it creates a new folder on the desktop.

You probably do a lot of new-folder making, so it might be a good idea to
memorize this command's keyboard shortcut, ⌘+N. It comes in handy later
because most software programs use the ⌘+N shortcut to create a new document, another thing you do a lot of.

If your memory is bad, use this mnemonic device: *N* is for *New.*

Most menu items, or at least most common ones, have keyboard shortcuts that
have a mnemonic relationship to their names. For example, New is ⌘+N, Open
is ⌘+O, Get Info is ⌘+I, and Make Alias is ⌘+M (which is good news because in
earlier versions of the Mac OS, you had no keyboard shortcut for Make Alias).

Open (⌘+O)

The File⇨Open command opens the selected item. Not much more to say,
except to remind you that, in addition to the menu command and its shortcut
⌘+O, a double-click also opens any icon.

Print (⌘+P)

The File⇨Print command, which prints the selected item, is active only if the
selected icon is a document. Furthermore, it works only if you have the

application that created the document on your hard disk. If you try to print (or open) a document when you don't have the application that created it, you see a dialog box like the one in Figure 4-6.

Figure 4-6:
What might
happen if
you try to
print or
open a doc-
ument when
you don't
have the
application
that
created it.

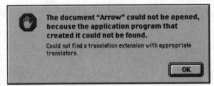

Notice the word *translators* in the message in Figure 4-6? I talk about translators when I discuss Macintosh Easy Open in Chapter 14. For now, leave it at this: If you select a document icon and then use the Open or Print command, the command works only if you have the application that created the document or another application that is capable of opening that type of document.

That's what translators do (refer to Figure 4-6 again). Many programs can open files created by another program, but only if the right translator is available. I'll save the details for later.

Move to Trash (⌘+Delete)

The File⇨Move to Trash command, new to Mac OS 8 and later and long needed, moves the selected icon to the Trash. Don't forget that the icon (that is, the item the icon represents) is not deleted from your hard disk until you choose the Empty Trash command from either the Special or contextual menu.

Close Window (⌘+W)

The File⇨Close Window command closes the active window. Don't forget, if you hold down the Option key before you click the File menu, the Close Window command changes to Close All.

You can read all about this command in Chapter 2, so let's move on.

Get Info (⌘+I)

When you select any icon and choose the File⇨Get Info command (or use its keyboard shortcut ⌘+I), a Get Info window opens, as shown in Figure 4-7.

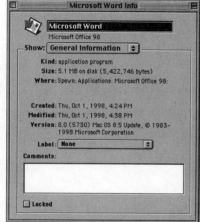

Figure 4-7:
A typical
Get Info
window
for an
application
(Microsoft
Word, in this
case).

The top portion of the window provides details about the icon, such as what it is (application, document, disk, folder, and so on), how big it is (in this case, 5.1 megabytes, which equals 5,422,746 bytes), where it is on the disk (in this example, Spawn: Applications: Microsoft Office 98), when it was created (October 1, 1998), when it was last modified (also October 1, 1998), and its version number (8.0 (5730) Mac OS 8.5 Update).

The bottom part is called the Comments box because that's where you type your comments about the icon. In earlier versions of Mac OS, these comments would disappear whenever you rebuilt your desktop or restored it from a backup. And, as I discuss in Appendix B, you should rebuild your desktop and back up your hard disk on a regular basis.

Since Mac OS 7.6, an icon's comments do survive rebuilding the desktop. The comments don't always survive restoration from backup, so use them at your own risk.

Near the top of the dialog box is the Show pop-up menu. In the figure, Show is set to General Information, so that's what the dialog box displays. The two other Show options are Memory and Sharing. Memory deals with the application's memory requirements. This stuff gets a little complicated, so I don't go into it here. (If you just can't wait, skip ahead to my dandy and easy-to-understand explanation in Chapter 11.) Sharing deals with file sharing, which you find out about in Chapter 10.

Artistic icons

The Get Info dialog box serves another more frivolous but fun function — it enables you to change any icon's picture to anything you like.

Don't like the Mac's folder icon? Give it a new one. Here's how: Find an icon you like, such as a guitar. Select it and choose the Get Info command. Now select the folder that you want to give the guitar icon to (for convenience, call it Boring Folder) and open its Get Info window. In the upper-left corner of the guitar icon's Get Info dialog box, you see the guitar picture.

Click the guitar. A box appears around the guitar icon indicating that it's now selected. Choose Edit⇨Copy.

Now click the Boring Folder icon in its Get Info window and choose Edit⇨Paste. The results of this last step are shown in the figure.

There you go! This technique works on any icon — disk, folder, application, or document. And if you can't find an icon you like, you can create a picture in any graphics program, select it, choose Edit⇨Copy, and then paste it into the Get Info dialog box of any icon. Furthermore, online services such as America Online as well as Macintosh user groups and the Internet offer humongous collections of icons for your pasting pleasure.

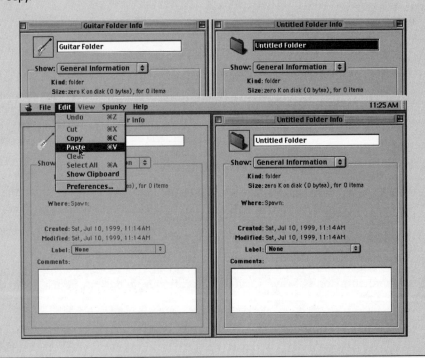

The last item in an application's Get Info dialog box is the Locked check box. When an application is locked, you can't change its name and you can't empty it from the Trash. (I mention locked files and the Trash briefly in Chapter 2.)

If you try to empty the Trash when a locked item's in it, you see a message telling you to hold down the Option key before you choose Special➪ Empty Trash. Holding down the Option key when you choose Empty Trash empties the Trash even if locked items are in it.

While I'm on the subject, do you hate the dialog box you see each time you try to empty the Trash? (You know, the one that reads: "The Trash contains X items. It uses X K of disk space. Are you sure you want to permanently remove it?") If you never want to see this pain-in-the-bottom dialog box again, select the Trash icon, invoke the Get Info command (⌘+I), and uncheck the Warn before Emptying check box.

Documents, folders, and disks each have slightly different Get Info dialog boxes. Folders and disks can't be locked by merely clicking a check box (see the following tip); documents and applications can.

Folders and disks can be locked. You just have to do it within the Sharing portion of the Get Info window by checking the option titled Can't Move, Rename, or Delete This Item (Locked).

Sharing enables you to decide who can share your files. So much can be said about Macintosh File Sharing that I could write an entire chapter about it. And in fact, I have. If you're interested, take a look at Chapter 10.

Label

Maybe it's just me, but I've never really gone much for the Label feature. And I hardly know anyone who uses it diligently, which is the only way it's useful. Anyway, the Label submenu, which looks a lot neater in color than it does in Figure 4-8, enables you to organize your files yet another way — by label.

To apply a label to an icon, select it and then choose the appropriate label from the Label submenu, as shown in Figure 4-8. Again, labels are more useful on a color screen, as they tint the icon the appropriate color. You can also choose a label from a pop-up menu in the icon's Get Info dialog box.

Because the Find command can search by label, you have reason to use labels. Still, unless you're very organized and remember to label every file (which, unfortunately, you must do in the Finder, not when you save from within an application, when it might actually be useful), labels aren't much use.

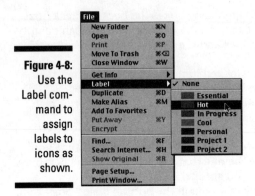

Figure 4-8:
Use the
Label com-
mand to
assign
labels to
icons as
shown.

The Dilemma: On one hand, several users (well, actually just two) took the time to write me and say they found labels useful. On the other hand, thousands of people didn't. On the other hand (that is, if you have three hands), severely obsessive, compulsive, or anal-retentive Mac users can have hours of pleasure assigning those pretty labels to their icons.

So labels: Yea or Nay? It's your call.

You can change the names and colors of your labels by using the Finder's Preferences dialog box, which I discuss in just a few pages (because it lives in the Edit menu, which is coming up really soon).

Duplicate (⌘+D)

File⇨Duplicate duplicates the selected icon. More precisely, it makes a copy of the selected icon, adds the word *copy* to its name, and places the copy in the same window as the original icon. Figure 4-9 shows the results of using the Duplicate command.

You may use the Duplicate command on any icon except a disk icon.

Figure 4-9:
The
Duplicate
command in
action.

Make Alias (⌘+M)

Aliases are a wonderful, fabulous organizational tool introduced with System 7. An *alias* is a tiny file that automatically opens its parent file. To create an alias for any icon, select the icon (the parent), and then choose File⇨Make Alias or press ⌘+M.

(By the way, you can also make an alias by ⌘+Option-dragging an icon, or you can Control-click an icon and choose the Make Alias command from the contextual menu that appears. Contextual menus, which are very cool, are covered in Chapter 5.)

When you open an alias, the parent opens.

An alias is different from a duplicated file. For example, my word processor, Microsoft Word 98, uses 5.1 megabytes of disk space. If I duplicated it, I would have two files, each using 5+ megabytes of disk space. An alias of Microsoft Word, on the other hand, uses a mere 3K.

Due to a variety of complicated and unimportant reasons having to do with sector size and hard disk size, your mileage may vary depending on the size of your hard disk. In general, the smaller the disk, the smaller the aliases will be.

When you make an alias, it has the same icon as its parent, but its name appears in italic type and the suffix *alias* is tacked onto its name. A tiny arrow also appears on its icon. Figure 4-10 shows an alias and its parent icon.

That tiny arrow is called a *badge*.

Figure 4-10:
An alias
icon and its
parent.

You can put aliases in convenient places such as the desktop or the Apple Menu Items folder (so that they appear in your Apple menu). You can also use the Add to Favorites command to automatically create an alias and place it in the Favorites folder so that it appears in the Apple menu (see the following section).

Aliases can help organize your Macintosh existence in at least a dozen ways, and I talk about all of them in Chapter 8.

Add to Favorites

The File⇨Add to Favorites command creates an alias of the selected item and puts it in the Favorites folder. Thereafter, it appears in the Apple menu's Favorites submenu.

Put Away (⌘+Y)

Choose File⇨Put Away to move the selected icon from your desktop to the window it was in before you moved it to the desktop. This command works even if it has been years since the icon was moved to the desktop and you don't remember which folder it came from.

The Put Away command is active only when an icon on the desktop is selected; it appears dimmed whenever any icon in a window is selected. Put Away appears dimmed also when the Trash icon is selected.

The Put Away command ejects a floppy or other removable disk and removes its ghost icon from the desktop. In other words, Put Away has the same effect on a removable disk as dragging its icon to the Trash does.

Encrypt

The Encrypt command works only with documents, so it appears dimmed on the File menu unless you click a document before you choose it. Encrypt allows you to password-protect a file quickly and easily. Just select the file, choose Encrypt from the File menu, and enter a password for your file.

If this is the first file you've encrypted — which is pretty likely if you're bothering to read this — you'll be asked whether or not you want to create a keychain. A *keychain* is a hidden file that stores passwords to encrypted files and other stuff you want to protect from prying eyes. When you create the keychain, you'll be asked to name it and give it a password. All those passwords won't do you much good if anyone can rifle through your keychain, now will they?

Find (⌘+F)

Use the File⇨Find command when you need to find an icon on your hard disk and you can't remember where you put it. This command is a Mac OS 9 feature that really kicks earlier versions' butts. It even has a new name: Sherlock 2.

You have three ways to invoke Sherlock 2 (here I go again with the ways):

✔ **Way #1:** Choose File⇨Find.

✔ **Way #2:** Use the keyboard shortcut ⌘+F.

✔ **Way #3:** Choose Apple⇨Sherlock 2.

Whichever way you choose, the next thing you see is the Sherlock 2 dialog box, as shown in Figure 4-11.

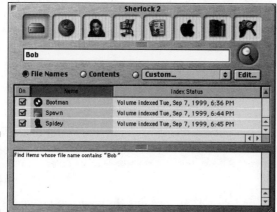

Figure 4-11:
The
Sherlock 2
dialog box.

First make sure the hard disk button at the top of the window — the leftmost one — is clicked. Then, in the field just below it, type the name of the file that you're looking for (Nanci in Figure 4-12), and then click the Find button or press the Return key. In a flash, you see every file on the disk you searched that matches the word you typed in the text entry box (see Figure 4-12).

In Figure 4-12, you can see that several items on my hard disk (Spawn) contain the word Nanci.

After I found all these files, I selected the one I wanted — nanci1.GIF. At this point, I have three ways to open the file:

✔ **Way #1:** Choose File⇨Open Item.

✔ **Way #2:** Use the keyboard shortcut ⌘+O.

✔ **Way #3:** Double-click the file in the top or bottom part of the Sherlock 2 window.

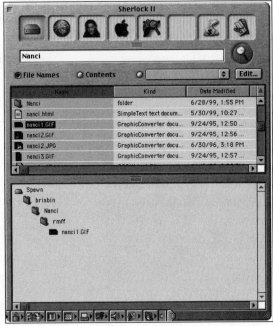

Figure 4-12:
Sherlock 2
showing the
items it
found.

If you prefer to open the folder that contains the item, you have three ways to do that:

✔ **Way #1:** Choose File➪Open Enclosing Folder.

✔ **Way #2:** Use the keyboard shortcut ⌘+E.

✔ **Way #3:** Double-click the folder in the bottom part of the Sherlock 2 window.

If searching by name alone finds too many files, you can narrow your search by clicking the Edit button in the Sherlock 2 dialog box and adding one or more additional criteria for the search. These criteria include the following: Size of file, Kind of file (application, alias, and so on), Label (see the Label menu section, earlier in this chapter), Creation Date (date the file was created), Modification Date (date the file was last saved), Version Number (is or is not a particular number), Lock Attribute (file is locked or is not), Folder Attribute (empty, shared, or mounted), File Type code, and Creator Type code.

Figure 4-13 shows the More Search Options dialog box that appears when you click the Edit button.

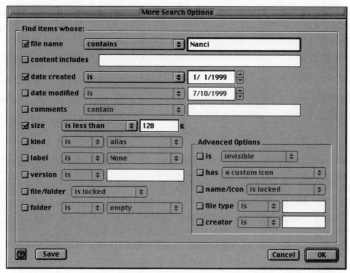

Figure 4-13:
The search finds only files that have *Nanci* in their name, were created before 1/1/99, and are smaller than 128K.

In addition to searching by file name and attributes, Sherlock 2 includes lots of other ways to find stuff by content and through the Internet.

Clicking the Contents option in the Sherlock 2 dialog box enables you to search for words within documents. So, for example, if you're looking for a letter that you wrote containing the phrase "You are a scumsucking dog," you can search for the word *scumsucking* in every document on your hard disk (or disks). You do need to index your disk before using this feature, but doing so is an easy (albeit slow) process. To index your disk, choose Find⇨ Index Volumes, click the disk you want to index, and click the Create Index button.

Because indexing takes a long time, you can schedule it to take place while you're not around. Click the Create Index button and then place a check mark next to the volume (that is, the disk) that you want to schedule for indexing. Now just click the Schedule button and choose a convenient time and day for the indexing to take place. Presto. As long as your Mac is on at that time, it creates the index automatically without any intervention from you.

If that process seems too complicated or you want to index your disk right this second, just click the Index Volumes button, click the volume (disk) that you want to index, and then click the Create Index button. Now go out for coffee.

The second nifty find feature in Sherlock 2 is the capability to search the Internet in a variety of ways. The large icons at the top of the Sherlock 2 dialog box perform different types of online searches. You can search the whole World Wide Web or just part of it. Sherlock 2's pointers lead to people-finder databases and Apple Web sites, as well as miscellaneous, entertainment, money, and news sites. Assuming that you have an available

Internet connection (see Chapter 17), the Sherlock 2 dialog box connects to the Internet, searches all the engines that you check under the various icons in the Sherlock 2 dialog box, and returns the results, along with summaries, in a new window — all without launching a browser. It's fast, it's fun, and it's one of Mac OS 9's most useful features.

And, unfortunately, in addition to whatever it is you're looking for, each search also brings you a scad of intrusive advertising that can't be turned off. Boo. Hiss.

I need to use another weasel-out here. I could write an entire chapter about using the new Sherlock 2 features, but one of the rules we ...*For Dummies* authors must follow is that our books can't run 1,000 pages long. So I'm going to give you the next best thing: Open the Help Center (by choosing Help⇨ Help Center from the menu bar) and search for the word *Find*. Searching for that term provides you with the information you need to get the most out of the new, improved Find command. It's almost as good as reading it here.

The Clipboard

Essential to your understanding of the Mac and essential to your understanding of the Edit menu is an understanding of the concept of the Macintosh Clipboard. In one sentence, the *Clipboard* is a holding area for the last thing you cut or copied. A *thing* can be text, a picture, a portion of a picture, an object in a drawing program, a column of numbers in a spreadsheet, or just about anything that can be selected. In other words, the Clipboard is the Mac's temporary storage area.

As a storage area, the Clipboard's contents are temporary. Very temporary. When you cut or copy an item, that item remains on the Clipboard only until you cut or copy something else. Then the Clipboard's contents are replaced by the new item, which remains on the Clipboard until you cut or copy something else. And so it goes.

To place the item that's on the Clipboard somewhere else, click where you want the item to go and then paste. Pasting does not remove the item from the Clipboard; the item remains there until another item is cut or copied.

Almost all programs have an Edit menu and use the Macintosh Clipboard properly, which means that you can usually cut or copy something in a document in one program and paste it into a document from another program. Usually.

The Clipboard commands in the Edit menu are relatively intelligent. If the currently selected item can be cut or copied, the Cut and Copy commands in the Edit menu are enabled. If the selected item can't be cut or copied, the commands are unavailable and appear dimmed. And when nothing is selected, the Cut, Copy, Paste, and Clear commands are dimmed.

The contents of the Clipboard don't survive a restart, a shut down, or a system error or crash, so when your Mac comes back to life, the Clipboard will be empty.

Search Internet (⌘+H)

So you wanna look for something on the Web, eh? The File⇨Search Internet command opens Sherlock 2's Internet window. Saves you a click, anyhow. Figure 4-14 shows the search engines you can choose from. Choose one or more of them by clicking the check boxes. When you select a search engine, keep in mind what you're searching for. There's not much point in searching CNET's Download.com, for example, for Web sites where you can buy cookware.

Most of the search engines included here are good choices for general searches. You could search all of them at once, if you wanted to. But that might be overkill if you're looking for something commonplace on the Web, like, oh, let's see, Web sites devoted to the Macintosh.

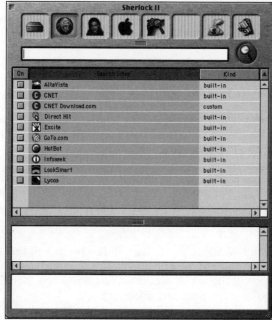

Figure 4-14: Choose a search engine or two and away you go.

If you're looking for something specific, try clicking one of the large icons at the top of the Sherlock 2 dialog box. The money icon, for example, includes search engines that are much more likely than the general search engines under Internet to turn up a hot stock tip. And the Apple Web site has lots of additional Sherlock 2 plug-ins to add new search capabilities to your Mac.

Show Original (⌘+R)

File⇨Show Original works only on aliases. Select any alias icon and then choose this command to reveal the parent file of the selected alias.

Page Setup

Choosing File⇨Page Setup opens the Page Setup dialog box, which is where you specify the type of paper in your printer (letter, legal, envelope, and so on), the page orientation (longways or wideways), and the scaling (100 percent = full size).

In addition to the command here in the Finder, you also can find a Page Setup command in almost every program you use. I devote a whole chapter to printing (Chapter 9, to be exact), so I'm leaving this topic alone here. (That's also why I didn't waste space here on a screen shot.)

Print Desktop/Print Window

The Print Desktop/Print Window command is a little tricky. If no windows are active, the command is called Print Desktop. If a window is active, the command's name changes to Print Window.

If you choose File⇨Print Desktop, your Mac prints a picture of your desktop, with its icons and Trash (but not the menu bar), exactly as you see them on-screen. This image generally requires two or more pieces of paper — unless you use the handy scale box in the Page Setup dialog box (see Chapter 9).

If you choose File⇨Print Window, your Mac prints a picture of the active window, showing all the icons it contains, even if you would need to scroll to see the icons on-screen. If the window contains a lot of icons, printing this document could require more than one sheet of paper.

And if a document is selected when you choose the Print command, the application that created the document launches automatically, and you see a Print dialog box. (Printing is covered in full and loving detail in Chapter 9, which is why no screen shot of this one appears either.)

The Edit Menu (Which Shoulda Been Called the Clipboard Menu)

In contrast to the File menu, which has commands that mostly deal with file management and are exclusive to the Finder, the Edit menu's commands and functions are available in almost every Macintosh program ever made (see Figure 4-15).

Because almost every program has an Edit menu and because almost every program uses the same keyboard shortcuts on its Edit menu, it behooves you to know these keyboard shortcuts by heart, even if you remember no others.

The Edit menu should have been called the Clipboard menu because most of its commands deal with the Macintosh Clipboard.

If you read the little sidebar about the Clipboard, you found out 75 percent of what you need to know about the Edit menu. Still, because IDG's paying me to be thorough, and because the Finder's Edit menu has a few commands that aren't Clipboard-related, I go through the Edit menu's commands one by one.

Undo (⌘+Z)

Undo is a great command! You're gonna love it. Undo undoes the last thing you did. Try it:

1. **Create a new folder in any window or on the desktop.**

   It's called *untitled folder*.

2. **Change the name *untitled folder* to *Undo Me*.**

3. **Without clicking anywhere else or doing anything else, choose Edit⇨ Undo or use the keyboard shortcut ⌘+Z.**

   The folder's name should magically undo itself and change back to *untitled folder*.

Neat, huh? Don't forget about this command 'cause it can be a lifesaver. Almost every program has one.

Now for the bad news: The Undo command is ephemeral, like the Clipboard. It undoes only your last action, and as soon as you do something else, you lose the ability to undo the original action. To see what I mean, repeat the exercise and change *untitled folder* to *Undo Me*. But this time, click another icon before you undo. What's that, you say? The Undo command appears grayed and isn't available anymore? I told you. When you clicked the other icon, you forfeited your chance to use Undo.

Unfortunately, Undo doesn't work with actions such as moving icons or copying files. In fact, as you find out more about using your Mac, you discover lots of actions that you can't undo. Still, Undo is a great command when it's available, and I urge you to get in the habit of trying it often.

Incidentally, the Undo command toggles (that is, switches back and forth) between the new and old states as long as you don't do anything else. So in the first example, if you chose Edit⇨Undo again without clicking anywhere else, the name would transform back to *Undo Me*. And if you chose Edit⇨ Undo again, it would change back to *untitled folder*. You can continue to undo and redo until you click somewhere else.

Cut (⌘+X)

The Edit⇨Cut command removes the selected item and places it on the Clipboard. Follow these steps to see this command in action:

1. **Create an untitled folder.**

2. **Select only the word *untitled*.**

    The word *untitled* should be black or colored with white letters; *folder* should be white with black letters.

3. **Choose Edit⇨Cut, or use the keyboard shortcut ⌘+X.**

    The word *untitled* disappears from the folder's name. Where did it go? You cut it! It's removed from the folder and is now waiting on the Clipboard.

You can, of course, use the Undo command at this point to make *untitled* reappear, as long as you haven't clicked anything else.

Show Clipboard

I know I'm not covering the commands in the order that they appear on the Edit menu, but there's a method to my madness. If you don't believe that the word *untitled,* which you cut in the previous section, is on the Clipboard, choose Edit⇨Show Clipboard. A window appears, telling you the type of item (text, picture, sound, and so on) on the Clipboard and displaying it if it can be displayed (see Figure 4-16).

Figure 4-16:
The Show
Clipboard
command
displays the
current con-
tents of the
Clipboard.

Here's another way to display the Clipboard's contents: Open the Clipboard icon in your System Folder. Because some programs don't have a Show Clipboard command, it's convenient to make an alias of the Clipboard file and put the alias in your Apple Menu Items folder so that it appears in your Apple menu. (Don't panic. I talk about the Apple menu in Chapter 6.) Then, even if you're in a program that doesn't have a Show Clipboard command, you can select the Clipboard alias from the Apple menu. This technique saves you two steps; without it you would need to first go back to the Finder and then choose Edit⇨Show Clipboard. Choosing the Clipboard alias from the Apple menu does both steps automatically.

Copy (⌘+C)

Edit⇨Copy makes a copy of the selected item and places it on the Clipboard. The original is not removed, as it is when you cut. Try it. Select your System Folder and choose Edit⇨Copy or use the keyboard shortcut ⌘+C. Now choose Edit⇨Show Clipboard. The Clipboard contains the text *System Folder*.

It's that simple.

Paste (⌘+V)

You've been cutting and copying but not doing much with the stuff on the Clipboard except looking at it to make sure that it's really there. Now, to use what you cut or copied, you need Edit⇨Paste. Do as follows:

1. **Create a new folder.**

2. **Change the folder's name to *Elvis Costello*.**

3. **Copy the word *Elvis* to the Clipboard.**

   (C'mon, you know how.)

4. **Create another new folder and select its name, which should be *Untitled Folder* if you've been following my instructions.**

5. **Choose Edit⇨Paste.**

   The new folder is now called *Elvis*. Pasting doesn't purge the contents of the Clipboard. Don't believe me? Choose Edit⇨Show Clipboard to confirm that Elvis is still alive and well and on the Clipboard.

Which is where he stays until you cut, copy, crash (the three Cs of Macintosh computing), restart, or shut down.

Clear

Edit⇨Clear deletes the selected item without involving the Clipboard. It works the same as pressing the Delete key on your keyboard. Use it when you want to make something disappear forever.

Clear can usually be undone as long as you haven't done anything else such as click, type, save, or use a menu.

Select All (⌘+A)

Edit⇨Select All selects all. If a window is active, Select All selects every icon in the window, regardless of whether you can see them. If no window is active, Select All selects every icon on the desktop.

Go ahead and try it a few times. I can wait.

Select All has nothing whatsoever to do with the Clipboard. So why is it on the Edit menu? Who knows? It just is and always has been.

Preferences

The Preferences item in the Edit menu combines a bunch of items (as shown in Figure 4-17) formerly found in the Views and Labels control panels, both of which were discontinued in Mac OS 8. You also get a few nifty new features that you meet in a second.

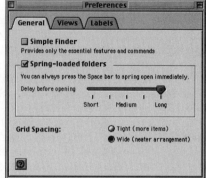

Figure 4-17:
The General
tab of the
Finder's
Preferences
dialog box.

Here's a quick tutorial of the Finder Preferences window.

General tab

Click the General tab at the top of the Preferences dialog box to access the following three features:

- Simple Finder
- Spring-Loaded Folders
- Grid Spacing

The Simple Finder check box emasculates your Mac and makes it harder to use by removing a lot of useful commands from its menus (see Figure 4-18).

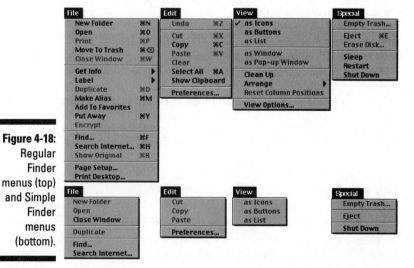

Figure 4-18:
Regular
Finder
menus (top)
and Simple
Finder
menus
(bottom).

Simple Finder is recommended only for absolute rank novices. As you can see in Figure 4-18, Simple Finder hides many useful menu items, such as Move To Trash and Make Alias, and thereby (at least in my humble opinion) reduces the usefulness of your Mac. If you have young children or old parents, this setting might be useful, but if your gray matter functions normally, just say no to the Simple Finder choice. In other words, unless you're computerphobic, don't bother with the Simple Finder for yourself.

The second feature on the General tab is the option for spring-loaded folders. This feature is turned on or off with a check box. *Spring-loaded folders* are a nifty feature that pops folders open when you hold an icon over them. They are opened only until you release the mouse button. Then they close automatically.

This option is easier to demonstrate than write about, so follow along with the following if you want to see a neat Finder feature in action:

1. **On the General tab of the Preferences dialog box, click to select the Spring-Loaded Folders check box.**

2. **Set the Delay Before Opening slider to Short.**

3. **Close the Preferences window.**

4. **In the Finder, click any icon and drag it on top of any folder that contains at least two subfolders — but don't release the mouse button yet.**

   The folder you've dragged the icon onto should spring open.

5. **Move the icon over one of the subfolders inside the original folder — but don't release the mouse button yet.**

   That folder springs open. If you were to release the mouse button right now, the original icon you clicked would be deposited in this subfolder.

6. **Move the icon so that it's not over any windows or folder icons.**

   Folders that have sprung open spring closed after you move the icon away from them.

In other words, spring-loaded folders let you move or copy an item deep into your folder hierarchy by automatically opening and closing folders for you with absolutely no double-clicking. Play around with this feature for a while and you'll wonder how you ever got along without it.

The third and last feature found on the General tab is Grid Spacing, which deals with an invisible grid that the Finder maintains for your convenience. The invisible grid is available only in icon views (which I cover in Chapter 5). Here in the Finder Preferences dialog box, you can choose from only Tight or Wide spacing.

TIP

The invisible grid can be turned on or off on a folder-by-folder basis using the View Options window (also explained in Chapter 5). Furthermore, if you have the grid turned off in View Options, hold down the ⌘ key when you drag any item to have it snap to the invisible grid. Alternatively, if you have the grid turned on in View Options, hold down the ⌘ key to temporarily disable the invisible grid and move the icon anywhere you like.

Views tab

Click the Views tab to set the Standard Views for your folders. These settings govern all folders unless you use View Options to customize the view of a specific folder. In other words, the settings you make in this tab become the default settings for all folders.

Because I explain these options in Chapter 5, I'll skip over them here. Just remember that the settings you make in the Preferences window apply to all folders except the ones that you changed using View Options.

Labels tab

The options on the Labels tab enable you to change the names and colors of the labels in the File menu's Label submenu.

To change the name associated with a label, double-click its name in the Finder Preferences window and type a new one. To change a label's color, click directly on the color itself and a Color Picker window appears (see Figure 4-19).

Figure 4-19:
A Color
Picker
window
appears
after you
click a color
in the Labels
tab of the
Finder
Preferences
dialog box.

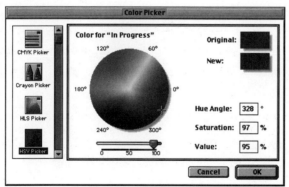

I know that all the colors in the Color Picker look gray in the picture, but on a color monitor, they're in color — I promise. To select a new color, just click the color wheel or change any or all of the Hue Angle, Saturation, and Value settings.

TIP

Color Pickers are a little hard to explain, but basically, they're just different windows that enable you to choose a color. The left side of the Color Picker window enables you to choose from six different types of Color Pickers. I generally use the HSV (hue, saturation, value) Picker shown in Figure 4-19, mostly because I consider it the easiest to use. But Apple now provides many other ways for you to choose colors. I recommend you play with all of them a little. Just click a Color Picker — Crayon Picker, CMYK Picker, and so on — on the left side of the window, and then play with the resulting controls on the right side of the window to choose a color.

Whee!

Chapter 5

Delectable Menus, Volume II

● ●

In This Chapter

▶ The View menu

▶ The Special menu

▶ Help and the Help menu

▶ The Application menu

▶ Contextual menus

● ●

*T*his is the middle stretch of our little menu trilogy. In Chapter 4, you find out what menus are and how they work and also meet the File and Edit menus. Here, you meet the rest of your menus: View, Special, Help, Application, and Contextual. In Chapter 6, you finish off the menu thing by exploring the powerful and timesaving features of your Apple menu.

A View from a Window: The View Menu

The View menu affects the icons in the active window or, if no window is active, it affects the icons on the desktop. The similar settings found in the Finder Preferences dialog box govern all windows except the ones that you use the View menu to modify.

The first two parts of the View menu have to do with what the icons and windows look like; the third part of the View menu has to do with how icons and windows are arranged and sorted.

The first part: As icons, as buttons, or as a list

Viewing by icon is the "Macintosh" view, the one most closely associated with the Macintosh experience. It's also, in my humble opinion, one of the two least useful views because those big horsey icons take up far too much valuable screen real estate. And, as you'll see in a minute, list view offers a nifty navigational extra and saves space as well.

The window in Figure 5-1 uses the icon view.

Figure 5-1:
My hard disk window, viewed as icons. Pretty, and very Mac-like, but a total waste of perfectly good screen real estate.

In all fairness, I must say that many perfectly happy Macintosh users love the icon view and refuse to even consider anything else. Fine. But as the number of files on your hard disk increases (as it does for every Mac user), screen real estate becomes more and more valuable.

By the way, if you like the icon view, they now make monitors as big as 21 inches.

Many users prefer the small icon view for their desktops. To change the desktop view, close all Finder windows, choose View⇨View Options, and click the small icon's radio button. This will make all the icons on your desktop — your hard disk, Sherlock 2, Mail, and so on — about half their present size.

The button view (shown in Figure 5-2) is no better and wastes just as much screen space as those blocky big icons. The biggest difference is that buttons require only a single-click to open them (as opposed to the double-click that opens normal icons).

Finally, the view I love and use most, the list view (shown in Figure 5-3). The only thing the icon and button views have over the list view is the capability to arrange the icons anywhere you like within the window. Big deal.

Figure 5-2:
The same
window,
viewed as
buttons.

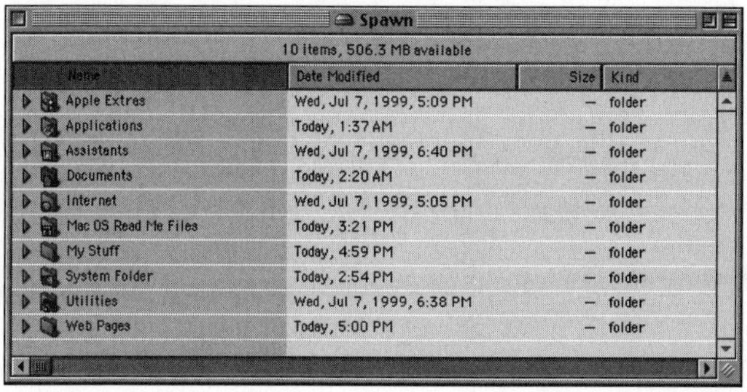

Figure 5-3:
The same
window,
viewed as a
list.

The triangles

In list view, folder icons have a little triangle to the left of their names. This is the outline metaphor, and it's available only in list view. You click the triangle to reveal the folder's contents right there in the same window.

I think that this is a much better way to get to an icon buried three or four folders deep than clicking through the folders themselves. Figure 5-4 shows the slow and tedious way of getting to the icon named NoseBlows Ch01.Nose Runs. Figure 5-5 shows the cool, savvy, and efficient way of getting to the same icon.

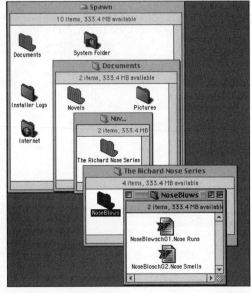

Figure 5-4:
Getting the
document
NoseBlows
Ch01.Nose
Runs the
usual way
by opening
windows.

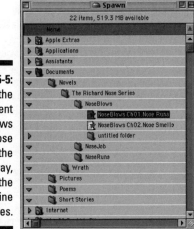

Figure 5-5:
Getting the
document
NoseBlows
Ch01.Nose
Runs the
fast way,
using the
outline
triangles.

In Figure 5-4, I had to double-click four folders to get to NoseBlows Ch01.Nose
Runs. When I got to it, I had four windows open on the desktop. In Figure 5-5,
I had to single-click four triangles to get to NoseBlows Ch01.Nose Runs. When
I got to it, only one window was open, keeping my desktop neat and tidy.

Easy copying and moving

The triangles-outline metaphor has other advantages. First and foremost, you can copy or move items from separate folders in one move, as Figure 5-6 illustrates.

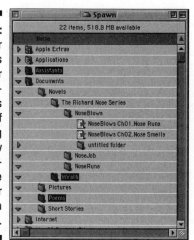

Figure 5-6: Moving or copying files from two or more separate folders is easy if you're using the list view (but impossible in the icon or button view).

In the list view, you can copy or move items from different folders with a single motion, without opening multiple windows. In either of the icon views, on the other hand, moving files from two or more different folders requires opening several windows and two separate drags.

Another feature of the triangles appears when you hold down the Option key and click a triangle. This action reveals all subfolders to the deepest level (see Figures 5-7 and 5-8).

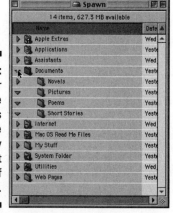

Figure 5-7: A regular click on the Documents triangle reveals only the next level of folders.

Figure 5-8:
An Option-
click on the
Documents
triangle
expands all
subfolders.

The bottom line is that almost all my windows are displayed in list view by name. And I almost always use the triangles to reveal the contents of folders, and rarely have more than a few windows open at one time.

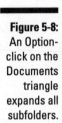

The View Options command, which I talk about in a moment, offers additional controls and enables you to choose stuff such as the size of the icons and which columns appear in list view. If you feel adventurous, go ahead and play with it a little now.

You can move among icons also by using the keyboard. If a window is active, make sure that no icons are selected and then type the first letter of a file's name. Regardless of which view you chose, the first icon that starts with that letter is selected. To move to the next icon alphabetically, press the Tab key. To move to the previous icon alphabetically, press Shift+Tab.

If no window is active, typing a letter selects the first icon on the desktop that starts with that letter. The Tab and Shift+Tab commands work the same with desktop icons as they do with icons in a window.

If you have many icons that start with the same letter, you can type more than one letter (for example, type *sys* to select the System Folder, even if you have folders called Stuff and Slime in the same window).

The second part: As window or as pop-up window

The second part of the View menu enables you to choose between regular old windows and nifty new pop-up windows, which enable you to arrange frequently used windows at the bottom of your screen for quick access (see Figure 5-9).

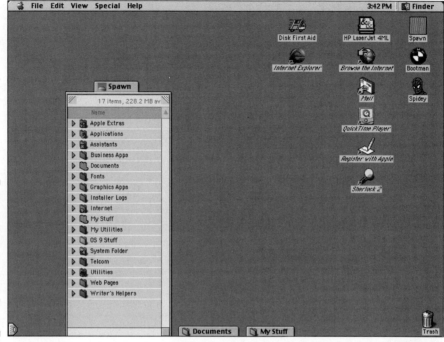

Figure 5-9:
I have three
pop-up
windows:
Spawn
(open),
Documents,
and My
Stuff.

You can create a pop-up window by dragging any window's title bar to the bottom of the screen. When it's all the way to the bottom of your screen, it automatically turns into a pop-up.

To open a pop-up window, click its name at the bottom of your screen; to shrink it back down, click its name again. When you open one pop-up window, any other open pop-up window closes automatically (but regular windows remain open).

You can drag any icon onto the name of a pop-up window at the bottom of your screen; the pop-up window will scroll open, revealing its contents.

Pop-up windows are a nifty new feature introduced in Mac OS 8. I recommend that you play with them a little now and decide whether they suit your work style. (I still haven't decided; I fluctuate between using them and not.)

The third part: Keeping things orderly

These last few commands on the View menu help you keep your stuff in order.

Clean Up

The Clean Up command aligns icons to the invisible grid; you use it to keep your windows and desktop neat and tidy. (If you like this invisible grid, don't forget that you can turn it on or off for the desktop and individual windows by using View Options.)

Clean Up is available only in icon views or when no windows are active. If no windows are active, the command instead cleans up your desktop.

If you're like me, you have taken great pains to place icons carefully in specific places on your desktop. Cleaning up your desktop destroys all your beautiful work and moves all your perfectly arranged icons.

Arrange

The command beneath Clean Up says Arrange (see Figure 5-10) if you're viewing icons. To see what it says when you're viewing a list, hold your horses until you get to the up-next "Sort List" section.

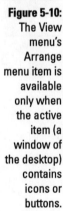

Figure 5-10:
The View menu's Arrange menu item is available only when the active item (a window of the desktop) contains icons or buttons.

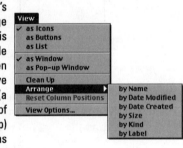

I'm going to talk about Arrange first. All Arrange options magically rearrange the icons in the active window (or on the desktop if no windows are open or active) in the following way:

- ✔ By alphabetical order — Arrange by Name
- ✔ With the most recently modified icon at top left and the icon modified longest ago at bottom right — Arrange by Date Modified
- ✔ With the most recently created icon at top left and the icon created longest ago at bottom right — Arrange by Date Created

✔ In descending order by size, with the largest item at top left and the smallest item at bottom right — Arrange by Size (Size, of course, referring to how much disk space the icon uses on your hard disk.)

✔ Applications in alphabetical order, documents in alphabetical order, and then folders in alphabetical order, from top left to bottom right — Arrange by Kind

✔ In the order in which labels appear in the File menu's Labels submenu, with icons in each label group arranged alphabetically — Arrange by Label

Use the Arrange by Date Modified view for folders with lots of documents in them. That way, the ones you use most recently are listed first. If that gets confusing, you can easily switch to the list view for a second to find things alphabetically.

Sort List

If you're viewing a window containing a list, the command beneath Clean Up says Sort List, as shown in Figure 5-11.

Figure 5-11:
If the active window contains a list (instead of icons or buttons), you can use the Sort List Command instead of Arrange.

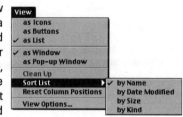

As you may expect, these items sort the contents of the active window.

Here's a shortcut for changing between sorting orders in list views. Notice how the appropriate column title is highlighted in Figure 5-12 — that is, how Name is dark and Date Modified, Size, and Kind are not? This highlight tells you which list view is in use.

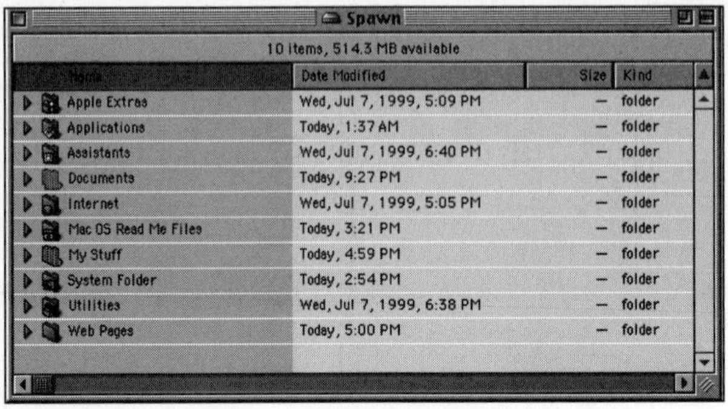

Figure 5-12:
This window
is sorted by
name, as
evidenced
by the word
Name high-
lighted at
the top of
the window.

Now for the shortcut: You don't need to use the Sort List submenu to switch between list views. Instead, just click directly on the column title, and the window's view changes. Go ahead, give it a try. The only proviso is that you must be in a list view in the first place (the column titles don't appear in icon views). In Figure 5-13, I've clicked the Date Modified column; the window is now sorted with the most recently modified items on top.

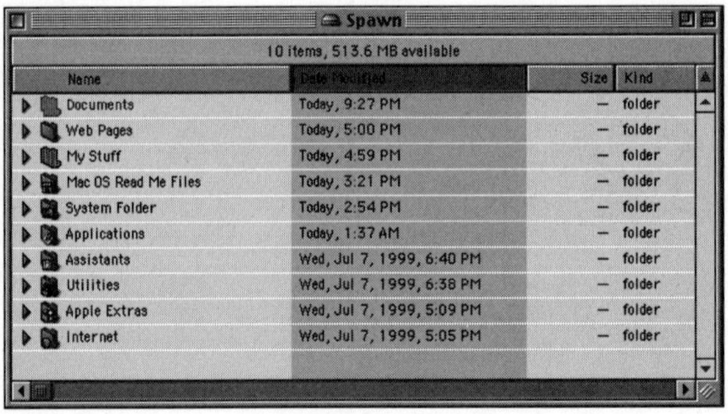

Figure 5-13:
I've clicked
Date
Modified at
the top of
the window.
As a result,
this window
is now
sorted with
the most
recently
modified
items at
the top of
the list.

In other words, clicking the title of the column is the same as using the Sort List submenu, only faster and easier.

Reset Column Positions

You don't know this, but you can change the order in which columns appear by clicking the title of the column and then dragging it to a new position. The only rule is that the Name column always appears first. Go ahead and try it. I can wait. . . .

The reason I give you this information here and now is that the Reset Column Positions command is a sort of Undo for changes you make in this manner. So if you move the columns around and decide that you don't like the new arrangement, you can use this command to put them back the way they were.

To make the columns narrower or wider, click between the headings. Just move the cursor over the little line between columns in the headings. The cursor changes shape to indicate it's in resize mode. Cool beans! Go ahead and try it. I can wait. . . .

View Options

The View Options command applies to the active window. If no window is active, it applies to the desktop. If icons or buttons are active when you choose View Options, you see a window like the one in Figure 5-14. If a window using list view is active, you instead see a window like that shown in Figure 5-15.

Figure 5-14:
View Options for icon or button views.

In View Options for icons and buttons (see Figure 5-14), choosing None for your icon arrangement turns off the invisible grid. Choosing Always Snap To Grid turns it on. And choosing Keep Arranged forces the Finder to constantly clean up the window according to the criteria you choose from the pop-up menu (by Name in Figure 5-14).

The Icon Size control enables you to choose between small and large icons.

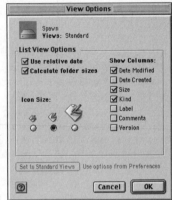

In View Options for lists (see Figure 5-15), different controls are available. The Use Relative Date option intelligently substitutes *yesterday* and *today* for numerical dates. Calculate Folder Sizes does just what its name implies — it enables you to see how much stuff is in each folder when you look at it in list view. The Show Columns check boxes govern which columns appear in the active window.

If you set your clock back a day and look at files you updated that day, before setting your clock back, the relative date will read *tomorrow*. Curious but true.

Finally, the Icon Size control enables you to choose between small, medium, and large icons in your lists. For my money, I think the smallest ones make windows appear noticeably faster; your mileage may vary.

If you have the Calculate Folder Sizes option turned on in View Options, the icons (including folder icons) in the active window are sorted in descending order from biggest to smallest when you sort by size.

If you don't have Calculate Folder Sizes turned on, icons other than folders are sorted by size, with all folders — regardless of their size — appearing at the bottom of the list.

Although sorting by folder size might seem convenient, I recommend that you keep this option turned off because I believe that Calculate Folder Sizes makes the Finder a bit sluggish. If you really need to know how big a folder is, select it and use the File⇨Get Info command (the keyboard shortcut is ⌘+I).

Finally, if you want your viewing options to apply to all folders, use the Finder Preferences dialog box. Conversely, if you want them to apply only to the active window, use View Options.

Something Special in the Menu Bar

The Special menu is a repository for a group of unrelated functions that don't fit in any of the other menus: cleaning up (rearranging) icons; emptying the trash; erasing and ejecting disks; and the Restart, Shut Down, and Sleep commands, to be precise.

Interestingly, only the Eject Disk command has a keyboard shortcut. One explanation might be that you wouldn't want to accidentally erase a disk or restart or shut down your Mac with something as easy to do as pressing the wrong key combination.

Empty Trash

I talk about the Trash in Chapter 2. And I talk about it in Chapter 4 when I show you the Get Info dialog box.

I've said it before and I'll say it again: Use this command with a modicum of caution. After a file is trashed and emptied, it's gone. (Okay, maybe Norton Utilities can bring it back, but don't bet the farm on it.)

Eject Disk and Erase Disk

See Chapter 3 for more information than you need on ejecting and erasing disks.

Sleep

The Sleep command puts your Mac and monitor into a state of suspended animation complete with lower power consumption. Waking up from sleep mode is much faster than restarting. You can control when your Mac goes to sleep automatically with the Energy Saver control panel, discussed in Chapter 14.

Restart

The Restart command shuts down your Mac briefly and then starts it back up. Why do you need such a thing? Every so often, Macs act wonky. By *wonky*, I mean that things don't seem to work right. You can't launch a program that used to launch fine. You can't rename an icon. You can't use the keyboard. Or something. That's when to use Restart.

You may also need to restart after installing certain types of new software, though most installer programs these days offer their own built-in Restart buttons if a restart is required.

You see, computer problems often disappear when you clear the computer's memory, which is one of the things that occurs when you restart.

One of the best pieces of advice I give people when they call me in a panic is to restart their Macs and try it again. At least half the time, the problem goes away and never comes back after restarting. I'm a little paranoid about things going wrong, so I often restart my computer in the middle of the day, just in case something is about to go wrong. It couldn't hurt.

Sometimes when your Mac gets really wonky, you may be unable to choose Special⇨Restart for one reason or another. If you can't because the cursor won't move or for any other reason, try pressing ⌘+Option+Escape. If things aren't too messed up, you should see a dialog box asking whether you're sure you want to force the current application to quit. You do. Your Mac is so wonked that you had to resort to the ⌘+Option+Escape technique, so click the Force Quit button. If it works, the current application (or the Finder) quits. If you're in the Finder, it relaunches itself automatically. You lose any unsaved changes in the application that you quit, but you might regain the use of your Mac. If you do, immediately save any documents you have open in other applications and restart. The Force Quit command leaves your Mac in an unstable state, and you should always restart as soon as possible after using it. After, of course, saving any unsaved documents.

If that trick doesn't work, try pressing both the ⌘ and Control (Ctrl) keys while you press the PowerOn key (the one with the little left-pointing triangle on it). This technique forces your Mac to restart. Unfortunately, it doesn't work all the time or on all Macintosh models.

If ⌘+Control+Power On doesn't work for you, look for the reset and interrupt switches on the front or side of your Mac and press the reset switch, which is the one with a triangle. This technique also forces your Mac to restart. Unfortunately, not all Macs have these switches.

If you're still having problems and still can't choose Special⇨Restart, turn off the power by using the power switch and leave your Mac off for at least ten seconds before you try to restart it.

Special note to iMac owners: Most of the preceding won't work on your computer. Because of the way the USB keyboard works, the keystrokes in the preceding paragraphs rarely work on an iMac. If your iMac is crashed, hung, or you are otherwise unable to restart or shut down, poke a straightened-out paper clip into the reset hole inside the little door on the right side of your iMac. (It's the little hole near the modem port, denoted by a tiny triangle.)

Shut Down

Shutting down is the last thing you do at the end of every session at your Mac. When you've finished using the machine, choose Special⇨Shut Down or press the Power On key and click the Shut Down button that appears.

Because I rag on endlessly in Chapter 1 about how important the Shut Down command is, I'm not going to do it again.

Use it or lose it.

Not Just a Beatles Movie: Help and the Help Menu

One of the best features about all Macs since System 7 is the excellent online help. And Mac OS 9 has online help in abundance.

Balloon Help is still available, but Mac OS Help goes it one (actually, a few) better.

Help Center

Choose Help⇨Help Center to open the Help Viewer.

Show Balloons

The Help⇨Show Balloons command turns on Balloon Help. When Balloon Help is on, pointing at almost any item on the screen causes a little help balloon to pop up and describe the item (as shown in Figure 5-16).

Figure 5-16:
Balloon
Help in
action.

After you choose Show Balloons, the command in the Help menu changes to Hide Balloons until you choose it again, at which time the command changes back to Show Balloons. And so on.

I rarely use Balloon Help myself, but if you're relatively new to the Mac, you might find it helpful. Most applications include Balloon Help, so don't forget that you can turn on balloons in programs as well as in the Finder and most Apple-supplied programs.

Mac OS Help (⌘+?)

In the beginning, little help was built into the Mac. In fact, before System 7, you had none. System 7 introduced Balloon Help, and it was good. Well, actually, it was kind of lame, and few developers implemented it at first, but it was better than nothing.

After most software started including Balloon Help, Apple raised the bar in System 7.5 with Apple Guide, an interactive step-by-step guidance system for accomplishing tasks on your Mac. But developers didn't cotton to it, so Apple Guide was replaced yet again with an HTML-based help system (that is, one that was created the same way you would create a Web page) called Mac OS Help.

Having Mac OS Help is like having a consultant at your side. But nothing opens your eyes quite like a demonstration, so here's how to have your new assistant, Mac OS Help, answer a question for you:

1. **Choose Help⇨Mac Help (or use ⌘+?).**

   The Mac OS Help window appears.

2. **Click the little button that looks like a house, and then click <u>Mac OS Help</u> (unless you want help with AppleScript, in which case you choose <u>AppleScript Help</u>).**

   (You can find more information about AppleScript in Chapter 15.) The Mac OS Help window appears, ready for use, as shown in Figure 5-17.

3. **In the list on the left, click any item.**

   I clicked the one marked <u>Shortcuts and tips</u>. A list of topics magically appears on the right, as shown in Figure 5-18.

4. **Click any item on the right to find out more about it.**

   That's it. You're finished.

5. **Close Mac OS Help.**

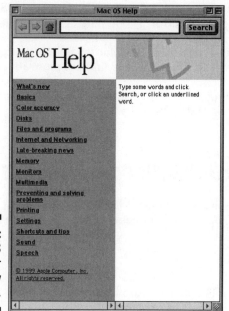

Figure 5-17:
Mac OS Help — your new assistant.

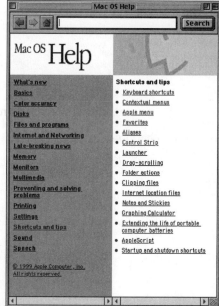

Figure 5-18:
A list of shortcuts and tips.

You can also type a word into the little box at the top of the Mac OS Help window, and then click the Search button to find help on a particular topic.

About the only thing you need to know to use Mac OS Help is that <u>underlined items</u> are hot links. Click any underlined item to find out more about the item.

Mac OS Help is an excellent resource, especially for those of you who are new to the Mac. I urge you to explore it further at your leisure.

Apply Yourself: The Application Menu

Last but not least is the Application menu (at least for menus in the menu bar; I talk about contextual menus in a moment). It's the one in the upper-right corner. Because all the functions in the Application menu are related, I'm going to skip describing its commands one at a time and try to convey the gestalt of the menu instead.

If the Finder is the active application, the Application menu displays a little Mac OS icon and the word *Finder,* as shown in Figure 5-19.

Figure 5-19:
The
Application
menu when
you're in the
Finder.

`11:04 PM` `Finder`

If another application is currently active, a little version of that application's icon (and its name) appears in the Application menu instead (see Figure 5-20).

Figure 5-20:
The
Application
menu when
you're in
Microsoft
Word.

`11:06 PM` `Microsoft Word`

The Application menu enables you to choose which program you want to use. As with windows, only one application is active at a time. Because Mac OS 9 enables you to open more than one application at a time (if you have enough RAM), the Application menu is one of the ways to switch between all currently running applications and the Finder. (I discuss the other methods near the end of this section.)

If a program is running, its name appears in the Application menu, and the Finder's name always appears in the menu. In Figure 5-21, I have two programs running in addition to the Finder: Microsoft Word and Adobe Photoshop.

Figure 5-21:
The
Application
menu itself.

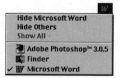

If the Finder is currently active and you want to switch to Microsoft Word, choose its name in the Application menu. Microsoft Word's menus appear in the menu bar, and if a document is open or you have an untitled new document, its window becomes the active window.

To switch back to the Finder, you choose Finder in the Application menu. Piece of cake, right?

Wrong. When you switch back to the Finder, Microsoft Word's document window may obscure items on the desktop. Finder windows aren't a problem — they float to the front. But icons on the desktop may be covered.

This situation is where the Hide and Show commands come into play. You can switch back to Microsoft Word and quit that program, but you have an easier way to free up desktop real estate. Choose Hide Others from the Application menu, and the Microsoft Word windows and toolbars are hidden from view. Microsoft Word is still running, but its window or windows and toolbars are hidden from view.

To make Microsoft Word visible again, choose Show All from the Application menu.

Open any application and play around with the Hide and Show commands on the Application menu. They're easier to understand after you play with them a little.

In Mac OS 8.5, Apple added the capability to tear off the Application menu and have it appear as a floating window. To tear off the menu and place it elsewhere on-screen, click the menu. Then, while still holding down the mouse button, move the cursor to the middle of the screen. The menu tears off and becomes a floating window, as shown in Figure 5-22. This window is always the frontmost window and is available regardless of which program you're currently using.

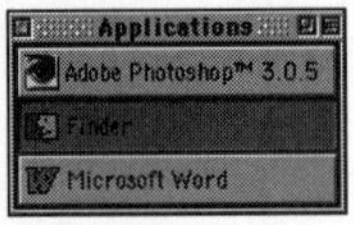

Figure 5-22:
The Application menu turns into a window after being torn off.

Here's a hot tip for you if you like Hide and Show. The Option key does three cool things:

✔ If you hold down Option when you choose an application from the Application menu, the current application will be hidden after the application switch occurs.

✔ If you hold down Option when you click an application in the tear-off Application menu, the current application will be hidden after the application switch occurs.

✔ If you hold down Option and click any window from another application, the current application will be hidden after the application switch occurs.

They're Sooo Sensitive: Contextual Menus

Context-sensitive menus are a neat new feature introduced in Mac OS 8. A contextual menu lists commands that apply to the item the cursor is over. Contextual menus appear in windows, on icons, and most places on the desktop when you hold down the Control key and click (see Figure 5-23).

If you click inside a window but not on any icon, the contextual menu contains actions you perform on a window. Notice how a contextual menu for a document differs from the contextual menu for a window (refer to Figure 5-23). That's why they call 'em *contextual*. Actions appear in contextual menus only if they make sense for the item you Control-click.

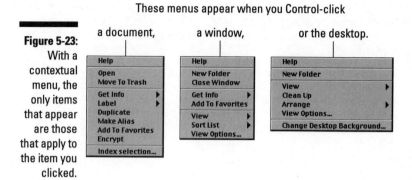

These menus appear when you Control-click

a document,   a window,   or the desktop.

Figure 5-23:
With a
contextual
menu, the
only items
that appear
are those
that apply to
the item you
clicked.

Don't believe me? Control-click the desktop (that is, click somewhere that's not in any window and not on any icon) and you see a contextual menu with different commands (and shown in Figure 5-23 as well).

Get in the habit of Control-clicking items. Before you know it, using contextual menus will become second nature to you.

Chapter 6

Polishing the Apple (Menu)

The Apple menu makes its appearance when you click the little Apple logo, an apple with a bite taken out of it, that graces the upper-left corner of your screen. The Apple menu gets its own chapter because, unlike the other menus, it's entirely configurable by you, the user. This menu embodies one of the finest features of the Mac — the capability to create your own customized file-launching and folder-accessing environment.

Mac OS 9, like all versions since 7.5, supports hierarchical submenus, which power users have loved in the form of Now Software's NowMenus and other similar programs for years. Finally, everyone else can see what the power-user elite has been raving about for so long. Submenus in the Apple menu are fantastic!

I show you the basics of configuring your Apple menu in this chapter, but I'm telling you in advance: For the really cool tricks, check out Chapter 13.

Before I talk about how to customize your Apple menu, I describe the stuff that's already in it: desk accessories, miniprograms (Key Caps, Calculator, and so on) that Apple thoughtfully included, and several special folders. I also show you how to use essential and useful desk accessories such as the Scrapbook and the Chooser, so don't think that all desk accessories are lame. Only most of them are.

Oh, and one last thing: At the end of this chapter, I let you in on a deep, dark secret that you probably figured out already.

About This Computer (Yours)

Before we do anything, let me tell you a bit about the Apple menu's only permanent item, About This Computer.

The first item on every Apple menu (at least if the Finder is the active application) is the About This Computer command. Take a peek at it from time to time — it tells you how much memory (RAM) is currently being used, how much of it is real RAM (random access memory) and how much of it is virtual memory, which programs are using it, and how much is left for programs yet to be launched. Those are good things to know. The command also tells you what version of the System software is running.

In Figure 6-1, you can see that my System software is using 18.3MB of RAM.

Figure 6-1:
A wealth of information about this computer.

18.3MB of RAM is a lot for System software. But I'm running all the options Mac OS 9 has to offer — QuickDraw 3D, QuickTime VR, File Sharing, AppleScript — the whole shebang. In Chapter 16, I show you how to turn this stuff off (or get rid of it completely) and give you advice on when you can safely do so. For now, just accept that your System software probably uses somewhat less RAM than mine does.

In Figure 6-1, the Stickies application is using 468K, and SimpleText is using 580K. The bar to the right of each program's name is especially meaningful. The right part of each bar reflects the amount of memory the program has grabbed (and corresponds to the number just to the left of the bar). The highlighted part of the bar shows how much of that memory the program is using at the moment. My System software looks like it's using all its allocation; SimpleText looks like it's using half. Stickies seems to be using about one-third.

What? You aren't willing to accept "about one-third" as an answer? Sigh. Okay. To find out exactly how much RAM Stickies is using, choose Help⇨ Show Balloons, and then point at the bar for Stickies. What you ought to see is shown in Figure 6-2.

Figure 6-2:
Stickies is
using
exactly 124K
of RAM.
Okay, so it's
a little under
one-third.

Why is the information in the About This Computer window important? First, you can see how much RAM is left (the Largest Unused Block) for launching additional programs. I have approximately 93 megabytes (wow!), but I have a lot of RAM (112MB of real RAM, plus 1 additional megabyte of virtual memory). If you try to launch a program that requires more RAM than the Largest Unused Block at any given time, your Mac politely informs you that it doesn't have enough memory to launch this program.

The other thing that's important is that I can see how SimpleText gobbled up 580K when I launched it, but it's using only 128K of its allocation at this time. (I found that out by using the Balloon Help tip.) So it's not using about 450K of precious RAM.

What can I do about it? Well, I can tell SimpleText to grab less RAM next time I launch it. Here's how:

Oops. Almost forgot. If SimpleText is open, quit before performing the following procedure. An application can't be running when you adjust its Preferred Memory Size.

1. **Select the SimpleText icon.**

2. **Choose File⇨Get Info, or use the keyboard shortcut ⌘+I.**

   The SimpleText Info window appears, as shown in Figure 6-3.

3. **From the Show pop-up menu, choose Memory.**

4. **Change the Preferred Size from 512K to a smaller number, somewhere between the Minimum and Suggested Size.**

   When I say "a smaller number," it's not because I don't want to tell you what number to use. I don't know the size of the documents you open with SimpleText, and that's what determines how much RAM it needs. Try 256K. If you someday discover that you can't open a document due to low memory (your Mac tells you so), increase this number a bit — to 384K or even 450K. You'll still save a little over the old setting of 512K.

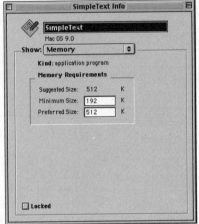

Figure 6-3:
Reduce the
Preferred
Size from
512 to
a lower
number (but
not lower
than the
Minimum
Size
above it).

5. Close the Info window.

The change doesn't take effect until the window closes.

Don't perform the preceding procedure haphazardly. Most programs run better with their preferred memory set higher than the suggested size. But (and it's a big but) if you're short on RAM for other programs and you can see that a program is using only a fraction of the RAM it requests, you can probably reduce its preferred size at least a little and maybe a lot.

From the Desk (Accessories) Of . . .

You use items in the Apple menu the same way you use any menu item — click the Apple and drag down to the item. After you release the mouse button, the item opens. If the item is a folder, it has a submenu; you can see its contents by dragging down until the folder is highlighted, and then stopping. Don't release the mouse button, or the folder pops open. To choose an item in the submenu, drag to the right.

If you haven't modified your Apple menu, it probably looks something like the one in Figure 6-4.

Ignoring the folders for now (I talk about them after I ridicule a few desk accessories), take a look at each desk accessory in turn.

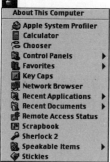

Figure 6-4:
A standard
issue, uncon-
figured,
fresh-from-
the-installer
Apple menu.

Technically, only a few of the items in the Apple menu are desk accessories (known affectionately as DAs), special types of miniprograms that are a little different from regular applications and are a holdover from System 6 and earlier. The rest of the menu items are regular old applications. Even so, most people refer to the programs Apple sticks under the Apple menu as desk accessories, and so do I. Desk accessories are basically miniapplications, and they're discussed further along with control panels and extensions in Chapter 14.

Profile THIS: Apple System Profiler

Apple System Profiler is a little program that gives you information about your Mac. What a concept. If you're curious about things such as what processor your Mac has or what devices are currently connected to it, give the Profiler a try. Poke around the Select menu and check it out; this little puppy is benign and won't hurt anything.

If you ever have occasion to call for technical support for your Mac, software, or peripherals, you're probably going to be asked to provide information from Apple System Profiler. So don't get rid of it just because you don't care about this kind of stuff.

A calculated risk: Calculator

The Calculator has been in the Apple menu as long as I can remember, and it hasn't changed one iota since it was introduced. (All right, it got a spiffy new icon when System 7 arrived, but that's the extent of it.) Figure 6-5 shows what the ol' Calculator (still) looks like.

Figure 6-5: The humble, and less-than-versatile Calculator DA.

The Calculator DA is the pixel (for picture element, the little dots that make up your screen) equivalent of the cheesy calculators that cheap companies give away — or the kind you see at the grocery store for $1.99. The Apple Calculator does have one feature that makes it different from all those Wal-Mart specials: Cheap calculators don't require a four-figure investment in computer equipment.

I'm kidding, of course. Although it's looking a little long in the tooth (Hey, Apple — how about a facelift for the old fellow? Maybe some pastel colors? More graceful looking buttons? A paper tape? And a Clear Entry button instead of only Clear All?), it still comes in handy more often than you might expect. For example, my wife used it to balance our checkbook for years (until she got hooked on Quicken).

The Calculator DA works just like a real calculator. Use the numeric keypad on your keyboard; the keys correlate to their on-screen counterparts.

Unfortunately, the Calculator lacks all but the most basic features. As noted, it doesn't have a paper tape, a Clear Entry key, or even a single memory recall. There are shareware and commercial calculators galore, with features galore. If you need a calculator DA, almost anything you can buy or download is better than the Calculator DA that comes with Mac OS 9.

Be a Chooser user

The Chooser is a desk accessory that enables you to choose at least two things: which printer to use and which computer(s) to share files with.

If you click a printer icon on the left side of the window, all the printers available on the network appear in a list on the right side of the window (see Figure 6-6).

The Chooser is also where you choose other Macs to share files with. If you click the AppleShare icon on the left side of the Chooser, every Mac on your network that has file sharing turned on appears in the list on the right.

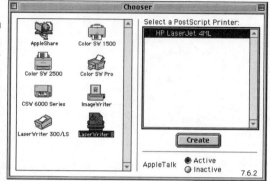

Figure 6-6:
The Chooser
lets you
choose
printers and
networked
computers
for file
sharing.

Finally, the Chooser is also where you create desktop printer icons.

You can read an entire chapter on printing (Chapter 9) and yet another one about file sharing (Chapter 10), so you've found out enough about the Chooser here.

The key to all your fonts: It's Key Caps

Want to know what every character in a font looks like? Or where the funny optional characters such as ´, ®, ©, æ, and ™ are hidden on your keyboard? Sounds like a job for Key Caps, a modest little desk accessory that shows you a lot about your installed fonts.

If you're not sure what a font is, choose Apple⇨Key Caps. The items in the Key Caps menu are your fonts. When you pull down the Key Caps menu you see a list of your installed fonts. To see what a particular font looks like, choose it in the Key Caps menu and type a few words. They appear in the white text entry box at the top of the Key Caps window. If you want to see what those words look like in another font, choose that font from the Key Caps menu.

Of course, you could do the same thing in any program that has a font menu. In fact, you can do more because Key Caps displays the font only in a single size, 12 points; other programs enable you to change the size as well as the font, and you can also apply character styles such as bold, italic, and outline.

So what good is Key Caps? It's the easiest way to find special symbols. Just open Key Caps, choose a font, and hold down the Option key. Key Caps displays the special symbols and characters on the keyboard. For example, to type ™ in your document, hold down the Option key and press the 2 key on your keyboard. Instant ™. You see something like Figure 6-7.

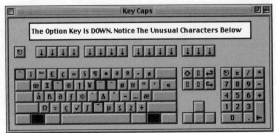

Figure 6-7:
The Key
Caps DA
shows you
all the cute
characters
in your fonts.

What Key Caps doesn't show you is how to create diacritical marks such as acute accents and umlauts. To type them, follow these instructions:

✔ To type a grave accent (`` ` ``), press Option+`` ` `` and then type the character. So to accent an e, you press Option+`` ` `` and then type e. It comes out looking like this: è. (The `` ` `` key is usually in the top row to the left of the 1 key.)

✔ To type an acute accent (´), press Option+e and then type the character. So to accent an e, you press Option+e and then type e. It comes out looking like this: é.

✔ To type a circumflex (^), press Option+i and then type the character. So to put a circumflex over an i, you press Option+i and then type i. It comes out looking like this: î.

✔ To type a tilde (~), press Option+n and then type the character. So to put a tilde over an n, you press Option+n and then type n. It comes out looking like this: ñ. I'm pretty sure that the n is the only character you can put a tilde over; I tried to put it over other characters, but they came out looking like this: ~b.

✔ To type an umlaut (¨), press Option+u and then type the character. So to put an umlaut over a u, you press Option+u and then type u. It comes out looking like this: ü, as in Motley Crüe.

Browse yer local area net with Network Browser

If your Mac is on a local area network, you can view a list of available network servers using the Network Browser in your Apple menu. You can also use the Network Browser to connect to listed servers and create a list of favorite servers for quick access.

If you want to know more about Network Browser, open Mac OS Help and search for Network Browser. You find a ton of interesting stuff that I don't have room for here.

Remote Access Status

Remote Access Status is a component of ARA (Apple Remote Access). See Chapter 10 for more.

The not-so-scrappy Scrapbook

You can use the Scrapbook to store graphics, text, QuickTime movies, and sounds. The Scrapbook uses an item metaphor for its pages. You move from item to item by using the scroll bar in the lower part of the Scrapbook window (see Figure 6-8).

Figure 6-8:
The Scrapbook is a repository for graphics, sounds, and text. You control it with the Cut, Copy, Paste, and Clear commands.

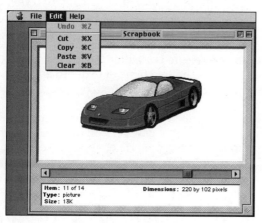

To put something into the Scrapbook, copy it to the Clipboard; then open the Scrapbook and choose Edit⇨Paste or use the keyboard shortcut ⌘+V. The pasted item becomes the item before the current item. So if you're looking at item 1 when you paste, the pasted item becomes item 1, and the former item 1 becomes item 2, and so on.

You can also drag and drop items — such as selected text in a document, a movie, or a picture — into the Scrapbook. Open the Scrapbook and drag the item onto the Scrapbook window.

Here are the various ways that you can use the Scrapbook:

 ✔ To remove an item from the Scrapbook and use it elsewhere, choose Edit⇨Cut or use the keyboard shortcut ⌘+X. This action removes the current item from the Scrapbook and places it on the Clipboard for pasting into another document.

✔ To use a Scrapbook item in another document without deleting it, choose Edit➪Copy or the keyboard shortcut ⌘+C. Then open a document and choose Edit➪Paste.

✔ To delete a Scrapbook item forever, choose Edit➪Clear or use the keyboard shortcut ⌘+B. Doing so deletes the item from the Scrapbook without placing it on the Clipboard.

You can't always paste a picture or sound into a document. The determining factor is the type of document you're trying to paste into. For example, you can't paste a picture into cells in spreadsheets or most fields in databases. And you usually can't paste a sound into a graphics file.

If you try to paste an inappropriate item into a document, your Mac either beeps at you or does nothing. If nothing happens when you paste, assume that the document can't accept the picture or sound you're trying to paste.

You can paste text into the Scrapbook, but it's probably easier to paste it into Stickies where you can select only a portion of it or edit it. After text is pasted into the Scrapbook, it can't be selected or edited, so if you want to change it, you'll have to copy and paste the entire chunk of text into an application that supports text editing (such as Stickies, SimpleText, or a word processor).

If you want to replace the old version of an item in the Scrapbook with a changed version, you have to copy the new version to the Clipboard and then paste it into the Scrapbook. Don't forget to delete the old version by scrolling until it appears and choosing Edit➪Clear (⌘+B).

Finder of lost files: Sherlock 2 (again)

Choosing Apple➪Sherlock 2 from the menu bar is the same as choosing File➪ Find in the Finder. The only advantage the Sherlock 2 DA has is that, because it's in the Apple menu, you can choose it even if the Finder isn't currently the active application. To find out how Sherlock 2 works, check out Chapter 4.

Don't be stuck up: Use Stickies

Stickies, which were new in System 7.5, are electronic Post-It Notes for your Mac. They're a convenient place to jot notes or phone numbers. Stickies are shown in Figure 6-9.

Stickies are supremely flexible. They can be moved around on-screen (just drag 'em by the title bar). They can display text in any font you desire. They can be collapsed by Option-clicking their grow boxes. They can be any color you like (if you have a color monitor, of course). You can import and export text files. And you can print Stickies.

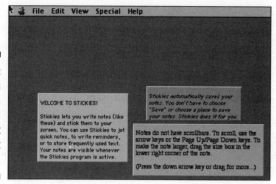

Anything you type on a Sticky is automatically saved as long as you keep that note open. But when you close a note (by clicking its close box, choosing File⇨Close, or using the keyboard shortcut ⌘+W), you lose its contents forever. Fortunately, Stickies gives you a warning and a second chance to save the note in a separate file on your hard disk.

If you like to live dangerously, you can turn the warning off by choosing Edit⇨ Preferences and unchecking the Confirm Window-Closing option. In the Preferences dialog box, you can also tell Stickies to save all notes every time you switch to another application (safer), set the zoom box so that it collapses the window without the Option key, and set whether Stickies should launch automatically at startup (if you check this item, Stickies creates an alias of itself and puts it in your Startup Items folder).

Those Interestingly Named Folders in the Apple Menu

A handful of folders in your Apple menu are spread out amongst the desk accessories. You may see little triangles to the right of their names (if you don't, I'll show you how to turn them on in a minute). A triangle indicates that the folder has a submenu; it will reveal its contents when you pull down the Apple menu and drag the cursor onto it. Submenus are a newish feature, introduced with System 7.5, though commercial programs such as ActionMenus and shareware programs such as MenuChoice have provided this functionality since the early days of System 7.

To select an item in the submenu, drag to the right and highlight it, as shown in Figure 6-10.

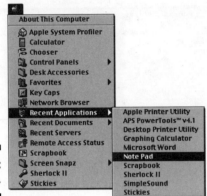

Figure 6-10:
A submenu.

To choose Note Pad (more on this little program later in this chapter) in the Recent Applications folder (refer to Figure 6-10), click the Apple, drag down until the Recent Applications folder is highlighted, drag to the right and down until Note Pad is highlighted, and then release the mouse button.

If you don't see the little triangles to the right of your folders, here's how to turn them on:

1. **Choose Apple⇨Control Panels.**

2. **Open the Apple Menu Options control panel.**

3. **Click the On option, as shown in Figure 6-11.**

Now that you know how submenus work, I'm going to talk about the folders you may see in your Apple menu.

What's a control panel, anyway?

Control panels are little programs that you use to adjust and configure your Mac. Each one has one or two specific functions — set the Mac clock (Date & Time), change menu blinking (General Controls), configure memory (Memory), adjust the mouse (Mouse) and keyboard (Keyboard), and so on.

Control panels go in the Control Panels folder inside your System Folder. The Installer automatically creates an alias of the Control Panels folder and puts it in your Apple menu for you when you install Mac OS 9.

If you get a new control panel (many screen savers and other utilities are control panels), simply drag it onto the System Folder icon, and Mac OS 9 automatically puts it in its proper place, the Control Panels folder. (Incidentally, Mac OS 9 is smart about extensions, fonts, and sounds as well. If you drag an extension, font, or sound onto the System Folder icon, Mac OS 9 puts it in its proper place automatically.)

If you want to read an entire chapter on control panels and how to configure them, see Chapter 14.

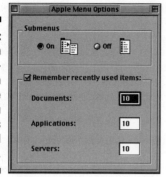

Figure 6-11:
Turning on
the sub-
menus in
the Apple
Menu
Options
control
panel.

The Control Panels folder

The Installer creates an alias of the Control Panels folder and puts it in your Apple menu so that you always have access to your control panels, even when you're using an application other than the Finder. Before submenus were introduced (1994), you had to choose the Control Panels folder from the Apple menu. That action would automatically switch you to the Finder (if you were in another application) and open the Control Panels folder's window. Then you had to open the icon for the control panel manually. Ugh. Mac OS 9, with its marvelous submenus, is much nicer.

Recent Applications, Recent Documents, and Recent Servers folders

I'll discuss the Recent Applications, Recent Documents, and Recent Servers folders together because they're related and work the same way.

If you don't see them in your Apple menu, open the Apple Menu Options control panel (choose Apple menu⇨Control Panels⇨Apple Menu Options) and check the Remember recently used items check box (refer to Figure 6-11). This action creates the folders in your Apple Menu Items folder as soon as you open an application, a document, or a server. If you never open a server (access another Macintosh over a network), the Recent Servers folder is never created.

Even if you do see these items in your Apple menu, you may want to use the Apple Menu Options control panel to change the number of applications, documents, and servers that the folders will remember. I find that 30 is a good number on my big 20-inch monitor: It's enough to ensure that the application or document (I rarely use the Servers folder) I'm looking for is still there, but not so many that the submenu scrolls off-screen.

These three folders track the last *x*-many applications, documents, and servers that you opened. Each time you open one of these three types of icons, the System makes a mental note of it and then creates an alias of that application, document, or server and pops it into the appropriate folder in your Apple Menu Items folder. The System also limits the number of items in each folder based on the Apple Menu Options control panel's settings. So when I open my 31st application, the oldest application alias in the Recent Applications folder disappears.

Why are these folders useful? Often the document or application you're looking for is one you had open earlier in the day or yesterday. These special folders in the Apple menu keep recently used items handy. Chances are, if you used it recently, you'll want to use it again soon. If so, look in one of these folders. (*Hint:* Use the submenu — it's faster.)

Favorites folder

The Favorites folder contains aliases of — what else? — your favorite files. If you use a particular program, document, or even folder more than a few times a day, you should add it to your Favorites for easy access.

To put an item into your Favorites folder, select it in the Finder and then choose File⇨Add to Favorites (or Control-click the item and choose Add to Favorites from the contextual menu).

Conversely, to get rid of an item from your Favorites folder, choose Apple Menu⇨Favorites. The Favorites folder opens, and ou can drag the unwanted item to the Trash.

The Favorites folder in your Apple menu is an alias of the actual Favorites folder, which lives right inside your System Folder. Don't believe me? Open the System Folder and look for yourself!

Roll Your Own: Customizing Your Apple Menu

Do you remember Figure 6-4, way back there at the beginning of the chapter? Can you say "Boooorrrring"?

The Apple menu is fully configurable. Whatever is in the Apple Menu Items folder appears in the Apple menu. It's that simple.

So start transforming your Apple menu from a dull repository for barely useful software to a turbocharged powerhouse that enables you to open any file in seconds. (See Chapter 13 to finish the transformation.)

Just open your Apple Menu Items folder (it's in your System Folder) and get ready to rock.

Before you do anything else, choose View⇨by Name. Now the contents of the Apple Menu Items folder reflect the order in which they appear in the Apple menu.

Doing the right thing with your desk accessories

As you've seen, most of the desk accessories are pretty lame and you probably won't use them very often. We're going to rearrange your Apple menu so that desk accessories don't take up so much space but you can still open them quickly. Here's how:

1. **Open the System Folder.**

   Double-click its icon. Or single-click its icon to select it and then choose File⇨Open, or press the keyboard shortcut ⌘+O.

2. **Open the Apple Menu Items folder (it's in the System Folder) and create a new folder inside it.**

   To create a new folder, choose File⇨New Folder or press ⌘+N.

3. **Name the new folder Desk Accessories.**

4. **Select all the icons in the window except the folders (see Figure 6-12).**

   You have two ways to do this: the easy way and the hard way. Easy way first: Press ⌘+A (or drag a selection box around the entire contents of the window) to select all the icons; then hold down the Shift key and click each folder. Hard way: Click Apple System Profiler, hold down the Shift key, click AppleCD Audio Player, hold down the Shift key, click Calculator, hold down Shift key, and so on until all the nonfolder icons are selected.

   This step illustrates one of the Finder's finer points. You can extend or unextend your selection by using the Shift key. In other words, if you hold down the Shift key and then click an icon, it is added to or subtracted from the selection; if you don't hold down the Shift key when you click an icon, only that single icon is selected.

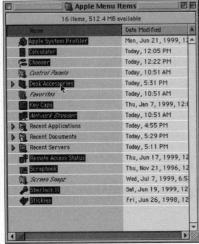

Figure 6-12:
Select all of
the icons
except the
folder and
folder alias
icons, and
drag them
into the
Desk
Accessories
folder.

5. **Drag these icons onto the Desk Accessories folder that you created in Step 2.**

After you release the mouse button, all the desk accessories, applications, and aliases that aren't folders move into the Desk Accessories folder.

6. **Pull down your Apple menu and revel in your handiwork.**

The menu should now look like the one in Figure 6-13.

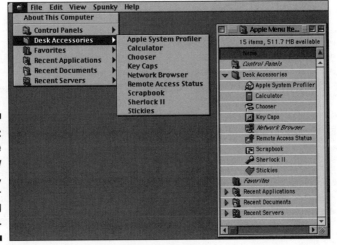

Figure 6-13:
Your Apple
menu is now
a lean,
mean file-
launching
machine.

Putting your stuff into the Apple menu

That last trick was pretty easy, wasn't it? Try one more thing before you move on. Why not add your favorite applications — the programs you use most often — to the Apple menu? Here's how:

1. **Find a favorite application on your hard disk, select it, and make an alias of it.**

   To make an alias, choose File⇨Make Alias or press ⌘+M.

2. **Move the alias to the Apple Menu Items folder.**

3. **Repeat Steps 1 and 2 for any additional applications that you want to appear in your Apple menu.**

Some Other Neat Stuff You Might Want in Your Apple Menu

If you have used previous versions of Mac OS, you probably noticed that a few items are missing from the Apple menu, most notably the AppleCD Audio Player, the Graphing Calculator, Note Pad, and SimpleSound. Never fear. Apple still provides them, they're just not installed in the Apple menu automatically.

You'll find AppleCD Audio Player, Graphing Calculator, and SimpleSound in the Applications folder that was installed with Mac OS 9. Note Pad can be found in the Apple Extras folder.

Since you've just read a little ditty about how to customize your Apple menu, you should have no problem installing these items if you so desire.

Sounds good to me: AppleCD Audio Player

The AppleCD Audio Player is a little program you use to play regular old audio CDs on your CD-ROM drive (see Figure 6-14). Just pop your David Garza CD into the CD-ROM drive, select AppleCD Audio Player from the Apple menu, and then click the Play button. Your room is filled with the mellow tones of Austin's own Dah-veed.

Figure 6-14:
AppleCD
Audio
Player is a
slick control
program for
playing
audio CDs in
your
CD-ROM
drive.

You may need to plug a pair of amplified stereo speakers into the stereo output jacks on some external CD-ROM drives. If you have an internal CD-ROM drive, you may need to select Internal CD from the Sound Input pop-up menu in the Monitors & Sound control panel before you hear music through your Mac's built-in speaker. Finally, you must have the Audio CD Access extension in the Extensions folder within your System Folder for the AppleCD Audio Player to function.

Because the internal speakers in most Macs stink, a nice pair of multimedia speakers is a good investment; then you can rattle the walls when you slap that David Garza CD in your drive.

A whole chapter (see Chapter 16) talks about every item in your System Folder and whether you need it. It also explains what an extension is, in case you're wondering. In any event, it should be obvious to you even now that this program isn't much use if you don't have a CD-ROM drive.

Fakin' it with Graphing Calculator (Power Macs only)

I still have no idea what the Graphing Calculator is really supposed to do, although I do enjoy running its demos for my friends and pretending I do know. If Graphing Calculator appears in your Apple menu, here's how to fake it. Choose Demo➪Surfaces. You should see something similar to Figure 6-15.

Figure 6-15:
The
Surfaces
demo in
Graphing
Calculator.

Click the Stop button and then use your mouse to spin the graph. Mumble something half-intelligibly about "PowerPC processors and real-time 3D surface-mapping capabilities." I guarantee you'll impress your friends.

Take note of the Note Pad

Note Pad is a handy, dandy, little note-taking utility that lets you store gobs of unrelated text items without saving a zillion different files all over your hard disk. Everything that you type into Note Pad is automatically saved in the Note Pad file, which is in your System Folder. Figure 6-16 shows Note Pad in action.

Note Pad uses a page metaphor. Click the dog-ear corner at the bottom left to change the page, or choose File⇨Go to Note and type the page number of the note that you want to go to.

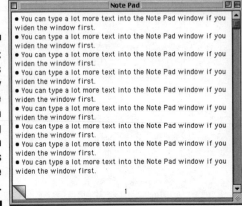

Figure 6-16:
Note Pad is
a handy
little
program
for jotting
random
thoughts
and phone
numbers.

The Note Pad in Mac OS 9 has several improvements over Note Pads of old. Most welcome is the Find command. And its window is resizable and has scroll bars. (Can you believe it took Apple until System 7.5 to add scroll bars and make its window resizable?) Finally, the pages seem to hold a lot more text than older versions. Oh, and you can choose a font in the Preferences dialog box; the older Note Pads gave a choice of Geneva or Geneva.

You can print notes, and Note Pad (like almost every Mac application ever made) includes full support of Cut, Copy, and Paste, so you can easily get text in and out of Note Pad by using the Clipboard.

Some people prefer Note Pad to Stickies (you read about Stickies earlier in the chapter), some people use both, and some people use neither. For a freebie, Note Pad is relatively well equipped. If you have a lot of random thoughts that you'd like to type, you might want to leave it open all day (it uses only a little RAM). It's also a good spot for frequently dialed phone numbers.

Sounds like . . . SimpleSound

SimpleSound is a simple little program for recording your own alert sounds. You need to have a proper microphone; contact your nearest Apple dealer for details. Just open SimpleSound, and click the Add button, the Record button, and then the Save button, and just like that you have a new beep sound.

SimpleSound has one other feature: Its Sound menu enables you to choose between CD Quality, Music Quality, Speech Quality, and Phone Quality sound. Frankly, I can't tell the difference, even using excellent amplified speakers. No SimpleSound on your Apple menu? Open up Applications. It's in there, I promise.

My Deep, Dark Secret

I can't go on with this charade any longer. I confess: The screen pictures you've been looking at aren't from my real hard disk at all. They're from a hard disk called Spawn that I borrowed from Apple to create the screen shots for this book. When I start up using my real hard disk, my Mac looks totally different.

I'm a power user. I have my Mac souped up and tricked out to the max. I have strange icons in the menu bar. I have a Trash alias behind the Apple menu (hidden in this shot). A slot machine is in my control strip.

I didn't want to confuse you, so I wrote the book using the Spawn hard disk, a disk that had nothing on it except Mac OS 9-related stuff. It makes for much cleaner screen shots so that I can avoid explaining every last difference between your Mac and mine. For the record, my Mac really looks like what you see in Figure 6-17.

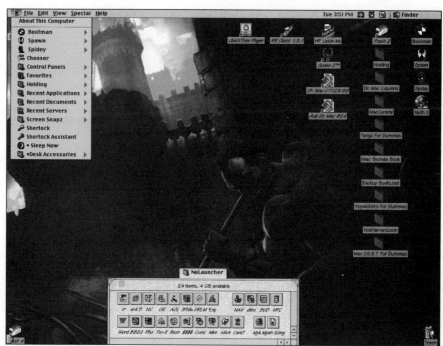

Figure 6-17:
My Mac.

I'll just point out a few highlights. The clock and telephone in the menu bar enable me to look at my appointments or phone book file without launching my calendar or contact database program (Chronos Software's excellent Consultant). The CC icon next to the Application menu is for Conflict Catcher, a kind of Extensions Manager on steroids from Casady & Greene (see Chapter 14). The background picture is Myth II, courtesy of Bungie Software. Finally, I have three aliases of the Trash can on my screen, so that I never have to drag trash very far.

I have three hard disks: Bootman (internal) and Spawn and Spidey (both external). Notice that I have aliases of all three in the Apple menu.

There. I feel better having gotten that off my chest.

P.S.: By the time you read this book, I'll be running the final released version of Mac OS 9 — in case you noticed that I was running OS 8.6 in Figure 6-17.

Chapter 7

Understanding the Save and Open Dialog Boxes

Mark my words, this may well be the most important chapter in this book. If you don't understand the Open and Save dialog boxes, the doohickeys that appear when you choose File⇨Open or File⇨Save, respectively, in most programs, you'll never quite get the hang of your Macintosh. Yet mastering these essential techniques is perhaps the biggest problem many users have. I get more phone calls that begin, "Well, I saved the file, and now I don't know where it went."

This chapter is the cure. Just pay attention, and everything will become crystal clear. And keep saying to yourself, "The Save and Open dialog boxes are just another view of the Finder." I explain in a moment.

Nested Folders and Paths

Before I get started, I need to remind you that you work with Open and Save dialog boxes within applications. I assume that you know how to launch your favorite application and that you know how to create a new document.

For the rest of this chapter, I use SimpleText as the sample application. SimpleText comes with Mac OS 9, so you should have it, too. In fact, you've probably already used SimpleText to read any Read Me files that came with Mac OS 9. (If you can't find a copy, ⌘+F gives you the Sherlock 2 dialog box. Search for Simple. I'll even bet you find more than one copy!)

So if you want to follow along, keystroke by keystroke, launch SimpleText and use File⇨New to create a new document. Type a few words in your document, such as "All work and no play makes Jack a dull boy." Or something like that. (Forgive me, Stephen King.)

Switch from SimpleText to the Finder. You may find the next part easier if you hide SimpleText while you work in the Finder. If you don't know how to do either, pull down the Application menu, the one at the far right; everything you need is right there. Then follow these steps:

1. **Open your hard disk's icon and create a new folder at the root level (that is, in your hard disk's window). Name this folder Folder 1.**

   That name reflects the fact that the folder is one level deep on your hard disk.

2. **Open Folder 1 and create a new folder in its window. Name this folder Folder 2.**

   And the Folder 2 name reflects the fact that this folder is two levels deep on your hard disk.

3. **Open Folder 2 and create a new folder in its window. Name this folder Folder 3.**

   Folder 3 is three levels deep on your hard disk.

You should now have a set of nested folders that look something like Figure 7-1.

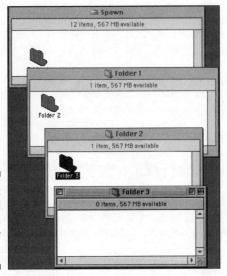

Figure 7-1:
Nested
folders,
going four
levels deep.

Let me make this perfectly clear: Stuff inside Folder 3 is four levels deep. Folder 3 itself is three levels deep. Folder 2 itself is two levels deep, but stuff inside Folder 2, such as Folder 3, is three levels deep. And so on. Got it?

What's important here is that you are able to visualize the path to Folder 3. To get to stuff in Folder 3, you open Spawn, open Folder 1, open Folder 2, and then open Folder 3. Remember this concept. You need it in the next section when you look at the Save dialog box.

An easy way to see the path to any open folder is to ⌘-click its name in the title bar of its window (hold down the ⌘ key before you press the mouse button). This action displays a drop-down path menu for that folder starting at the desktop level, as shown in Figure 7-2.

Figure 7-2:
The drop-down path indicates that Folder 3 appears when you press the name in the title bar while holding down the ⌘ key.

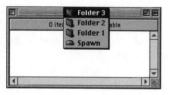

This path menu is live, so you can choose another folder from it by sliding the cursor to the folder's name and releasing the mouse button.

Try out this feature with Folder 3. ⌘-click its name in the title bar, move the cursor down until Folder 1 is highlighted, and then release the mouse button. Folder 1 pops to the front and becomes the active window. Try to remember this shortcut because ⌘-clicking title bars can save you lots of time and effort.

Okay, our preparatory work in the Finder is finished. Use any of the techniques you know to make SimpleText the active application. And don't forget what that path to Folder 3 looks like.

Save Your Document Before It's Too Late

Okay, back in SimpleText, it's time to save your masterpiece. Choose File⇨ Save or press ⌘+S. This command displays the Save dialog box shown in Figure 7-3. Don't panic. These dialog boxes are easy as long as you remember that they're just another view of the folder structure in the Finder.

Figure 7-3:
The Save dialog box for SimpleText after clicking the Desktop button.

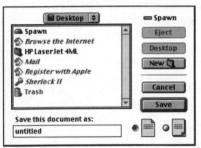

When the Save dialog box appears, the first thing I want you to do is click the Desktop button to view the icons on your desktop.

Let's talk about the Save dialog box for a moment. It contains that other view of your hard disk I mention at the beginning of the chapter. You're looking at the icons on your desktop right now. You know that they're the icons on your desktop because the active item is the desktop. Its name appears on the drop-down menu at the top and center.

In programs other than SimpleText, the Save dialog box may look slightly different because it contains additional options. Don't worry. The Save dialog box always works the same, no matter what options are offered. When you can navigate with the SimpleText Save dialog box, you can navigate with any program's Save dialog box. So don't worry if the one you're used to seeing doesn't look exactly like Figure 7-3; just follow along.

In the scrolling list (known as the file list box), click the name of your hard disk (mine is Spawn), and then click the Open button or press the Return or Enter key on your keyboard. (In all dialog boxes, the Return or Enter key activates the default button, which is the one with the heavy border around it.) Double-clicking the name of your hard disk opens it as well.

Open Folder 1 the same way. Open Folder 2 the same way. Open Folder 3 the same way. Your Save dialog box should look like Figure 7-4.

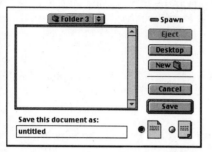

Figure 7-4:
If you save now, the document will be saved into Folder 3 and named *untitled*.

You navigate folders in the Save dialog box the same way you navigate folders in the Finder: by opening them to see their contents.

In the Save dialog box, the name at the top in the drop-down menu is the name of the active item (a folder, a disk, or the desktop). Think of the active item in a Save dialog box as the active window in the Finder. That's where your file is saved if you click the Save button. This concept is important. The file is always saved in the active folder (or the active disk or the desktop) whose name appears at the top of the dialog box in the drop-down menu.

To make comprehension easier, think back to when I asked you to remember the path to Folder 3 in the Finder. Now look at the current path to Folder 3 in the Save dialog box by clicking the drop-down menu. Like the drop-down path menu in the Finder (⌘-click the window's name in the title bar), the drop-down menu in the Save dialog box is also live, so if you slide the cursor down to another folder (or Spawn or the desktop), that item becomes the active item. See Figure 7-5.

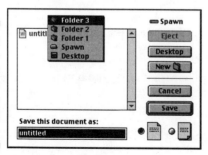

Figure 7-5:
The drop-down menu shows the path to the current folder.

The Save (and Open) dialog boxes treat disk icons and the desktop in the same way that they treat folders. Although the desktop and root level (your hard disk's window) are not really folders, you can save items to them.

You always move through the hierarchy in the same way. The desktop is the top level. When you're at the desktop level, you can see all mounted disks and any folders on the desktop. If you open a disk icon, you see its folder structure.

You always navigate up and down the tree. Your most deeply nested folders are at the very bottom; the desktop is at the very top.

That metaphor is correct — the desktop is at the top of the hierarchy of folders; your most deeply buried file is at the bottom. So why are the drop-down menus in the Open and Save dialog boxes upside down? The desktop appears at the bottom of the menu. But that's wrong. If the dialog box were correctly following the rest of the metaphor, the desktop would appear at the top of the menu, wouldn't it? Grrrrr.

If you have more than one disk mounted, make sure that the disk name, which appears in the top right next to a little disk icon (hard disks have a hard disk icon; floppies have a floppy disk icon), is correct. If it's not, navigate back up to the desktop level and choose the correct disk.

Get into the habit of noticing the disk name in the Open and Save dialog boxes if you often have multiple disks mounted. Nothing is more frustrating than saving a file to the wrong disk and not being able to find it later.

Your file is saved to the active item in the drop-down menu when you click Save. In other words, when the desktop is the active item (as it is in Figure 7-3), your document is saved on the desktop if you click the Save button. When Spawn is the active item, your document is saved in the Spawn window if you click the Save button. When Folder 3 is the active item, your document is saved in Folder 3 if you click the Save button.

Here's how it works:

1. **In the Save dialog box, navigate to Folder 3.**

   That is, make Folder 3 the active item.

2. **Select (highlight) the word *untitled* and type a more descriptive name.**

   I called mine Love Letter to Lisa.

3. **Click the Save button (or press the Return or Enter key).**

   That's it. If you switch to the Finder and open up Folder 3 (if it's not already open), you can see that the file is saved right there in Folder 3.

Congrats. That's all there is to it. You now know how to navigate in a Save dialog box.

Remember the path I asked you to remember, the one you saw when you ⌘-clicked the name in the title bar of Folder 3's window? Just remember that the path in the Save dialog box's drop-down menu (shown back in Figure 7-5) is the same.

If that information makes sense to you, you're golden. If you're still a little shaky, go through the exercise again and keep trying to understand the relationship between the three folders you created (one inside the other inside the other) and the drop-down path menus you see when you ⌘-click Folder 3's title bar or click its name in the drop-down menu in the Save dialog box. Keep reviewing the figures. Eventually it'll just click, and you'll slap yourself in the head and say, "Now I get it."

Don't read on until you get it. This idea of paths and navigating is crucial to your success as a Macintosh user.

There's a little more to understand, but if you get it so far, you're home free.

The rest of what you should know about Save dialog boxes

One thing you need to know is that the file list box and the file name field are mutually exclusive. Only one can be active at a time. You're either navigating the folder hierarchy or you're naming a file. When a Save dialog box first appears, the file name field is active, ready for you to type a name, as shown on the right in Figure 7-6.

Active file list box   Inactive file list box

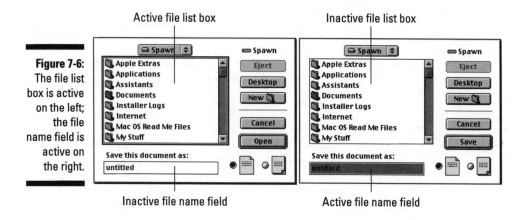

Figure 7-6:
The file list box is active on the left; the file name field is active on the right.

Inactive file name field   Active file name field

Notice the border around the file list box when it's active. Also notice how the bottom button changes from Open to Save when the file name field is active. You can read more about this phenomenon in a few pages.

When you want to navigate, click anywhere in the file list box to make it active. In Figure 7-6, this box is displaying the folders beneath the active item (Spawn). When you click anywhere in the box, it becomes active and displays a double-line border around it. If you type something while the file list box is active, the list scrolls and selects the folder that most closely matches the letter(s) you typed. Go ahead and give it a try. It's easier to experience than explain.

For what it's worth, you can also type the first letter or two in any Finder window to select the icon closest alphabetically to the letter or letters you typed.

When the file list is active, the letters you type do not appear in the file name field. If you want to type a file name, you have to activate the file name field again to type in it. Here's how. Regardless of which box or field is active at the time, when you press the Tab key on your keyboard, the other becomes active. So if the file name field is active, it becomes inactive when you press Tab, and the file list box becomes active. Press Tab again and they reverse — the file name field becomes active again.

If you don't feel like pressing the Tab key, you can achieve the same effect by clicking either the file list box or the file name field to make it active.

Try it yourself and notice how visual cues let you know which is active. When the file list is active, it displays a border; when the file name field is active, the file list has no border and the file name field is editable.

The buttons

SimpleText's Save dialog box contains five buttons: Eject, Desktop, New Folder, Cancel, and Open/Save. The first four are straightforward and almost explain themselves, but the fifth requires a bit of concentration. I describe them all.

Ejector seat

The Eject button is active only when an ejectable disk is selected in the file list box. It's mostly used to save a file to a different floppy or other removable disk than the one currently in the drive. Use the Eject button to eject that disk so that you can insert another. When you insert a disk, it becomes the active item automatically. You can tell because its name appears in two places (see Figure 7-7):

  ✔ At the top right of the Save (or Open) dialog box above the buttons

  ✔ In the drop-down menu above the file list box

Figure 7-7:
The floppy
disk auto-
matically
becomes
the active
item.

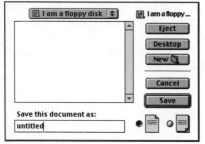

Do it on the desktop

The Desktop button takes you rocketing up the hierarchy of folders to the very top level, as high as you can go. When you click the Desktop button, the desktop becomes the active folder (I know that the desktop isn't really a folder, but play along) in the Save dialog box. From here, you can navigate your way down into any subfolder.

If you get lost in a Save (or Open) dialog box, the best thing to do is click the Desktop button and start from the top (the desktop), which should make it easy to find your way to the folder you want. Just remember to navigate down through folders in the same order you would in the Finder.

Something new: The New Folder button

The New Folder button is a nice touch. If you click this button, a new folder is created inside the active folder in the Save dialog box. You can then save your document into it. Not every program has this button; in fact, many don't. So don't get too used to it.

What usually happens is that you don't think about needing a new folder until the Save dialog box is on-screen. And in most Save dialog boxes, you can't do a thing about it.

What I do in these cases is to save my file on the desktop. Later, when I'm back in the Finder, I create a new folder in the proper place on my hard disk and then move the file from the desktop to its folder.

That's an 86: Cancel

The Cancel button dismisses the Save dialog box without saving anything anywhere. In other words, the Cancel button returns things to the way they were before you displayed the Save dialog box.

The keyboard shortcut for Cancel is ⌘+period (the Esc key sometimes works, too). ⌘+period is a good command to memorize. It cancels almost all dialog boxes, and it also cancels lots of other things. If something is going on (for example, your spreadsheet is calculating or your database is sorting or your graphics program is rotating) and it's taking too long, try ⌘+period. It works (usually).

The Open/Save button: The exception to the rule

If you've been paying extra-careful attention to the illustrations, you've no doubt noticed that the button near the bottom sometimes is Save and other times is Open. I even called your attention to it a few pages ago. So? What gives?

In particular, how do you save something when there's no Save button, as in Figure 7-8? Suppose I want to save the Love Letter to Lisa file in Folder 1. I navigate my way to Folder 1, and I see Folder 1 at the top of the drop-down menu. I'm ready to save, but there's no Save button.

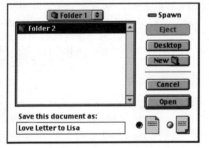

Figure 7-8:
How do you save when this is what you see?

That's because Folder 2 is selected in the file list box, and if a folder is selected in the file list box, the button says Open, not Save. To deselect Folder 2, click anywhere in the file list box except on Folder 2 or press the Tab key. When Folder 2 is no longer selected in the file list box, the Open button becomes the Save button, and you can now save, as shown in Figure 7-9.

I know. It doesn't really make sense, but that's how it works. Try it a few times. It's not as straightforward as other parts of the Mac interface, but once you get it, you get it for life.

I could have just as easily pressed the Tab key instead of clicking. The result would be the same — the Open button would change to the Save button.

Figure 7-9:
The Open
button
changes to
the Save
button,
which
allows me to
save Love
Letter to
Lisa in
Folder 1.

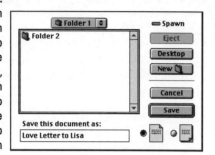

If this little section confuses you, look again at Figures 7-8 and 7-9. Folder 1 is where I want to save the file. But there's no Save button in Figure 7-8 because a folder, Folder 2, is currently selected. When I click anywhere in the file list box (anywhere except on Folder 2) or press the Tab key on my keyboard, Folder 2 is deselected, the Open button changes into the Save button, and I can save the Love Letter to Lisa file in Folder 1.

If you still aren't sure what all this stuff means, try it. It's not particularly intuitive, but it's relatively easy to get the hang of:

1. **In the file list box of the Save dialog box, select Folder 2.**

   Folder 1 is the active folder.

2. **Click the file list box anywhere but on Folder 2.**

   Notice the Open or Save button before and after you click.

3. **Press the Tab key.**

   Notice the Open or Save button before and after you press Tab.

When the button says Save and you click the button or press Return or Enter, the file is saved in Folder 1. When the button says Open (because Folder 2 is selected) and you click the button or press Return, you move down one level and Folder 2 becomes the active folder.

Got it?

It Looks Like Save and It Acts Like Save, So Why Is It Called Save As?

The Save As command, which you can find in the File menu of almost every program ever made, lets you save a file that has already been saved and give it a different name.

Why might you want to do that? Suppose you have two sisters, Jodie and Zelda. You write Jodie a long, chatty letter. You save it as Letter to Jodie. Now you decide you want to send it to Zelda, too, but you want to change a few things. So you change the part about your date last night (Zelda isn't as liberated as Jodie) and replace all references to Steve (Jodie's husband) with Zeke (Zelda's husband). Aren't computers grand?

You've made those changes to Letter to Jodie, but you haven't saved again since you decided to make the changes. So now the document on your screen is actually a letter to Zelda, but its file name is still Letter to Jodie. Think of what would happen if you were to save now.

I'll tell you: If you save now, the file named Letter to Jodie will reflect the changes you just made. The stuff in the letter that was meant for Jodie will be blown away and replaced by the stuff you said to Zelda. If you save now, the file name Letter to Jodie will be inaccurate.

That's what Save As is for. If you use Save As now (it's a different command from Save — look on the File menu and see), you get a Save dialog box where you can type a different file name. You can also navigate to another folder, if you like, and save the newly named version of the file there.

Now you have two files on your hard disk — Letter to Jodie and Letter to Zelda. Both contain the stuff they should.

That's what Save As is for.

Open (Sesame)

You already know how to use the Open dialog box; you just don't know you know yet.

Using the Open dialog box

Guess what? If you can navigate using a Save dialog box, you can navigate using an Open dialog box. They work the same except for a few minor differences.

Save early, save often = no heartache

This is as good a time as any to talk about developing good saving habits. Needless to say, saving your work every few minutes is a very good idea.

Here's my advice:

✔ Always save before you switch to another program.

✔ Always save before you print a document.

✔ Always save before you stand up.

If you don't heed this advice and your Mac crashes while switching programs, printing, or sitting idle (which, not coincidentally, are the three most likely times for it to crash), you lose everything you did since your last save.

⌘+S is the keyboard shortcut for Save in almost every program I know. Memorize it. See it in your dreams. Train your finger muscles to do it unconsciously. Use it (the keyboard shortcut) or lose it (your unsaved work).

First, there's no file name field. Of course not. This dialog box is the one you see when you want to open a file! There's no need for the file name field because you're not saving a file.

There's also no New Folder button. You don't need it when you're opening a file. (It sure comes in handy when you're saving a file, though, doesn't it? I sure wish every program had one.)

Anyway, that's it. Those are the differences. Navigate the same way as you would in a Save dialog box. Don't forget your mantra, "The Open and Save dialog boxes are just another view of the Finder."

Figure 7-10 shows two different ways of viewing the same file. In the Open dialog box, at top, I navigated to the Love Letter to Lisa file in Folder 3. I clicked the drop-down menu in the Open dialog box to show you the path to the Love Letter to Lisa file. Below the Open dialog box is the Finder view of the path to the file Love Letter to Lisa.

If you aren't 100 percent comfortable with the relationship between the two views, please go back and try the exercises earlier in this chapter again. Please. Keep reviewing the pictures and instructions until you understand this concept. If you don't, your Mac will continue to confound and confuse you. Do yourself a favor — don't read any further until the Open and Save dialog boxes feel like the most natural thing in the world to you.

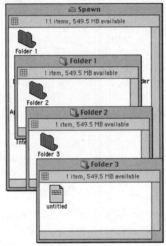

Figure 7-10:
The Open dialog box, like the Save dialog box, is just a different view of the Finder.

A really big show — Show Preview

Okay, something else about the Open dialog box is different. As you can see in Figure 7-10, the Open dialog box for SimpleText has a check box called Show Preview. What does this little box do? It lets you create little previews for PICT, GIF, and other formats, which are the type of files created by many popular graphics programs.

Click the Show Preview check box. You'll probably see a little picture of the file you've selected, as shown in Figure 7-11. If you don't, click Create. The picture appears after a moment. From now on, every time that file is high-lighted in an Open dialog box, its preview picture automatically appears (as long as the Show Preview check box remains checked).

As you might guess, previews are a nice feature. Many graphics programs include previews in their Open dialog boxes.

Figure 7-11:
The Preview area in this Open dialog box shows a small picture of what the macOS.gif file looks like.

Weird folder or file names

Every so often, you see some weird folder names — such as Move & Rename or Network Trash Folder or Desktop DB or DF or VM Storage — in the Open dialog box, but you don't see these folders when you look at the corresponding windows in the Finder. Don't worry. It's perfectly natural.

Here's what's going on. Move & Rename and VM Storage are invisible files. You aren't supposed to see them. The System uses them to keep track of stuff that you don't need (or want) to know about. They're invisible when you look in your hard drive's window, but they show up in some applications' Open dialog boxes. This anomaly is known as a bug. You shouldn't be able to see those files. Just ignore them, and they won't bother you. If you're lucky, you won't even see them on your Mac (many people don't).

The last thing you need to know

Selectively displaying certain items in Open dialog boxes is a feature of most applications. When you use a program's Open dialog box, only files that the program knows how to open appear in the file list. In other words, the program filters out files that it can't open, so you don't see them cluttering up the Open dialog box. Pretty neat, eh?

On the other hand, not seeing every item in an Open dialog box can be a little disconcerting when you're trying to envision the correlation between the Finder and the Open dialog box. Just remember this: Stuff you see in the Finder doesn't always appear in the Open dialog box. That's why I showed you the Save dialog box first. It always includes everything. In a Save dialog box, items that you can't select appear grayed, but they do appear. Open dialog boxes usually show only files that you can select and open with the current application.

So . . . if you know something is in a particular folder but you can't see it in the Open dialog box, consider the possibility that the program you're using isn't capable of opening that kind of document (not every program can open every document).

File Exchange, a standard part of the Mac OS, can often allow one program to open documents created by another program. If you can't see the document in the Open dialog box, quit the current program and find the file in the Finder (that is, open the folders it's in). When you open the document in the Finder, File Exchange kicks in and offers you a list of programs on your hard disk that can open that particular type of document.

New-Style Open and Save Dialog Boxes?

One other thing. Really. Then you're finished with opening and saving stuff. Ever since Mac OS 8.5, there has been a new style of Open and Save dialog boxes. The new-style dialog boxes are movable, are resizable, have little expansion triangles like windows in the Finder do, and include buttons for shortcuts, recent items, and favorites. Although they look a little different (see Figure 7-12), they work pretty much the same as I describe in this chapter.

Figure 7-12:
A new style of Open dialog box. Notice the buttons at the top right. They are (left to right) shortcuts, recent stuff, and favorites.

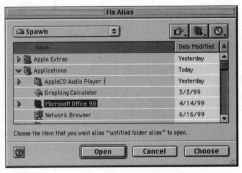

That's the good news. The bad news is that I know of few programs at present (summer 1999) that use them. The reason why is that programs need to be updated (revised/upgraded/rewritten/and so on) to display the new style of dialog boxes for opening and saving. And not that many have been updated to support them yet.

I did find one place where you can look at a new-style Open dialog box — in the Fix Alias dialog box. To see it for yourself:

1. **Create a folder.**

2. **Make an alias of it.**

3. **Drag the original folder to the Trash, and then empty the Trash.**

4. **Double-click the alias.**

5. **Click the Fix Alias button.**

You should see something that looks like Figure 7-12.

Hey, do you notice the title bar on top of the dialog box? That's a sure sign that in addition to opening or saving files here, you can move that sucker around the screen. This comes in handy if you need to glance at a folder or document that's sitting behind your dialog box before you click the Open/Save button.

We'll see a lot more dialog boxes like this as third-party software programmers update their software to use this nifty new Mac OS feature. In the meantime, check out these new-style dialog boxes whenever you see them — with their pop-down menus and movability, they're much better than the old ones.

Part II
Making It Purr

In this part . . .

*T*he chapters in this part show you how to perform important hands-on tasks. But don't get all worked up: This stuff is easy. In fact, I think of this part as "The Lazy Person's How-To Guide."

Chapter 8 deals with how to organize your Mac. You discover, among other things, how to do routine file-management and navigating tasks the easy way.

Next is the how-to-print chapter, Chapter 9. It includes info on how to decipher Print options and plenty of other hows and whys that will help you become a modern-day Gutenberg.

In Chapter 10, you find out how to share. Files, that is. It's easy, it's convenient, it's free, and it beats the heck out of sneakernet.

Finally, there's a wonderful chapter (numbered, conveniently enough, 11) on how to manage memory (and other seemingly complicated arcana) — an easy-to-understand, almost jargon-free primer on how the whole memory thing works.

Chapter 8

File Management Made Simple

• •

In This Chapter

▶ Launching Launcher

▶ Organizing

▶ Using aliases

▶ Working with spring-loaded folders

• •

*I*n other parts of the book, you discover the basics about windows and icons and menus. Here, you begin a never-ending quest to discover the fastest, easiest, most trouble-free way to manage the files on your Mac.

I can help. I'm not a doctor, but I play one in books and magazines. I've been wrangling with the Macintosh interface for more than twelve years now, and I've learned a lot about what works and what doesn't — at least what works for me. This chapter will spare you at least part of the ten-year learning curve.

Remember, I'm talking about Mac OS here. And I'm talking about developing your own personal style. There is no right way to organize your files, no right way to use aliases, no right way to use the Apple menu, and no right way to use drag-and-drop. The only thing for sure is that these features are useless if you don't use them.

Please take the time to understand these wonderful features. They make your Mac so much easier to use. I'll show you how, and it's easy. After absorbing that info, you'll have all the ammunition you need to create your own personal Macintosh experience: a Mac environment designed by you, for you.

Launcher or Not

Launcher is a control panel that was introduced in System 7.5. It creates a window in the Finder with single-clickable icons that launch (open) frequently used files.

If you don't see Launcher, choose Apple menu⇨Control Panels⇨Launcher. If you want Launcher on all the time, choose Apple menu⇨Control Panels⇨ General Controls and click the box marked Show Launcher at system startup.

The advantage of Launcher is that the icons in the Launcher window can represent items in many different folders on your hard disk. (See Figure 8-1.)

Figure 8-1:
Launcher makes frequently used items available in a single convenient window, even if the items are in different folders as shown.

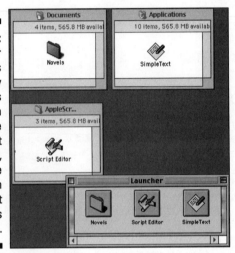

So Launcher, at least in theory, saves you time by saving you from rooting through folders every time you need one of those items.

Launcher is easy to configure. Just drag anything you want to add to Launcher onto the Launcher window.

Here's what happens when you drag an icon onto the Launcher window: Your Mac creates an alias of that icon and places that alias in the Launcher Items folder, which you'll find in your System Folder. (See Figure 8-2.)

If you want something to appear in the Launcher window, put an alias of it in the Launcher Items folder or drag its icon onto the Launcher window. To remove an item, hold down the Option key and drag it to the Trash. That's it. The whole enchilada.

Well, almost the whole enchilada. I feel obligated to mention one other feature. You can create categories for Launcher by creating folders in the Launcher Items folder and starting their names with the bullet character (•, which you create by pressing Option+8). This creates categories with different buttons for different stuff, as shown in Figure 8-3.

Figure 8-2:
If an item's alias is in the Launcher Items folder, the item appears in the Launcher window.

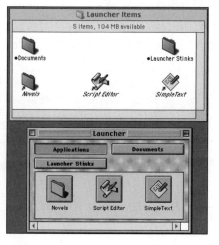

Figure 8-3:
The secret for creating categories in Launcher is folders that start with a bullet.

For what it's worth, I couldn't find anything about Launcher in my Apple manual, but I got a great demo of this trick by searching for Launcher in Mac OS Help. Yet another reason for you to check out Mac OS's cool Help system.

I think I've been objective up to this point. Now I'll tell you why I think Launcher stinks:

> ✔ It doesn't float in front of other Finder windows, so it's easy to lose behind other windows.

> ✔ It has only an icon view, so it wastes valuable screen real estate. (Hint: You can change the size of the icons by ⌘-clicking anywhere on the Launcher window except on an icon. But its smallest buttons are still larger than the smallest buttons you can have in Finder windows.)

> ✔ It can't be chosen from the Application menu.

✔ It's no different from a regular window in View as Buttons mode except for the stupid categories feature.

✔ Like the stupid View as Buttons view, Launcher uses single clicks to open icons, a clear violation of Macintosh Human Interface Guidelines, the bible of Macintosh interface design.

Gasp. So why did Apple start including Launcher, first with the old Performa models and now in OS 9? And why, after ten years of rabid insistence that double-click means open, did Apple change its mind?

My take on it is that Apple is afraid that new users are too stupid to grasp the concept of double-clicking to open a file. And too stupid to realize that you can do everything Launcher does and more by customizing your Apple menu (as you can see later in this chapter).

I don't think you're that dumb. I say get rid of the lame-o Launcher. (See Chapter 16 for complete instructions on shuffling Launcher off this mortal coil.) And, for the most part, I eschew the Button views mostly on the grounds that it's too easy to accidentally open something by single-clicking it.

With what I present in this chapter, you can instead create your own customized environment, which I promise will let you find and launch items faster and more flexibly than Launcher or the clunky Button view.

On the other hand, if for some unfathomable reason you like Launcher or even the Button view, by all means enjoy them. Launcher doesn't use all that much disk space or RAM, so there's no great advantage to trashing it.

No advantage, that is, besides never seeing Launcher again (which I consider a big advantage). If a single-click file launcher tickles your fancy, plenty of excellent commercial and shareware utilities make Launcher seem even crummier.

Getting Yourself Organized

I won't pretend to be able to organize for you. Organizing your files is as personal as your taste in music. You develop your own style with the Mac. So in this section, I give you some food for thought, some ideas about how I do it, and some suggestions that should make organization easier for you, regardless of how you choose to do it yourself.

And it's root, root, root for the root level

Root level refers to the window you see when you open your hard disk's icon. It's the first level down in the hierarchy of folders. How you organize the root level is a matter of taste, but let me try to give some guidance.

KISS: Keep It Simple, Stupid

I find that less is more when it comes to organizing files and folders. I try to use the simplest structure that meets my needs. For example, if I have more than a handful of icons at the root level, I begin to look for ways to reorganize. I shoot for no more than ten items at the root level; fewer are better.

At the very least . . .

The root level must contain the System Folder. It won't work properly if you put it somewhere else (like in another folder or on the desktop). Beyond that, what you place on the root level is up to you.

I think most people should start with two other folders, Applications and Documents, at the very least, but even these don't have to go at the root level. The desktop is an equally good place for them, as you can see in a later section.

A full installation of Mac OS 9 leaves a bunch of folders at the root level in addition to your System Folder. To keep things tidy, create a new folder at the root level called Mac OS 9 Stuff and put these folders inside it, as shown in Figure 8-4.

Do NOT put the System Folder in this (or any other) folder. The System Folder must reside at root level or it won't work. If you drop the System Folder into any other folder, it will break. And your Mac won't start up. So don't do that, okay?

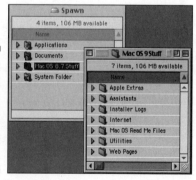

Figure 8-4: Reducing clutter on your hard disk with a Mac OS 9 Stuff folder.

Documentary evidence: The Documents folder

Remember, you don't need to have a Documents folder. If you do have one, though, here are some tips for organizing it:

- ✔ Don't create subfolders (within the Documents folder) until you need them.

- ✔ Creating a bunch of empty folders because you think that you might need them someday is more work than creating them when you need them. You end up opening an empty folder when you're looking for something else — a complete waste of time.

- ✔ I recommend saving everything in the Documents folder for a week or two (or a month or two, depending on how many new documents you save each day). Once a decent-size group of documents has accumulated in the Documents folder, take a look at them and create logical subfolders to put them into.

- ✔ Let your work style decide the file structure.

You should create the subfolders based on a system that makes sense to you. Here are some ideas for subfolders:

- ✔ **By type of document:** Word-Processing Documents, Spreadsheet Documents, and Graphics Documents

- ✔ **By date:** Documents May-June, Documents Spring '99

- ✔ **By content:** Memos, Outgoing Letters, Expense Reports

- ✔ **By project:** Project X, Project Y, Project Z

When things start to get messy and you start noticing some folders swelling (that is, becoming filled with tons of files), subdivide them again using a combination of the methods I just mentioned.

For example, suppose you start by subdividing your Documents folder into four subfolders — Expense Reports, Letters, Memos, and Other Documents (as shown in Figure 8-5). A few months later, when those folders begin to get full, you might subdivide them in one or more ways, as shown in Figure 8-6.

The folder called Other Documents hasn't required subdividing yet, as it only contains four items so far.

Figure 8-5:
A Documents folder containing four subfolders.

Figure 8-6:
The same
Documents
folder
several
months
later,
with new
subfolders
for three
of the
original four
subfolders.

The point is that your folder structure should be organic, growing as you need it to grow. Let it happen. Don't let any one folder get so full that it's a hassle to deal with. Create new subfolders when things start to get crowded.

How full is too full? That's impossible to say. If I find more than 15 or 20 files in a single folder, I begin thinking about ways to subdivide it. On the other hand, some of my subfolders that contain things I don't often need, such as my Correspondence 1992 folder, contain more than 100 files. Because I don't use the folder all that much (but want to keep it on my hard disk just in case), its overcrowded condition doesn't bother me. Your mileage may vary.

After almost ten years of growth, my Documents folder contains only about 20 subfolders, most of which contain their own subfolders. (See Figure 8-7.) Being a nonconformist, I call my Documents folder Stuff.

Other folders at the root level

You can follow the preceding philosophy for other folders at the root level, subdividing them as needed. If you use a particular folder a great deal, move it from the Documents folder to the root level or to the desktop (more about that in a few pages) to make it easier to use. For example, if you write a lot of letters, keep your Correspondence folder at root level or on the desktop. And so on.

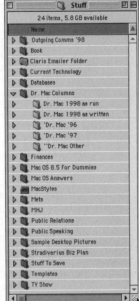

Figure 8-7:
My
Documents
folder
and its
subfolders.

The only thing I want to caution you against is storing stuff in the System Folder that doesn't belong there. There's no harm in it, but the System Folder is already the repository for many files used by System software and by applications. For most people, the System Folder is the most crowded folder on their disk, so sticking items that don't belong in it would only cause further clutter. Word-processing documents and spreadsheets (and indeed almost all documents) don't belong in the System Folder. You know how the file system works. Create a folder somewhere else for your documents.

Other than that, the only rule is that there are no rules. Whatever works for you is the best way. And don't forget Find File if you lose something!

Apply here: The Applications folder

I recommend having an Applications folder for all your programs. The best place for this folder is either at the root level or on the desktop. Your Applications folder can also be subdivided when the need arises. Given what I do for a living, I have a lot of programs, so my Applications folder has subfolders for business programs, graphics programs, writing tools, utilities, toys, and online (modem) stuff, as shown in Figure 8-8.

Figure 8-8:
My Apps folder contains six subfolders.

It'll probably be a while before you need so many subfolders — unless you're like me and try a lot of new software. Either way, organize your applications the same way you organize your documents — in a way that makes sense to you. Follow this advice, and I promise that you'll always be able to find what you're looking for.

The Greatest Thing Since Sliced Bread: Aliases

When System 7 first arrived several years ago, many of its features were heralded as breakthroughs. But of these features, none has proved to be more useful than the alias.

An *alias* is a quick opener for another file. With aliases, a file can seem to be in two (or more) places at once. When you create an alias of a disk, a file, or a folder, opening its alias is the same as opening the item. And an alias takes up only the tiniest bit of disk space.

Why is this feature so great? First, it lets you make items appear to be in more than one place, which on many occasions is exactly what you want to do. For example, keeping an alias of your word processor on your desktop and another in your Apple menu is convenient. You may even want a third alias of it in your Documents folder for quick access. Aliases let you open your word processor quickly and easily without navigating into the depths of your Applications folder each time you need it.

Here's another example: If you write a memo to Fred Smith about the Smythe Marketing Campaign to be executed in the fourth quarter, which folder does the document go in? Smith? Smythe? Marketing? Memos? 4th Quarter?

With aliases, it doesn't matter. You can put the actual file in any of the folders and then create aliases of the file and place them in all the other folders. So whichever folder you open, you'll be able to find the memo.

Finally, many programs need to remain in the same folder as their supporting files and folders. Some programs won't function properly unless they are in the same folder as their dictionaries, thesauruses, data files (for games), templates, and so on. Ergo, you can't put those programs on the desktop or in the Apple Menu Items folder without impairing their functionality.

Icons on the desktop

How about a little hands-on training? You can create an alias for your favorite application and put it on the desktop, a very good place for it.

1. **Find your favorite application — AppleWorks, Microsoft Word, Myth II Soulblighter, whatever — and select its icon.**

   Be sure to select the program's icon, not the folder that it's in.

2. **Choose File⇨Make Alias or press ⌘+M, as shown in Figure 8-9.**

   An alias of the application appears next to the original. The alias's file name is the same as the original's, except that it's in italics and has the word *alias* added at the end.

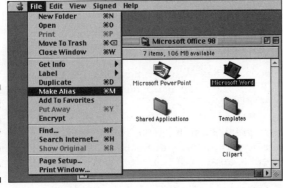

Figure 8-9:
Make an alias of your very favorite program.

3. **Drag the alias onto the desktop and move it to a convenient place.**

   Under your hard disk icon is one prime location. (See Figure 8-10.) Along the bottom of the screen is another.

Figure 8-10:
Right under
your hard
disk icon is
an excellent
place to put
a frequently
used alias.

There. You've just made it easier to use your favorite program. Next time you need your favorite program, just open its alias right there on your desktop instead of opening several folders and cluttering up your screen.

Frequently used folders or documents are good candidates for aliases on the desktop. In fact, any icon you use more than a few times a day is a good candidate for an alias on the desktop.

Remember, aliases don't take up much disk space (a measly 3K or 4K each), so there's no penalty for making an alias and later deciding that you don't like it. Big deal. Drag it to the Trash (which, by the way, deletes only the alias, not the original file).

The temporary alias theory

I use a lot of temporary aliases on my desktop. When I first create a file, I save it in its proper folder inside my Documents folder somewhere. If it's a document that I plan to work on for more than a day or two, such as a magazine article, I make an alias of the document (or folder) and put it on the desktop. When I've finished the article and submitted it to my editor, I trash the alias. The original file is already stashed away in its proper folder.

With bigger projects such as books, which have multiple subfolders of their own, I keep an alias of the parent folder on the desktop for easy access. When I submit the last chapter, the alias goes into the Trash.

Incidentally, a similar technique can be used without the aliases. Just save all your new documents on the desktop (click the Desktop button in the Save dialog box or use the shortcut ⌘+D). Later, when you're finished with the documents, you can file them away in their proper folders.

My point is that the desktop is an excellent place to keep the things you need most often — whether you use aliases of documents or save the actual files on the desktop until you figure out where you want to store them. Keep frequently used programs on the desktop forever and use the desktop as a temporary parking place for current projects.

Whatever you do, I encourage you to do it on the desktop.

What a drag it is not to drop

Macintosh drag-and-drop deals with dragging text and graphics from one place to another. But there's another angle to drag-and-drop, one that has to do with documents and icons.

You can use drag-and-drop to open a file using a program other than the one that would ordinarily launch when you open the document. This concept is easier to show than to tell, so follow along on your own computer:

1. **Make a screen shot picture of your desktop by pressing ⌘+Shift+3.**

   You hear a cute snapshot sound, and a document called Picture 1 automatically appears in your hard disk's root level window.

2. **Open Picture 1.**

   Assuming that a copy of SimpleText is on your hard disk, SimpleText launches and displays Picture 1.

   But you don't want to use SimpleText. SimpleText can open and display a picture file but can't make changes to it. You want to open the picture with a program that can edit it. What do you do? Use drag-and-drop.

3. **Quit SimpleText.**

4. **Drag the icon for Picture 1 onto the alias of your favorite program, which you created a few paragraphs back.**

   Figure 8-11 shows how I made changes to Picture 1.

If the alias of your favorite program didn't get highlighted when you dragged Picture 1 on top of it, or if dragging Picture 1 onto the alias launched the program but didn't open Picture 1, your favorite program isn't capable of opening picture files.

Your solution if your favorite program can't open Picture 1: Get a different favorite program. Just kidding. The solution is to try dragging Picture 1 onto other program icons (or aliases of program icons) until you find one that opens it. When you do, you might want to put an alias of that application on the desktop, too.

What happens if you don't have a copy of SimpleText on your hard disk when you try to open Picture 1? Mac OS File Translation kicks in and offers you a choice of other programs that can open your picture, as shown in Figure 8-12.

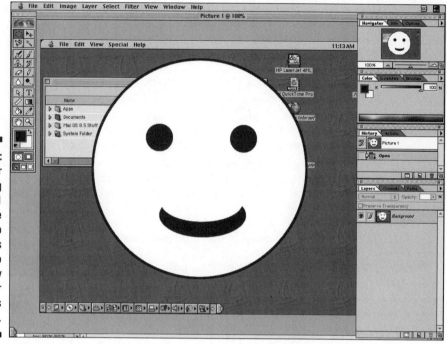

Figure 8-11:
After
dragging
Picture 1
onto the
Photoshop
icon, I was
able to
make a few
minor
changes
to it.

Figure 8-12:
Mac OS File
Translation
lets you
choose from
compatible
applications
if you try to
open a
document
created by a
program you
don't have
on your hard
disk.

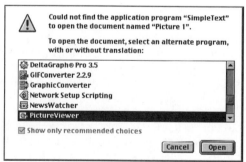

When I trashed SimpleText and tried to open Picture 1, Figure 8-12 is what I saw. In a more technical book, I would go on to explain about file types and creator codes and how they have to do with which program gets launched when you open a document. But this is *Mac OS 9 For Dummies,* so I won't.

Suffice it to say that Mac OS 9 is smart enough to figure out which applications on your hard disk can open what documents and offer you a choice. Earlier versions weren't that smart.

Spring has sprung: Meet your nifty new spring-loaded folders

Speaking of dragging and dropping, Mac OS 9 has a little feature that makes dragging and dropping less of a drag: the useful and usable spring-loaded folders. Spring-loaded folders make folders spring open temporarily when you hold an item over them.

To turn on spring-loaded folders and give them a try:

1. **Make the Finder the active application.**

2. **Choose Edit⇨Preferences.**

3. **Click the General tab at the top of the window, and then click the Spring-Loaded Folders check box.**

4. **Set the Delay before Opening slider to Short (at least for this demo).**

Now grab any icon in the Finder, and drag it onto the System Folder icon. Don't release the mouse button. There. See how the System Folder springs open automatically when you hold an icon on top of it? That's a spring-loaded folder in action.

If you can stand more excitement, drag the icon you're holding onto the Preferences folder (or any other subfolder in the System Folder) without releasing the mouse button. That folder springs open. Finally, without releasing the mouse button, drag the icon away from any windows or folder icons or drag it into the menu bar. All sprung folders should magically spring shut.

One other nice thing about spring-loaded folders is that you can use them without even dragging any icons. Just do what I call a "one-and-a-half-click" on any icon when spring-loaded folders are turned on. To do this, click once on the target icon (folder or disk only, please) and then click again quickly, but do not release the mouse button the second time. If you keep holding the button down, the cursor turns into a magnifying glass and you can cruise through your folders, spring-loaded style. (See Figure 8-13.)

Figure 8-13:
A click and
a half gives
me the mag-
nifying glass
cursor that
indicates
that I'm
browsing
through
spring-
loaded
folders.

Smart Apple menu tricks

Remember when I called the Launcher *lame* earlier in this chapter? Here's something way better. I talk a bit about the Apple menu in Chapter 6; now I show you how to make it work for you.

First, make sure that you've turned on the wonderful submenus in the Apple Menu Options control panel. If you don't see little black triangles to the right of all the folders in the Apple menu, the submenus are not turned on.

The hard-disk-alias-in-the-Apple-menu trick

Now do something useful. Make a file launcher that enables you to open every file on your hard disk from a single Apple menu item:

1. **Select your hard disk icon, and then select your hard drive and choose File⇨Make Alias or use the shortcut ⌘+M.**

   You just made an alias of your hard disk.

2. **Put the alias of your hard disk in the Apple Menu Items folder (which is in your System Folder).**

3. **Pull down the Apple menu and admire your handiwork.**

If having your hard drive on the Apple menu is too overwhelming for you, consider putting an alias of your Documents folder or your Applications folder in the Apple menu. It's easy, fast, and convenient. Get in the habit of putting frequently used items in the Apple menu — it's not just for desk accessories and folders anymore. You'll be glad you did.

A quick trick for adding an alias to the Apple menu

The following automatically creates an alias of the selected item and puts it in the Apple Menu Items folder:

1. **Select the icon of the item that you want to appear in the Apple menu.**

2. **Choose Apple menu⇨Automated Tasks⇨Add Alias to Apple Menu.**

The old alias-of-the-Apple-Menu-Items-folder-on-the-desktop trick

Are you growing fonder of your Apple menu? You should be. It's a great resource and it's easy to customize. If you find yourself customizing yours a lot, make an alias of the Apple Menu Items folder and put it on your desktop for easy access.

If you make frequent changes to your Apple menu, this tip saves you at least one step. And here's another tip: You can also put an alias of the Apple Menu Items folder in the Apple menu so that you can select it even if a window is covering the alias on your desktop.

When you put an alias of the Apple Menu Items folder in your Apple menu, it won't have subfolders, which makes sense when you think about it. If it had subfolders, they would create an endless loop.

By the way, I reveal some more very cool Apple menu tricks in Chapter 13.

Chapter 9

Publish or Perish: The Fail-Safe Guide to Printing

. . . .

In This Chapter

▶ Choosing a printer

▶ Using Page Setup

▶ Printing to most printers

▶ Using desktop printers

▶ Fonts and font stuff

. . . .

*P*rinting is like being. It just is. Or at least it should be. It should be as simple as pressing ⌘+P and then pressing the Return or Enter key. And usually that's how it is. Except when it isn't, and printing turns into a raging nightmare.

You won't be having any nightmares. If you get your printer and printing software configured properly, printing is simple as can be. And that's pretty darn simple.

So this is a chapter about avoiding nightmares. I go through the entire process as if you just unpacked a new printer and plugged it in. If you upgraded from an earlier version of Mac OS and can print with Mac OS 9 already, you can probably skip some of the steps. The objective here is to familiarize yourself with the printing process from start to finish.

 I suggest that you read the documentation that came with your specific printer. Hundreds of different printer makes and models are available for the Mac, so I may contradict something that your printer manual says. If you run into this discrepancy, try it the way the manual says first. If that doesn't work, try my way.

Another thing you need to know is that every application can use its own Print and Page Setup dialog box. Although many look like the ones in this chapter, others don't. For example, the Print and Page Setup dialog boxes for

Microsoft Word include choices I don't cover in this chapter, such as Even or Odd Pages Only, Print Hidden Text, and Print Selection Only. If you see commands in your Print or Page Setup dialog boxes that I don't explain in this chapter, they're specific to that application and should be explained in its documentation. I use Apple's SimpleText program for this demonstration.

Don't forget about Balloon Help and Mac OS Help. Many programs support these excellent Apple technologies; they can be the fastest way to figure out a feature that has you stumped.

I'll get started then. In previous editions of this book, I said, "Begin by connecting the printer to the Printer port on the back of your Mac (with both the Mac and the printer turned off, of course — but you knew that, didn't you?)." These days I have to change it to "Begin by connecting the printer to the appropriate port. . . ." That's because these days printers don't always connect to the Printer port. Some printers connect to the Ethernet port. Others connect through the USB port. So read the instructions that came with your printer and plug it into the appropriate hole in your Mac.

If you don't have a cable (and many Apple printers don't come with cables), contact your printer manufacturer and ask where it is. Plug the printer into an outlet. Turn it on. If the printer came with software, install it on your hard disk, following the instructions that came with the printer. That's it.

Ready, set, print!

Ready: Choosing a Printer in (What Else?) the Chooser DA

The path to printing perfection begins with the humble Chooser DA. Many of the steps involving the Chooser require that the printer be turned on and warmed up (that is, run through its diagnostics and startup cycle), so if yours isn't, it should be. Do that now so that you can choose a printer.

From the Apple menu, select the Chooser. The Chooser desk accessory opens. If you have previously chosen a printer, its icon is selected when the Chooser opens. If you've never printed before, the Chooser appears with no printer icon selected.

The Chooser is also where you choose network connections. You see an icon for AppleShare and maybe one for your fax modem. Don't mess with them yet. I talk about file sharing in Chapter 10.

If no icon is selected in your Chooser, click the printer icon that matches
your printer. If you have an Apple printer, one of the icons should match it. If
you have an Apple printer and none of the icons match your printer, try clicking the one that sounds most like your printer.

If you have a non-Apple printer, see its manual for instructions on installing
printer drivers for your printer. Or try clicking one of the Apple printer drivers.
(If it's a laser printer, try LaserWriter 8; if it's an inkjet, try Color SW 1500.)

Most of the icons in the Chooser represent printer drivers. Printer drivers
translate between your Mac applications and your printer, ensuring that what
you see is what you print. Technically, a printer driver is a special piece of
software called a Chooser extension. When you drag a printer driver onto
your System Folder, Mac OS 9 automatically places it in the Extensions folder
for you. As long as a printer driver is in the Extensions folder, you should see
an icon for it in the Chooser.

If you have a printer made by someone other than Apple, you may want to
contact the manufacturer about getting the latest, greatest driver. Many
printer manufacturers are offering new drivers with enhanced functionality. If
you have a modem, you may find new drivers for your printer on America
Online or the Internet. Check with your printer manufacturer for details.

Apple printer drivers are installed automatically when you install the Mac OS.
You remove them by dragging them from the Extensions folder to the Trash.
It's perfectly safe to remove printer drivers for printers that you never intend
to use. Removing unneeded printer drivers can free up more than a megabyte
of hard disk space.

Now I want to get down to business. The left side of the Chooser should be
displaying a selection of printer icons; the right side of the Chooser should
be displaying either your printer's name (see Figure 9-1) or a pair of icons
(see Figure 9-2).

Figure 9-1:
The Chooser
DA as it
appears
when you
select an
AppleTalk
printer.

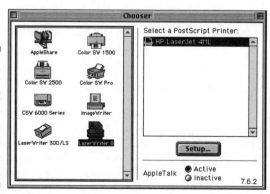

If you've never used a printer with Mac OS 9, you may see a warning box that says, "If the printer you wish to use has not been set up, please click the Setup button." If that happens, do what it says. If there's an "Auto Setup" button there, use it.

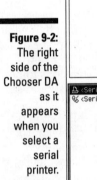

Figure 9-2:
The right side of the Chooser DA as it appears when you select a serial printer.

If you have an AppleTalk printer

If you have an AppleTalk printer, click your printer's name on the right side of the Chooser to select it — even if only one name appears, as shown in Figure 9-1.

If you have a serial printer

If you have a serial printer, you'll see two icons on the right side of the Chooser instead of a printer name. Choose whichever port — Printer or Modem — the printer cable is connected to on the back of your Mac.

If you have a USB printer

If you have a printer connected directly to an iMac, it's probably a USB printer. Look for the flat, rectangular ports on new PowerBooks and blue-and-white PowerMacs, too. If you have a USB printer connected, you'll need to install its driver software before you can print. Apple doesn't currently sell USB printers, so there are no icons for them in the Chooser until you install drivers. When you click the printer's icon, you may see the names of the USB ports on your Mac, or you may simply see an empty pane on the right side of the Chooser.

If you have a SCSI, an Ethernet, a USB, or a server-based printer

If you have a SCSI, an Ethernet, a USB, or a server-based printer, you're on your own. What you see on the right side of the Chooser depends on the printer's manufacturer or your server's setup. I couldn't beg or borrow any of the preceding devices, so I don't know what you'll see. With luck, you'll figure it out.

My printer is a Hewlett Packard LaserJet 4ML — a compact, inexpensive, 300-dots-per-inch PostScript AppleTalk laser printer. I've had the HP for more than three years now and it has performed like a champ. At some point I plan to upgrade to a 600- or 800-dpi printer, but it's not mission-critical as long as the faithful HP keeps chugging along.

The AppleTalk Active/Inactive options

Okay. Here's something I can help you with. Should AppleTalk be active or inactive? My answer: Inactive unless you need it.

How do you know if you need AppleTalk? Well, for starters, if you're on a network and use file sharing, you need AppleTalk. If your printer is an AppleTalk-only printer (many are), you need it. If you're in neither of these situations, you probably don't need AppleTalk. There's no reason to keep it turned on if you don't need it.

If in doubt, just give it a try. You'll know that your printer works with AppleTalk inactive if your printer spits out a page.

That's it for the Chooser. When you close it, a desktop printer is created automatically on your desktop for the printer you chose. I talk much more about those desktop printers later in the chapter. For now, just know that if for some strange reason you hate it, you can trash it later. (But, much like the proverbial bad penny, it'll keep coming back every time you select a printer in the Chooser.)

Not all printers can be turned into desktop printers. Most can, but a few — such as my tech reviewer's Epson Stylus Photo 1200, for example — can't.

Before you close the Chooser . . .

I go through the rest of this exercise using an AppleTalk printer as the example. If you have a different kind of printer — a serial, USB, SCSI, or server printer — and you can print to your printer at this point, everything in the rest of the chapter should work the same for you. (To see whether you can print to your printer, close the Chooser, open a document, and choose File↪ Print. If the document comes out of the printer, you're all set.)

Set: Setting Up Your Page with Page Setup

You did the hard part. Now you should be able to print a document quickly and easily. Right? Not so fast, bucko. Although you may not need the Page Setup dialog box right this second, you do need to know about it.

Almost every program that can print a document has a Page Setup command on its File menu. Some programs call it Page Setup and others call it Print Setup. (Print Setup is the quaint, old-fashioned term, more popular in the System 6 era than today.) Either way, this dialog box lets you choose paper type, page orientation, scaling percent, page flipping, and page inverting.

Your Page Setup dialog box should look like Figure 9-3.

Portrait Landscape

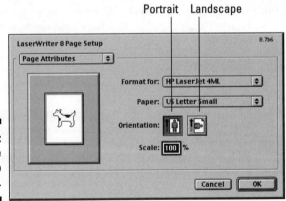

Figure 9-3:
The Page
Setup
dialog box.

Paper type

The objective here is to choose the type of paper currently in the paper tray of your printer or the type of paper that you're about to feed manually.

To do so, click the Paper pop-up menu (see Figure 9-4) and choose the type of paper you plan to use for your next print job.

Figure 9-4: Choosing a paper type in the Page Setup dialog box.

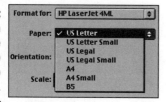

Page Setup dialog box settings remain in effect until you change them. So if you are printing an envelope this time, don't forget to change back to US Letter before trying to print to letter-size paper.

Page orientation

Page Orientation lets you tell the printer whether the page you're about to print is a portrait-oriented (letter, longways) page or a landscape-oriented (spreadsheet, sideways) page. Check out Figure 9-5.

Figure 9-5: Portrait (left) and land-scape (right) pages.

The Page Setup dialog box offers a choice of portrait or landscape (labeled in Figure 9-3).

Scale

The Scale control lets you enlarge or reduce your image for printing. Just type a new value into the Scale text entry box, replacing the number 100. I typed 200, as shown in Figure 9-6. In old-style Page Setup dialog boxes, you can also use the arrow buttons next to the Scale box to change the value.

Figure 9-6:
The setting (200%) doubles the size of the printout.

Scale: 200 %

The range of scaling is 25 percent to 400 percent. If you try to enter a higher or lower number, your Mac beeps at you and changes the number automatically to the closest acceptable number. Nice touch.

To see actual numbers on the left in your Page Setup dialog box, just click the dog. Click again to see them in centimeters.

PostScript options

But wait, there's more. The Page Setup dialog box offers two additional sets of options if you choose PostScript Options from the pop-up menu: Visual Effects and Images & Text. Check out Figure 9-7.

Figure 9-7:
PostScript Options in the Page Setup dialog box.

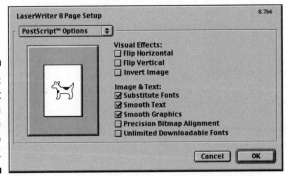

The tail of the dogcow

The dogcow has appeared in the Page Setup dialog box since time immemorial. He's a kind of unofficial Macintosh mascot. His name, they say, is Clarus. His bark, they say, is Moof.

Clarus is more than just a mascot. He's an elegant way to give you visual feedback on your choices. Look at Figure 9-8. It works.

Visual Effects

Flipping the page vertically or horizontally merely requires that you check the appropriate check box. The dogcow on the miniature page reflects your choices. (See Figure 9-8.)

Checking the Invert Image option inverts your page, making light areas dark and dark areas light, like a photograph negative.

Figure 9-8:
The miniature page featuring Clarus the Dogcow (Moof!) provides visual feedback for your choices of Visual Effects.

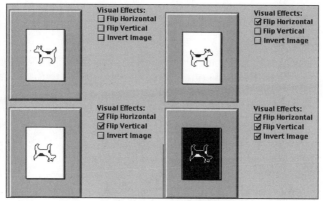

Note that the Invert Image option generally uses a lot of toner or ink. And printing a large number of inverted pages could cause a laser printer to overheat or an inkjet printer to clog. Use this feature sparingly.

I suppose that the Invert Image option is useful for creating artsy effects or making negative images of documents that will be printed to film. I've never used it in the 15 years I've used a Mac.

Image & Text

The next five options are thrilling. I could spend two pages explaining them, but I'm going to invoke a weasel-out and tell you to look at the Balloon Help to find out what they do. While the Page Setup PostScript Options dialog box is on the screen, choose Show Balloons from the Help (question mark) menu, and point at each of the five check boxes, as shown in Figure 9-9.

Figure 9-9: Balloon Help explains these five check boxes almost as well as I could. It'll save a tree (part of one, at least), too.

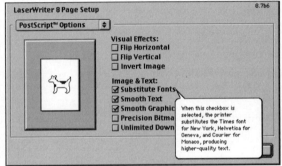

One last thing . . .

Most programs also offer their own Page Setup choices. To see them (if your program offers them, of course), choose the program from the pop-up menu below the words "LaserWriter 8 Page Setup." Adobe Photoshop and Microsoft Word have them (see Figures 9-10 and 9-11, respectively); SimpleText doesn't.

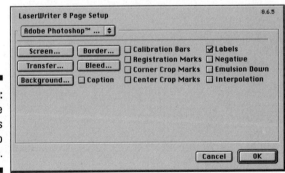

Figure 9-10: Adobe Photoshop's Page Setup choices.

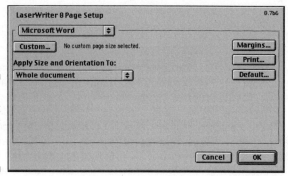

Figure 9-11:
Microsoft
Word's
Page Setup
choices.

Go: Printing to Most Printers

Now I come to the final step before that joyous moment when your printed page pops out of the printer. It's the Print dialog box, and it's the last thing standing between you and your output.

Although most of you will see Print dialog boxes that look like the ones in this chapter, others won't. The features in the Print dialog box are strictly a function of the program with which you're printing. Many programs choose to use the standard-issue Apple dialog boxes as shown in this chapter, but others don't. If a feature isn't explained in this chapter, chances are it's a feature that's specific to the application you're using and is explained in that program's documentation.

Your printer is chosen in the Chooser. Your page is set up in Page Setup. If, up to this point, you haven't been working with a document that you want to print, find one now and open it because it's time to . . .

1. Choose File⇨Print (⌘+P).

One of the best things about the Mac is that Apple has published a set of guidelines that all Mac programs should use. Consistency among programs is one of the Mac's finest features. Notice how 99 percent of all programs have Open, Close, Save, Save As, Page Setup, Print, and Quit commands in their File menus and Undo, Cut, Copy, and Paste commands in their Edit menus. That's the kind of thing the Macintosh Human Interface Guidelines recommend.

According to Apple's guidelines, the Print command should always appear in the File menu, which is good. Macintosh Human Interface Guidelines also say that the keyboard shortcut ⌘+P should be reserved for plain text (the way ⌘+B is often used for bold and ⌘+I for italic). This is bad.

Fortunately, software developers listened to Apple about the first item and ignored Apple about the second, so ⌘+P is almost always the shortcut for the Print command in the File menu.

Every so often you come across a program that doesn't follow these conventions, but I would say at least 90 percent of commercial Mac programs put the Print command in the File menu and use ⌘+P for its keyboard shortcut.

The point is that there's a slight chance that Step 1 won't work for you. If the Print command is on a different menu, if there's no Print command, or if the keyboard shortcut is anything but ⌘+P, you'll have to wing it. Then write the software company a brief note mentioning that they could make things easier on everyone by putting the Print command in the proper place and using the generally-agreed-upon keyboard shortcut.

Anyway, the Print dialog box looks like Figure 9-12 when it first appears.

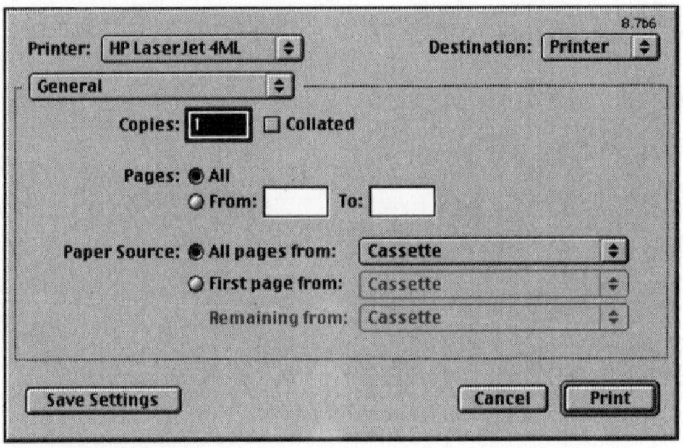

Figure 9-12:
The general
Print
dialog box.

The Print dialog box has a pop-up menu that offers seven options. (See Figure 9-13.) I go through these options and their suboptions one at a time.

Figure 9-13:
The Print
dialog box's
pop-up
options
menu.

The Print⇨General dialog box

The choices you make in the Print⇨General dialog box are

- How many copies to print
- Which page numbers to print
- Automatic or manual feed paper
- Which printer to use for this print job
- Which destination to use: printer or PostScript file
- Whether to save these settings permanently

Try pressing the Tab key and watching what happens. The active field jumps to each of the text fields in the dialog box in rotation. Shift+Tab makes the active field jump backward. Try it; you'll like it.

Copies

How many copies do you want to print? The Print dialog box defaults to one copy in most applications, so you'll probably see a 1 in the Copies field when the dialog box appears. Assuming that's the case, don't do anything if you want to print only one copy. If you want to print more than one copy of your document, select the 1 that appears in the Copies field and type a new number.

Pages

Which pages do you want to print? All of them? Or just some? This option is easy. If you want to print your entire document, click the All option. If you want to print only a specific page or range of pages, type their numbers in the From and To text entry boxes.

For example, suppose you have a 10-page document. You print the whole thing and then notice a typo on page 2. You correct the typo and then print only page 2 by typing a 2 in both the From and To fields, as shown in Figure 9-14.

Figure 9-14:
Here's how to print only the selected page of a document.

You can type any valid range of pages in the From and To fields.

Paper source

Your choices for paper source are Paper Cassette or Manual Feed for your first page or all your pages. If you plan to use the paper in your printer's paper tray, choose Cassette. If you plan to feed a single sheet, choose Manual Feed.

If you want the first page to come from one place and the remaining pages to come from another, click the appropriate option and make the appropriate choices from the pop-up menus.

It's that simple.

Destination

The pop-up menu in the dialog box's upper-right corner lets you choose to print to your printer or create a PostScript file on disk instead. When you choose File, the Print button becomes a Save button. When you click the Save button, a standard Save dialog box appears.

Save Settings

The Save Settings button saves the current settings and makes them the default for future print jobs. If everything is just as you like it, click this button and all future print jobs will use these settings.

The Print⇨Background Printing dialog box

Choosing Background Printing from the Print dialog box's pop-up menu lets you turn background printing on or off and set a print time if you so desire. (See Figure 9-15.)

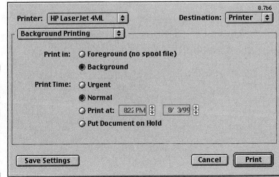

Figure 9-15:
The Print dialog box's Background Printing options.

Print in foreground or background

Background printing has been around for a while. It's the thing that allows you to continue using your Macintosh while it's printing. Wonderful stuff.

Under Mac OS 9, background printing is turned on unless you specifically turn it off. You may notice your Mac feeling a little twitchy or jerky when a document is printing in the background. That's normal. Ignore it. After a while, you hardly notice it at all. And it's much better than the alternative — being unable to work until your print job is finished.

Print time

To set a printing time for your document (see Figure 9-15), click the option next to your desired print time priority. Here's what the priorities mean:

- ✔ The Urgent option prints the document now and places it ahead of any documents in the print queue.

- ✔ The Normal option prints the document now. If other documents are in the print queue, the document takes its place behind documents printed before it.

- ✔ The Print At option lets you choose a specific time. When you click this option, you can adjust the time and date.

- ✔ The Put Document on Hold option lets you prepare a document for printing but not print it at this time.

The Print⇨Color Matching dialog box

In the Color Matching dialog box, you get to choose from Black and White, Color/Grayscale, ColorSync Color Matching, or PostScript Color Matching for your output. (See Figure 9-16.) Use your best guess.

Figure 9-16:
The Print dialog box's Color Matching options.

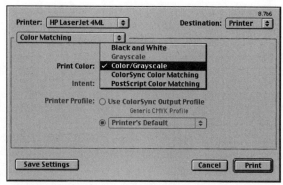

The Print⇨Cover Page dialog box

In the Cover Page dialog box, clicking the Before Document or After Document option (see Figure 9-17) adds a page at the beginning or the end, respectively, of your print job.

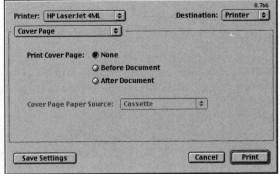

Figure 9-17:
The Print dialog box's Cover Page options.

The cover page contains your name, the program and document names, the date and time, and the printer name. In other words, the cover page looks pretty much like this:

User: Bob LeVitus

Application: Microsoft Word

Document: Great American Novel

Date: Wednesday, Aug 12, 1999

Time: 3:54:02 PM

Printer: HP LaserJet 4ML

I may have used this feature once in the past ten years. I suppose if you're on a network sharing a printer, you may have a reason to waste trees by printing useless pages with hardly anything on them. But unless you must have a cover page, leave the None button selected.

The Print⇨Font Settings dialog box

Here's another option your probably won't use much: The Font Settings dialog box lets you choose the type of fonts (Type 1 or TrueType) you want to use, and whether to download needed fonts when you print.

The Print⇨Job Logging dialog box

In the Job Logging dialog box, you can keep track of PostScript errors when they occur and generate reports on print jobs. You might use the error-reporting features if you have problems printing to a laser printer. Chances are that you won't do any job logging unless you're working in a copy shop or other business where you need to assign costs to your print jobs.

The Print⇨Layout dialog box

In the Layout dialog box, you can choose the number of pages per printed sheet and whether or not you prefer a border. (See Figure 9-18.)

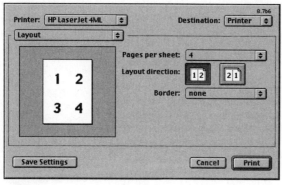

Figure 9-18:
The Print dialog box's Layout options.

The Print⇨Save As File dialog box

In the Save As File dialog box, you can save your file as a PostScript file on disk. One pop-up menu lets you choose between raw PostScript and several flavors of Encapsulated PostScript.

Another pop-up menu lets you include no fonts, all fonts, or only nonstandard fonts. (Nonstandard fonts are fonts other than the ones the Install Mac OS program installs.) Choose whichever setting is appropriate for the recipient of your document.

The safest bet is to include all fonts, just in case. The downside to this solution is that the PostScript file will be much larger than the original. For example, a SimpleText file of mine uses only 5K of disk space in its original form (that is, saved as a SimpleText document). When I save it as a PostScript file with all fonts included, it grows more than fifteenfold, requiring a whopping 80K of disk space.

Several things can inflate the size of a PostScript file. Including all fonts adds a lot of K. High-resolution images add a lot of K. And long documents use a lot of K. It's common for color artwork or page layout documents printed to disk as PostScript files to be larger than a high-density floppy disk. So if you plan to save a PostScript file to your hard disk and then copy it to a floppy disk, you may have to use a backup or compression utility to segment the file so that it will fit on several floppy disks. Another option is to use a Zip disk or some other high-capacity storage option.

I can't tell you much about the PostScript Level and Data Format choices; ask the people to whom you're sending the file if they have a preference.

One last thing . . .

StyleWriter and StyleWriter II users, as well as users of other inkjet printers or non-PostScript printers, may see slightly different versions of the Print and Page Setup dialog boxes. The differences should be minor enough not to matter.

Desktop Printers

Desktop printers are unique and a huge improvement over earlier printing schemes. The new architecture for printing makes the entire experience easier.

What is a desktop printer, anyway?

A *desktop printer* is an icon on your desktop that represents a printer connected to your computer. It's created automatically when you select a printer in the Chooser DA. To print a document, drag its icon onto a desktop printer, as shown in Figure 9-19.

Figure 9-19:
Drag-and-drop printing with desktop printer icons.

In Figure 9-19, when I release the mouse, Great American Novel will start printing.

Technically, Microsoft Word, the application that created the Great American Novel document, will launch, and its Print dialog box will open automatically. Click the Print button, or press Return or Enter, and the document will print and then Word will quit automatically. What if Word isn't available? If you have a translator that can open Word documents, you see a dialog box where you can choose another application. If you don't have a compatible application or translator, you see an error message telling you that the document cannot be opened.

You create new desktop printers with the Chooser.

Using desktop printers

Before I talk about using desktop printers, I need to tell you why you should use desktop printers. Three words: They save steps. Instead of opening a document, choosing File⇨Print, and diddling around in the Print dialog box, you can drag that document onto a desktop printer, click Print (or press Return or Enter), and then go out for a Jolt cola or whatever. In a word, it's easy. No muss, no fuss. Just drag-and-drop and click (or press), and in a few moments, paper starts popping out of your printer.

So basically, you use a desktop printer by dragging a document onto it. As long as the application that created the document is available, it will be printed after you click Print (or press Return or Enter) with no further ado.

Another handy use for desktop printers is to create desktop printers for special kinds of print jobs. For example, create one for envelopes that uses landscape, manual feed, and black-and-white settings. Create another for grayscale portrait-mode printing. And so on. Just drag your file onto the appropriate desktop printer (be sure to give it a descriptive name) and you avoid all those messy adjustments in the Page Setup and Print dialog boxes.

But there's more to using desktop printers than just drag-and-drop. When you select a desktop printer (by single-clicking it), a new printer menu appears in the menu bar, as shown in Figure 9-20. To view the print queue, open the desktop printer icon. (In case you forgot, you open an item by double-clicking its icon or by selecting its icon and choosing File⇨Open.)

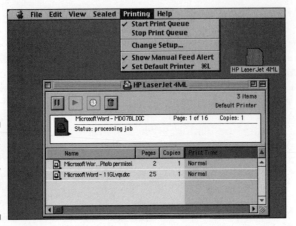

Figure 9-20:
The custom
printer
window and
more.

You'll notice a set of tape recorder–like icons in the desktop printer window. From left to right, these are Stop the Print Queue, Start the Print Queue, Set the Print Time for the Selected Item or Items, and Delete the Selected Item from the Queue. Also note that you can click any column head — Name, Pages, Copies, or Print Time — to change the sorting order of the items in the list.

In Figure 9-20, three Microsoft Word documents are in the queue. MDO7BL.DOC is currently printing. Clicking the stop button would suspend the printing of MDO7BL.DOC until I chose to resume. Clicking the delete button would permanently remove MDO7BL.DOC from the printing queue, and it would never print.

So what do the menu commands do?

✔ Start Print Queue and Stop Print Queue are like the play and pause buttons on your VCR. To pause the printing process and be able to resume where you left off later, choose Stop Print Queue. To resume, choose Start Print Queue.

✔ Change Setup lets you choose another PPD (PostScript Printer Description) file for this printer.

✔ Show Manual Feed Alert lets you decide whether or not your Mac pauses to ask you to insert a sheet of manual feed paper before a manual feed print job. A check mark beside this item means it's turned on.

✔ Set Default Printer lets you decide, if you have more than one printer attached, which one will be the default printer (that is, the one that's selected when you choose Print) in the Print dialog box.

One last thing about these here desktop printers: You can choose your desktop printers from the pop-up menu in the Print dialog box! That's right, the Print To pop-up menu in the Print dialog box gives you a choice of any printer that appears on your desktop. No more trips to the Chooser! Hooray!

Font Mania

To a computer user, *font* means typeface. Although professional typographers will scream, I'll go with that definition for now.

Each font looks different. Tens of thousands of different fonts are available for the Macintosh. You can buy single fonts and font collections anywhere you can buy software. Plenty of shareware and public domain fonts are also available from online services and user groups. Some people have thousands of them.

Installing fonts

This is a very short section. To install any font except a Type 1 font, drag it onto your System Folder icon. To install a Type 1 font, drag all of its files — the "printer font(s)" and the "screen font" — onto your System Folder. Note that your Type 1 font might have more than one printer font file.

When you drag any font onto your System Folder icon, your Mac asks whether you want to place the font in the Fonts folder. Click OK. When you click OK, the deed is done and the font is installed.

To remove a font, drag it out of the Fonts folder (which is in the System Folder). After a font is installed, it appears in the Font menu of all your applications.

You can store fonts anywhere on your hard disk, but a font is available in an application only if it's in the Fonts folder when you launch that application.

Types of fonts

You need to know about three types of fonts:

- ✔ Bitmap fonts, unlike other font formats, come in different sizes. You need a separate bitmap file for each size of the font that you want to display or print.

- ✔ TrueType fonts come with Mac OS 9. They are the Apple standard-issue fonts and are in wide use on Macs as well as on Windows machines. These fonts are *scaleable,* which means that there is only a single outline for the font, and your Mac makes it bigger or smaller when you choose a bigger or smaller font size in a program.

- ✔ Type 1 fonts, sometimes referred to as PostScript Type 1 fonts, are the standard for desktop publishing on the Mac. Tens of thousands of Type 1 fonts are available. (Not nearly as many TrueType fonts exist.)

  Type 1 fonts come in two pieces, a bitmap font suitcase and a second piece, called a printer font. Some Type 1 fonts come with two, three, or four printer fonts, which usually have related names.

Font advice in brief

You don't need to know a thing about font types. Really. When you get a font, just drag it (or all of its parts) onto your System Folder icon.

If you have a lot of fonts and need help managing them, try ATM Deluxe from Adobe or SuitCase 8 from Extensis.

Chapter 10

File Sharing for the Rest of Us

Computer networking has a well-deserved reputation for being complicated and nerve-wracking. The truth is, there's nothing scary or complicated about sharing files, folders, and disks (and printers, for that matter) among computers — as long as the computers are Macintoshes.

If you have more than one computer, file sharing is a must. It's fun, it's easy, and it's way better than SneakerNet. (SneakerNet is the "moving of files from one computer to another via floppy disk or other media such as Zip, Jaz, Orb, CD-R, and so on" according to the *Dr. Macintosh Unabridged Dictionary*.)

Your Macintosh includes everything you need to share files and printers. Everything, that is, except the printers and the cables. So here's the deal: You supply the printers and cables, and I supply the rest.

This chapter is unusual. I don't show you how to actually share a file until the next-to-the-last section. The first four sections provide an overview and tell you everything you need to know to share files successfully. Trust me, there's a method to my madness. If you try to share files without doing all the required prep work, the whole mess becomes confusing and complicated — kind of like networking a pair of PC clones.

So just follow along and don't worry about why you're not sharing yet. You'll share soon.

What It Is

Macintosh file sharing lets you use files, folders, and disks from other Macs on the network as easily as if they were on your own local hard disk.

Devices connected directly to your computers, such as hard disks or CD-ROM drives, are *local*. Devices you access (share) over the network are *remote*.

File sharing also lets any computer on the network access (if you desire) your files, folders, and disks as easily as if they were on someone else's local hard disk.

Finally, file sharing lets you link programs on your computer to programs on other computers. Why would you want to do that? You'll find out.

For our purposes, a *network* is two or more Macs connected by LocalTalk-compatible cables, Ethernet, or AirPort wireless networking.

This chapter assumes you're working on a small network, the kind typically found in a home or small business. There are also huge corporate networks, spaghetti-like mazes with thousands of computers and printers connected by cable, phone, infrared link, and ISDN, complete with confusing-sounding hardware such as routers and hubs and hublets and transceivers and net modems. That type of network is complicated, even if the computers are Macs. This chapter isn't about that subject.

If you're part of a mega-monstrous corporate network and you have questions about your particular network, talk to the P.I.C. (person in charge, also known as your network administrator).

If you're trying to build one of these mega-networks, I regret to inform you that you'll need a book a lot thicker than this one.

Portrait of a LocalTalk Network

This chapter describes my office network. It consists of two Macintoshes and a network laser printer. (By the end of the chapter, that's not all I'll be sharing, if you know what I mean.)

This two-person network is merely an example. In real life, a network can and often does have dozens or hundreds of users. Regardless of whether your network has two nodes or 2,000, the principles and techniques in this chapter are the same.

My little network looks like the one shown in Figure 10-1.

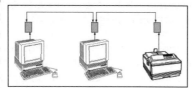

Figure 10-1:
My Mac,
Lisa's Mac,
and the
printer.

The black lines between the devices are cables; the gray box near each device is a connector. You need one connector for each device and enough cable to run between them. We happen to use the Apple LocalTalk Locking Connector Kits (part number M2068) and Apple Locking Cable Kits (M2066). LocalTalk connectors look something like Figure 10-2. The plug coming from the far side goes into the printer or modem port of your Mac. The two holes (ports) on the rear side are where you connect your Apple locking cables. Don't laugh. I drew the picture myself.

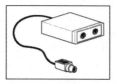

Figure 10-2:
This is what
a LocalTalk
connector
looks like.

I could have used PhoneNet connectors from Netopia (they used to be Farallon) instead of the Apple connectors. The big difference is that PhoneNet connectors use regular telephone cord from Radio Shack (or Target or anywhere) instead of expensive Apple Locking Cables. PhoneNet connectors are also less expensive than Apple LocalTalk connectors. Finally, PhoneNet connectors perform as well as (if not better than) Apple's LocalTalk connector. So why did I use the Apple cables? Because they were here. They came with my loaner computer. Otherwise, I would have gone with PhoneNet instead.

When discussions of networks take place, you're likely to hear the words *AppleTalk, EtherTalk* (or *Ethernet*), *TokenTalk,* and *LocalTalk* bandied about with great regularity. The last, LocalTalk, is a collection of wires and connectors. I talk more about this aberration in a moment. The others are protocols, a kind of language that networks speak.

Support for the AppleTalk protocol is built into every Mac. Almost all Macs (excluding the iMac and some newer PowerBooks) include ports for LocalTalk. Your Mac includes all the software you need to set up an AppleTalk network; all you have to provide are LocalTalk-compatible cables and connectors (such as the Apple or Netopia products I mention earlier).

LocalTalk is an aberration. It's not a protocol even though it sounds like one. In the old days, Apple referred to both the wires and the protocol as AppleTalk. Then one day a few years ago, Apple decreed that AppleTalk was a protocol and LocalTalk was the wires and connectors.

I suppose disassociating the protocol and the wires makes sense. Still, LocalTalk sounds like a protocol (AppleTalk, EtherTalk, TokenTalk), even though it's not. Anyway, LocalTalk refers to the physical connections that an AppleTalk network uses.

Got it? AppleTalk, EtherTalk, and TokenTalk are protocols, the languages that the network speaks. LocalTalk is a collection of physical parts — connectors (LocalTalk connectors), ports (like the modem or printer port), and cables (LocalTalk-compatible cables) — that hook the machines together.

Like I said, iMacs and new PowerBooks are the only Macs that don't include LocalTalk ports. Instead, they have Ethernet ports — they look like phone jacks but take a cable with a slightly larger connector. To network Macs with Ethernet, you need a little box called an Ethernet hub. Cables from each Mac or printer connect to the hub. You can also network two devices (an iMac and a PowerBook, say) with a special kind of Ethernet cable called a crossover cable. Go to your local electronics store to get one. They'll know what you're talking about, even if you don't. With a crossover cable, you can plug one end into each Ethernet device and, voila, you have a network.

Getting Turned On

No network activity can take place until AppleTalk is on. That means the first thing you need to do is turn on AppleTalk:

1. **Open the Chooser (Apple menu⇨Chooser).**

2. **Click the Active option to turn on AppleTalk.**

   See Figure 10-3.

3. **Close the Chooser by clicking its close box in the upper-left corner.**

   You could, instead, choose File⇨Close (⌘+W).

Figure 10-3:
The
AppleTalk
option.

4. **Open the AppleTalk control panel (Apple menu⇨Control Panels⇨ AppleTalk) and choose the appropriate connection from the pop-up menu.**

   See Figure 10-4. If you're using a small network, that's all you need to do to get started. If your network has multiple zones, you also have to choose a zone at this time.

   You can turn AppleTalk on and off also by using the AppleTalk module in your control strip.

Figure 10-4:
Choose the
connection
from the
AppleTalk
control
panel.

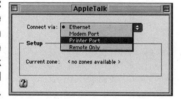

Zones are mininetworks connected together. When a network gets to about 50 users, zones help network managers keep network traffic under control. If you have zones, someone is probably around to ask whether you need to know more.

5. **Close the AppleTalk control panel by clicking its close box in the upper-left corner.**

   Or choose File⇨Close (⌘+W).

Setting Up File Sharing

Okay. AppleTalk is on, and you're ready for a quick game of Name That Mac before you turn file sharing on:

1. **Choose Apple menu⇨Control Panels⇨File Sharing.**

   The File Sharing control panel appears, as shown in Figure 10-5.

2. **In the Network Identity section at the top, type all three pieces of information: your name, a password, and a name for your Mac.**

   • *Owner Name:* This one should be self-explanatory — type your name.

   • *Owner Password:* Your password can be any combination of up to eight letters and numbers. When you click anywhere outside the Owner Password field, the letters or numbers in your password turn into bullets, as shown in Figure 10-5.

   • *Computer Name:* Select a computer name that's unique and memorable. *Lisa's Macintosh,* for example, is a better choice than *Mac.*

You can press the Tab key to move from field to field in the File Sharing control panel.

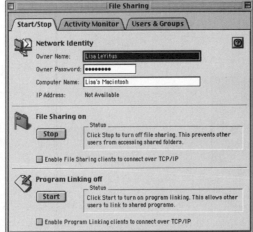

Figure 10-5:
The File
Sharing
control
panel for
Lisa's Mac.

If you ran the Mac OS Setup Assistant when you first installed OS 9 (or when you first got your Mac), you may have already entered this information.

Turn file sharing and program linking on

File sharing and program linking each have a Stop/Start button. If file sharing or program linking is turned on, the button reads Stop. If sharing or linking is not turned on, the button reads Start. Turn file sharing and program linking on (if they're not on already) by clicking each section's Start button.

The status of file sharing and program linking appears to the right of their buttons, as shown in Figure 10-5. File Sharing is presently on; Program Linking is presently off. How do I know? Well, first, it says right on the screen,

"File Sharing On" and "Program Linking Off." In addition, the buttons read Stop (for File Sharing) and Start (for Program Linking). Finally, the status boxes to the right of the buttons explain how to change them.

You want your File Sharing control panel to look like Figure 10-5, so if file sharing and program linking aren't on, click their Start buttons. (Click each one once.) In other words, if your buttons say Start, click them. If they say Stop, don't click them.

Program linking lets certain Macintosh programs exchange information with other programs. Programs implement linking in various ways, and not all programs can link. See the documentation that came with your program to find out whether linking is supported and how to use it.

There may be some performance penalty for having Program Linking turned on, so I have turned it off on my Macs. I can't recall ever needing it anyway. You allow or disallow program linking for specific users in the Users & Groups control panel (more on that subject in a second).

If program linking is not on in the File Sharing control panel, other users on your network cannot program link even if the Allow User To Link To Programs On This Computer check box is checked in the appropriate user window of the Users & Groups control panel.

Sharing and linking with TCP/IP

In most cases, folks who connect to your computer with file sharing or program linking will use AppleTalk. They can also use another network protocol, called TCP/IP, if both your Mac and theirs are set up to use it. If that's the case, and you want to let others connect with TCP/IP, click the matching check boxes under the File Sharing and Program Linking sections of the File Sharing control panel.

TCP/IP is the network protocol used on the Internet. It lets Macs, PCs, and other computers connect to one another using a number-based addressing system that's standard all over the world. You can (and most big companies do) use it to communicate in offices and over the Internet. I have more to say about setting up TCP/IP for the Internet in Chapter 17. If you need to know more about using it to connect to computers on your network, talk to the system administrator or the network geek in charge of these things where you work.

Users and Groups and Guests (Oh My!)

Macintosh file sharing is based on the concept of users and groups. Shared items — disks or folders — can be shared with no users, one user, or many users. Other people's access to items on your local hard disk is entirely at your discretion. You may configure your Mac so that no one but you can share its folders and disks, so that only one other person can share its folders and disks, or so that many people can share its folders and disks. People who share folders and disks are called *users*.

Users

Before you can go any further, you need to create user identities for the people on your network. You perform this little task with the Users & Groups control panel. I'm going to demonstrate on Lisa's Mac:

1. **Open the File Sharing control panel if it's not already open.**

   To do so, choose Apple menu⇨Control Panels⇨File Sharing.

2. **Choose Sharing⇨Users & Groups.**

   A Users & Groups window appears, as shown in Figure 10-6. If you haven't previously created users or groups, two users appear in the window:

   • *Owner* lets you configure sharing for the owner of your Mac, the person whose name appears in the Owner Name field of the File Sharing control panel. This icon should have your name on it.

   • *Guest* lets you configure a guest account for your Mac.

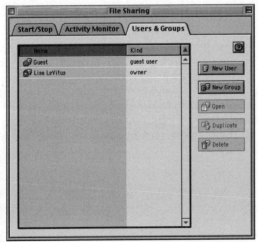

Figure 10-6:
The Users &
Groups
window.

3. **Click the New User button to create a new user.**

4. **Rename the new user's name to something meaningful.**

   When you create a new user, you have the option of assigning a password. If network security is unimportant to you (if only people you trust use the network), it's okay to leave the password field blank. You can also use the Allow user to change password check box to give your new user more control over his or her password. If you leave this box unchecked, the owner of the Mac has control over this user's password.

5. **Click the Users & Groups window and then open the item that has your name on it.**

   I'm referring to the name you typed in the Owner Name field of the File Sharing control panel.

6. **Pull down the pop-up menu at the top of the window and choose Sharing.**

7. **Open the item for the new user you created in Steps 3 and 4, and choose Sharing from the pop-up menu.**

   If you arrange the screen so that you can see both users' windows, you should see something similar to Figure 10-7. Use the following descriptions to determine how to configure the check boxes.

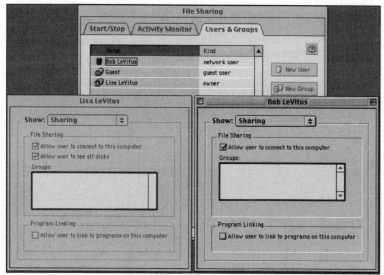

Figure 10-7:
The user privileges windows for Lisa and me.

The check boxes set the privileges of each user. Because Lisa and I are partners and want full access to each other's computers, we check both choices:

- *Allow user to connect to this computer:* Lets the user connect to this Mac from a remote Mac (as long as he or she knows the proper password).

- *Allow user to see all disks:* This choice is available only for the owner of the Mac. It means that you can see every file on your hard disk if you connect from a remote machine.

8. **Close the user window.**

That user is registered.

In a forthcoming section, I discuss the three categories of users on the network; registered users are one of the three.

Groups

Groups are a convenient way to deal with a bunch of users at once. In the preceding example, I set privileges for a single user, Lisa. Suppose I want to create a group so that I can assign the same privileges to everyone in our family: Lisa and myself as well as our daughter, Allison, and our son, Jacob, who occasionally use our computers.

First, I open the Users & Groups control panel (Apple menu⇨Control Panels⇨ Users & Groups). Next, I create new user items for Allison and Jacob. Then I create a new group (by clicking New Group) and name it The LeVitus Family. Finally, I drag the icons for Lisa, Bob, Jacob, and Allison onto the group icon as shown in Figure 10-8. The group icon inverts.

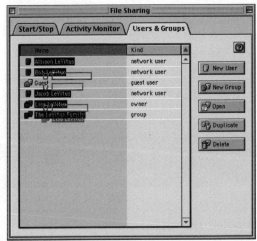

Figure 10-8:
Creating a
group for
the LeVitus
family.

If you open a group window and look inside, you see items representing the individual users. (See Figure 10-9.) Opening one of the user items is the same as opening it in the Users & Groups window. In other words, the Jacob LeVitus item in the LeVitus Family group window is like an alias of the Jacob LeVitus item in the Users & Groups window.

Figure 10-9:
Opening
either Jacob
LeVitus
item — from
the Users &
Groups or
The LeVitus
Family
window —
displays the
user
privileges
window for
Jacob
(lower
right).

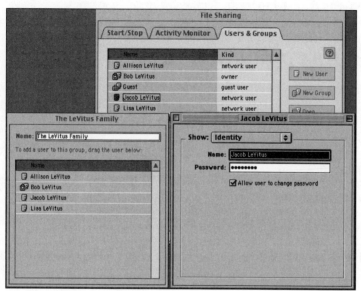

Giving privileges to a group is the same as giving those same privileges to each individual member of the group.

Be our guest

Did you notice the icon in your Users & Groups window called Guest? The Guest icon represents any users who haven't been assigned individual access privileges. Use this icon to allow or disallow guests to connect to your shared folders or disks. Even when guest access is turned on, no one but you has access to any of your folders or disks until you specifically share them. I talk about assigning access privileges to disks and folders in the next section.

Removing users or groups

To remove a user or group item from the Users & Groups window, drag it to the Trash. It's that simple.

Access and Privileges (Who Can Do What)

Now that file sharing is on and you've created users and groups for your network, you're ready to begin deciding who can use what.

Sharing a folder or disk

To share a folder or disk with another user, take the following initial steps:

1. **Select the folder or disk icon, and choose File⇨Get Info (or use the keyboard shortcut ⌘+I).**

   The Get Info window for the selected item opens.

2. **From the Show pop-up menu at the top of the window, choose Sharing.**

3. **Click the Share This Item and Its Contents check box.**

   If you want to be the owner of the folder, leave the Owner pop-up menu alone (more about ownership in a sec).

4. **Choose a user or group from the User/Group pop-up menu.**

   The LeVitus Family group is shown in Figure 10-10.

Figure 10-10:
This window controls access privileges for the Documents folder on Spawn.

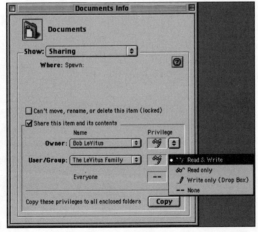

5. **For the owner and each user or group, choose access privileges from the pop-up menus.**

   The categories of access privileges are explained in the following sections.

You may not see exactly what's in Figures 10-9 and 10-10 on your screen. Well, of course you won't. I would be surprised if your network's users were named LeVitus. But there are other differences you may see as well:

✔ If you've selected a folder inside another shared folder, the check box near the middle says "Use enclosing folder's privileges" instead of "Share this item and its contents."

✔ If you've selected a folder on another computer, the Owner and User/Group areas are text entry boxes, not pop-up menus.

✔ If you've selected a folder that someone else owns, all the pop-up menus are dimmed.

Setting access privileges

The pop-up menus to the right of the Owner and User/Group pop-up menus control access. In other words, they control who can use what and how much they can use it.

Three categories of users are on the network:

✔ **The owner:** The owner of a folder or disk can change the access privileges to that folder or disk at any time. The name in the Owner Name field of the File Sharing control panel is the default owner of shared folders and disks on that machine. Ownership may be given away (more on that in a moment).

✔ **A registered user or a registered group:** A registered user has access to shared folders and disks over the network as long as the user or group has been granted access by the folder or disk's owner. A registered user is any user who has an entry in the Users & Groups control panel. A registered group is nothing more than a bunch of registered users.

✔ **Everyone:** This category is an easy way to set access privileges for everyone at once — the owner, registered users and groups, and guests.

The access privileges pop-up menus (the ones with icons, to the right of the Owner, User/Group, and Everyone items) let you control how much access each type of user has to the shared folder or disk. If you click one, you see the privilege description that corresponds to the icon.

You can choose from four types of access for each user or group:

✔ **Read & Write:** A user with read and write access can see, add, delete, move, and edit files just as if they were stored on his or her own computer.

✔ **Read only:** A read-only user can see and use files that are stored in a shared folder, but can't add, delete, move, or edit them.

✔ **Write only (Drop Box):** It's like the label says: A user with write-only access can drop files into your shared folder or disk.

✔ **None:** With no privileges, a user can neither see nor use your shared folders or disks.

Useful settings for access privileges

Here are some ways you can combine access privileges for a folder or disk.

Allow everyone access

Figure 10-11 shows the settings that allow access for everyone on a network. That means everyone can open, read, and change the contents of this shared disk or folder.

Figure 10-11:
Allow every-
one access.

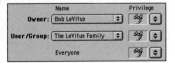

Allow nobody but yourself access

Figure 10-12 shows the appropriate settings that allow only the owner access. No one but the owner can see or use the contents of the shared disk or folder.

Figure 10-12:
Allow no
one but
yourself
access.

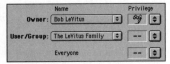

Allow one person or one group access

Figure 10-13 shows the settings that allow only a single user or a single group (in addition to the owner) access to see, use, or change the contents of the shared disk or folder.

Figure 10-13:
Allow one
person or
one group
access.

Allow others to deposit files and folders without giving them access (a drop box)

Figure 10-14 shows the settings that allow users to drop files or folders of their own without being able to see or use the contents of the shared disk or folder. After a file or folder is deposited in a drop folder, the dropper cannot retrieve it, because he or she doesn't have access privileges to see the items in the drop folder.

Figure 10-14:
Allow others
to deposit
files and
folders, but
do not allow
them
access.

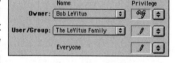

Read-only bulletin boards

Figure 10-15 shows the settings that let everyone open and read the files and folders in this shared folder or disk, but only the owner can make changes.

Figure 10-15:
Allow every-
one read
access.

The two other privileges

The access privileges window has two more items. At the top, the Can't Move, Rename, or Delete This Item check box protects the folder from being moved, renamed, or deleted by users whose privileges would otherwise allow them to move, delete, or rename that folder. (This check box doesn't appear in the access privileges window for disks.)

The Copy These Privileges to All Enclosed Folders option, at the bottom of the access privileges window, does exactly what its name implies. This feature is a fast way to assign the same privileges to many subfolders at once.

The Actual Act of Sharing

Okay, this is the moment you've been waiting for. You did everything leading up to the big moment: Sharing is set up, users and groups are registered, and access privileges are assigned.

If you've been following along, you know how to do all the prep work and more. So make sure that you've shared at least one folder on your hard disk and that you have full access privileges to it. Now go to another computer on the network, and I'll show you how to access that folder remotely.

Interestingly, file sharing doesn't have to be activated on the other machine. If file sharing is turned off, you can't create users and groups or assign access privileges, but you can access a remote shared disk or folder if its owner has granted you enough access privileges.

If file sharing is turned off on your Mac, though, others won't be able to access your disk or folders, even if you've shared them previously.

Connecting to a shared disk or folder

Continuing my little network example, I'm going to access the Documents folder on Lisa's Mac, which Lisa owns but has granted me full access to. (See Figure 10-16.)

On my computer, I choose Apple menu⇨Chooser and then click the AppleShare icon.

Figure 10-16:
The
Documents
folder on
Lisa's Mac. I
have full
privileges so
I'm able to
access the
folder from
my (remote)
computer.

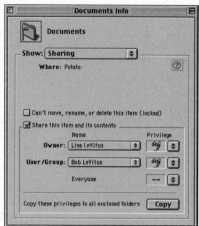

AppleTalk, of course, is active on my machine. If it's not, I won't be able to use the network. Although file sharing doesn't have to be turned on for me to access a remote disk or folder, AppleTalk does.

In the Chooser's file server list, I select Lisa's Mac and then click OK, as shown in Figure 10-17.

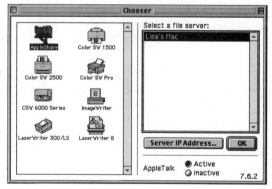

Figure 10-17:
The Chooser
on my Mac
as I connect
to Lisa's
Mac.

After I click OK, the Connect dialog box appears. Because I'm the owner of this Mac, my name appears in the Name field. I type my password and then click Connect, as shown in Figure 10-18.

Figure 10-18:
The Macintosh owner's name appears automatically.

I now encounter another dialog box where I can select one or more items to use. Because that single folder, Documents, is the only folder on Lisa's Mac that has been shared with me, it's the only one that appears in Figure 10-19.

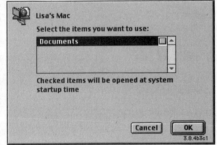

Figure 10-19:
The last dialog box before the Documents folder on Lisa's hard disk appears on my desktop.

I click OK, and the Documents icon appears on my desktop, as shown in Figure 10-20. This icon represents a shared folder from Lisa's hard disk.

Figure 10-20:
The Documents icon represents a shared folder.

The icon for the Documents folder clearly indicates that this is a shared folder accessed over the network. (Those are wires coming out of the bottom of the icon.) This icon is what you see whenever a remote disk or folder is mounted on your desktop.

If multiple items appear in the item selection dialog box (refer to Figure 10-19), you may select more than one. Click the first item, hold down the Shift key, and click once on each item that you want to add to the selection. After you've selected all the items you want to use, click the OK button, and they are all mounted on your desktop.

Connecting automatically at startup

If I wanted the Documents folder, which is on Lisa's Macintosh, to appear automatically on my Mac's desktop every time I turn it on, I would click the check box to the right of Documents in Figure 10-19.

I expect to use this folder only occasionally, so I won't click the check box.

Reopening the remote Documents folder quickly and easily

Now that I've mounted Lisa's Documents folder on my desktop for the first time, I can make it easier to use in the future by creating an alias for it. Next time I want to use the Documents folder, I open the alias, and the Connect dialog box appears. I type my password and the folder appears (is mounted) on the desktop. No Chooser, no other dialog boxes, no muss and no fuss.

If you use remote folders often, mount each one on your desktop, create an alias for each one, and put the aliases in a folder called Remote Folders. Move the Remote Folders folder to your Apple Menu Items folder and you'll be able to mount these remote folders on your desktop almost instantly.

If you're on a small network like this and always expect to have full access to stuff on the other computer, configure the computers so Guest access is set to full on — that way, when you get to the point of mounting the remote Mac's stuff, you don't need to enter a password. Just click the Guest button, and then click OK.

With the new Keychain Access feature, you can add a remote drive to a keychain. Then you can open the drive by choosing Open Keychain Access from the Keychain Control Strip Module, selecting Get Info on the drive in question, and clicking the Go There button. If you've configured the keychain to not issue a warning, the drive mounts without another question. You find out more about the Keychain in Chapter 12.

Connecting to your own computer from a remote computer

Because Lisa is the owner of her computer, if she walks over to my computer, she can mount her entire hard disk on my desktop. She has checked the Allow User to See All Disks check box in the Sharing pane of her user item in the Users & Groups control panel. In other words, after she opened the icon representing herself in her Users & Groups control panel, she gave herself the privilege of seeing her entire disk remotely by choosing the appropriate options.

Anyway, if Lisa were at my Mac and wanted to use her hard disk, she would do almost the same things that I did to mount the Documents folder on my desktop, with one small difference.

Here's how she would do it: First, she would walk over to my Mac. Then she would select Apple menu⇨Chooser. In the Chooser, she would select her Macintosh from the list of servers. Now, here's where the procedure is a little different: When the Password dialog box appears, it has the owner's name in it, as was shown in Figure 10-18. She would delete the "Bob" part and replace it with "Lisa." Then she would type her password and click Connect. Then, instead of seeing a list of folders, she would see her hard disk in the next dialog box. (If Lisa had logged on as a guest or used my name and password, she would have seen the Documents folder instead of her hard disk in the dialog box.)

Here's a great tip for Lisa. There's an even easier way for her to use her hard disk while working at my Mac. Before she leaves her computer, she should make an alias of her hard disk and copy it to a floppy disk. When she gets to my computer, all she has to do is insert that floppy and open the alias of her hard disk. The Connect dialog box appears, and as long as she types the correct password, her hard disk will mount on my desktop. Neat.

This technique is often called office-on-a-disk. If you work in a largish office and find yourself trying to connect to your hard disk from someone else's computer, carry one of these office-on-a-disk floppies with you at all times.

What? No floppy? Just because your iMac has no floppy drive doesn't mean you can't use a disk alias. The first time you mount your hard disk on a remote Mac, make an alias of the mounted disk. Leave it on the desktop or some other convenient location, and you can use it to quickly mount the disk.

Disconnecting from a shared folder or disk

When you finish using the shared disk or folder, close any open files or programs on the shared disk or folder and then disconnect using one of these three methods:

- Select the shared disk or folder icon and choose File⇨Put Away (⌘+Y).

- Drag the shared disk or folder icon to the Trash.

- If you've finished working for the day, choose Special⇨Shut Down. Shutting down automatically disconnects you from shared disks or folders.

A Few Other Things You Ought to Know

That's the gist of it. But you still may want to know about a few more aspects of file sharing. For example, how do I know who is using the network? How do I change my password? How can I unshare a folder or disk? And how do I connect to my shared computer remotely via modem?

The answers to these and other fascinating questions await you. Read on.

Monitoring file sharing

When file sharing is on, you can see what's going on out on the network with the Activity Monitor in the File Sharing control panel. (See Figure 10-21.)

A list of connected users appears at the top, and a list of shared folders and disks appears at the bottom. To disconnect a user at any time, select his or her name in the list and then click the Disconnect button. A dialog box appears, asking you how many minutes until the selected user is disconnected.

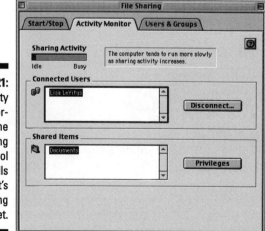

Figure 10-21: The Activity Monitor portion of the File Sharing control panel tells you what's happening on the net.

Type a number and click OK. When that amount of time has passed, the user is disconnected. The shared disk or folder icon appears grayed on the user's desktop, indicating that the item is no longer available. The disconnected user sees a dialog box saying that he or she has been disconnected.

If you type 0 (zero) in the disconnect dialog box, and then click OK, the user is disconnected immediately.

The Activity Monitor at the bottom of the screen tells you how much activity is on the network. If yours is always up in the busy range, you may need to rethink your network strategy.

AppleShare file servers or hardware add-ons such as hubs and routers can ease network traffic. If your network appears busy in the Activity Monitor most of the time, you should beef up your network with one or more of the aforementioned items.

Changing your password

You can change your password at any time. Just follow these steps:

1. **Open the File Sharing control panel from your own computer.**

   To do so, choose Apple menu➪Control Panels➪File Sharing.

2. **If the Activity Monitor tab still shows, click the Start/Stop tab to get back to the main file sharing window.**

3. **Delete your old password.**

4. **Type a new password.**

5. **Close the File Sharing control panel.**

Your new password is now in effect.

Unsharing a folder or disk

To unshare a folder or disk you own, merely select it, choose File➪Sharing, and uncheck the Share This Item and Its Contents check box. The folder or disk becomes inaccessible over the network as soon as you close the Sharing window.

Logging on remotely via modem

The Mac OS includes Apple Remote Access at no extra charge. It used to be an "additional-cost add-on." This change is a very good thing.

What remote access means is that if you're at another location with a Mac and modem, and your Mac has a modem that has been configured for remote access (I show you how in a moment), you can access your home hard disk from the remote Mac!

Preparing your Mac for remote access

Preparing your Mac so that you can log on to it remotely is simple. Because remote access uses the same Users & Groups and File Sharing control panels as network file sharing, if you've followed along so far in this chapter, you're almost ready for remote access. You have just one last thing to do:

1. **Open the Remote Access control panel.**

2. **From the Remote Access menu, choose Modem.**

   The Modem control panel opens automatically.

3. **Turn your modem speaker on or off by clicking the appropriate option, as shown in Figure 10-22.**

Figure 10-22:
The Modem control panel.

4. **Select your dialing method by clicking the appropriate option.**

5. **Leave the Ignore Dial Tone check box unchecked.**

   If you can't make things work, try checking it later.

6. **Close the Modem control panel.**

7. **In the Remote Access control panel, choose Remote Access⇨Answering.**

8. **In the Answering window (see Figure 10-23), click the Answer Calls option to allow others to dial into your Mac.**

When your modem receives a call, Remote Access will answer it and allow registered users to connect to your computer.

Figure 10-23:
Use the
Answering
window to
tell Remote
Access how
to handle
incoming
phone calls
from other
Macs.

9. **Close the Answering window.**

10. **In the Remote Access control panel, click the Options button.**

11. **Click the Protocol tab.**

This is where you tell Remote Access what kind of network connection to make.

12. **From the Use Protocol pop-up menu, choose ARAP, and click OK to close the window.**

That's it! Your Mac is now ready for registered users to access it remotely.

The ARAP protocol you chose in the last step is one of two that Remote Access uses to make connections with other computers. ARAP stands for Apple Remote Access Protocol (clever, huh?) and is primarily used for Mac-to-Mac connections. PPP (Point-to-Point Protocol) is the other choice, and is usually used to connect your computer to the Internet. You can read more about PPP in Chapter 17.

Getting files from your Mac while you're on the road

Upon arriving in your remote location, use the Remote Access control panel to make a connection to the hard disk of your home Mac. Launch Remote Access. Fill in the fields for your name, your password, and the phone number of the modem connected to your home Mac, as shown in Figure 10-24. Click the Options button, and then click the Protocol tab. Be sure that the Protocol pop-up menu says either ARAP or Automatic.

Figure 10-24:
Fill in the
blanks and
then click
Connect to
mount your
home com-
puter's hard
disk on the
remote
computer's
desktop.

If you expect to use this connection again, Save it by choosing File⇨Save (⌘+S).

If you click the Save My Password option, you don't have to type your password when you connect. On the other hand, people who get their hands on
the remote computer or the file that stores the passwords can connect to
your home computer and wreak havoc with your files. So don't check it
unless you're certain that you won't misplace the disk with the Remote
Access Client document on it.

That's it. Almost. You need to know two other things before you're a Ph.D. in
remote access: the Options dialog box and the DialAssist control panel.

You've already met the Options dialog box (shown in Figure 10-25,), but
there's more to it than choosing a protocol. Here, you specify whether and
when to redial, choose an alternate phone number, and specify whether and
when you want to be reminded of your connection if you forget.

Figure 10-25:
Remote
Access's
Options
dialog box.

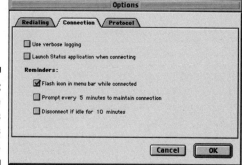

DialAssist is a control panel that helps you remember and dial complicated phone number sequences. If you choose DialAssist from Remote Access's Remote Access menu (or choose Apple menu⇨Controls Panel⇨DialAssist), the DialAssist control panel opens, as shown in Figure 10-26. (You can also choose Dial Assist from the Control panel's submenu in your Apple menu as well.)

Figure 10-26:
The DialAssist control panel helps you remember and dial stuff like your credit card or long-distance access number.

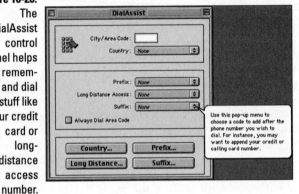

If dialing home involves anything more complicated than dialing a 9 before your phone number — a country code, a long-distance access number, a credit card number, or whatever — check out DialAssist.

Note that DialAssist has Balloon Help, so if you need to know more about how a feature works, turn it on. A nice touch.

After you've used DialAssist's pop-up menus to create your custom dialing string, you can preview the results in the Remote Access Client window.

There. That's it! You know how to share files with the best of them, no matter where you are.

Chapter 11

Memory and Other Seemingly Complicated Arcana

$$\bullet\ \bullet$$

In This Chapter

▶ Running out of RAM

▶ Finding out about the Memory control panel

▶ Discovering the disk cache

▶ Unveiling virtual memory

▶ Working with the RAM disk

▶ Memory-related troubleshooting

$$\bullet\ \bullet$$

The Mac lets the user — that's you — get along fine without knowing much about memory. You could go through your entire life with a Macintosh without knowing anything more than "it has 32 megs in it."

On the other hand, a working knowledge of the way your Mac's memory works can be invaluable in getting the most out of your Mac.

In other words, you don't have to know this stuff, but it's likely to come in handy someday. It's not particularly complicated or particularly technical, so it wouldn't hurt to just jump right in.

Baby, Baby, Where Did Our RAM Go?

RAM is the TLA (three-letter acronym) for random access memory. RAM is a special kind of memory where your System software and applications live while your Mac uses them. System software (including most extensions and control panels) loads into RAM on startup; applications load into RAM when you open them.

Your Mac probably came with 32, 64, or more megabytes of RAM. Depending on what you want to do, that amount may or may not be enough.

If you never plan to do anything more than use a single program that doesn't require a massive amount of RAM (that is, not Photoshop, which requires at least 16MB of RAM) and never plan to use two or more programs at once, a 32-meg Mac may let you squeak by.

If you have 32MB or less of RAM, read this chapter and Chapter 16 very, very carefully. The less RAM you have, the more important it is to manage it wisely.

If you want to keep a word processor, a calendar, a phone book, and a graphics program open at the same time, or if you like to play fast-action games, a 32MB Mac may not have enough RAM for you. I consider 64MB the functional minimum for using Mac OS 9 effectively. If you have less RAM than that, buy more.

The simple rule is that the more stuff you want to run at once, the more RAM you're gonna need. If you have programs that require a lot of RAM, you need enough RAM to run them and your System software simultaneously. You need even more RAM if you want to keep several programs open at the same time.

Essentially, you should remember that three things use RAM:

- ✔ The System and Finder
- ✔ Extensions and control panels
- ✔ Applications

Go ahead: Add more RAM

You can add more RAM to most Mac models easily and relatively inexpensively. (32MB is going for less than $100 today, and 128MB DIMMs can be had for less than $400. But prices change quickly, so check around before you buy.)

If you are so inclined, you can install RAM yourself with a minimum of technical skills. Memory comes mounted on cute little printed circuit boards called SIMMs (a fancy acronym for Single In-line Memory Module) or DIMMs (a fancy acronym for Dual In-line Memory Module) that snap into little printed-circuit-board holders inside your Mac. Installing RAM yourself might void your warranty. (On the other hand, if your

Mac is more than 366 days old, it doesn't have a warranty.)

If you're technologically challenged and never want to lift the lid off your Mac (I don't blame you), you can have RAM installed for you at any Apple dealer. But this service costs significantly more than doing it yourself.

I'm a klutz. I don't repair things around the house. But I've managed to install RAM upgrades in several Macs without incident. It's not terribly difficult, and it doesn't require soldering or other specialized skills. If you can turn a screwdriver, you can probably handle the task.

You have no control over the first pair, the System and Finder. That dynamic duo is going to chew up almost 15-or-so megabytes of RAM no matter what you do.

You do have control over extensions, control panels, and applications, however, and you can use this control to make the most of the memory you have.

Okay. RAM is used primarily for three things. Other stuff — PRAM (parameter RAM), debuggers, rdev and scri files — could be rattling around in there, using up small amounts of RAM. But their impact on the amount of RAM you have to work with is negligible, so they're not important to this discussion. Besides, most people never need to know what a scri file is.

Sigh. Okay, just this once. A scri file is a special type of extension that automatically loads before all other extensions. The old System Update 3.0 that you should have been using with System 7.1 (but don't need with Mac OS 9) is a scri file. So is Speed Doubler 8.

System software memory

To observe how RAM is being used on your Mac, look at the About This Computer window (Apple menu⇨About This Computer).

Figure 11-1 shows a Mac running Mac OS 9. No extensions or control panels are loaded. The System software uses 15.2MB of RAM.

Figure 11-1:
Mac OS 9
alone,
with no
extensions
or control
panels
loaded, uses
15.2MB
of RAM.

How do you get Mac OS 9 alone to load, without loading any extensions or control panels? Easy. Hold down the Shift key during startup until you see the "Extensions Off" message on the Welcome to Mac OS 9 screen. Memorize this tip; it's good to know. If you run into memory problems (that is, if you see error messages with the word *memory* in them), starting up with extensions turned off will enable you to run your Mac so that you can pinpoint problems related to control panels or extensions.

After the System software eats up its share of RAM on my Mac (which has 128MB of RAM), 112.2MB of RAM is available for extensions, control panels, and applications.

Your mileage will vary, and you'll probably see a slightly different number on your Mac. Don't worry about it. The System software for each Mac model requires a slightly different amount of RAM.

When I restart my Mac the old-fashioned way, without holding down the Shift key, the extensions and control panels load as usual, and the System software expands to take up a whopping 29.8MB, as shown in Figure 11-2. See what I mean about 32MB being the functional minimum? If you had less than 32MB of RAM, you would have no RAM left for running applications. That's not good. You'll need more RAM or virtual memory (which I cover soon).

Figure 11-2:
Mac OS 9, with its full complement of extensions and control panels loaded at startup, uses 29.8MB of RAM.

This situation often causes confusion. When you look at the bar for System software in the About This Computer window, it displays not only the RAM used by your System and Finder but also the RAM used by the extensions and control panels that load at startup.

There's no way to tell how much of that bar consists of the System and Finder and how much consists of the extensions and control panels. The important thing is that the System software bar tells you how much combined RAM the System, Finder, extensions, and control panels use.

If you're good at math, you can figure out that loading the full complement of Mac OS 9 extensions and control panels costs almost 15MB of RAM.

29.8MB - 15.2MB = 14.6MB.

On my 128MB Mac, I'm left with slightly less than 100 megabytes available for applications.

You can free up a bit more RAM for applications by turning off extensions and control panels in the Extensions Manager control panel. Read Chapter 16 for details on exactly how much RAM each extension and control panel uses and what happens if you turn them off.

Application memory

If you haven't read the first part of Chapter 6, which explains the About This Computer item in the Apple menu and provides you with your first glimpse of memory management, you should do so now. I discuss an important technique there — how to adjust Application memory — and I'm not going to waste space repeating it.

Well, I guess I have to repeat at least part of it. This is, after all, a chapter about memory management.

When you launch an application, the application grabs a chunk of memory (RAM). You can see how big a chunk of RAM it grabs by going back to the Finder after you launch it and choosing Apple menu⇨About This Computer. (See Figure 11-3.)

Figure 11-3: Microsoft Word, being somewhat of a RAM hog, grabs 16.6MB of RAM when launched.

The beginning of Chapter 6 has a lengthy discourse on changing the amount of RAM a program grabs when you launch it and why you may want to do so. You diddle a program's RAM usage by selecting its icon and either choosing File⇨Get Info or using the keyboard shortcut, ⌘+I. (See Figure 11-4.)

Figure 11-4:
Microsoft
Word
grabbed
16.6MB of
RAM when I
launched it
because
that's what
its Preferred
Memory
Size was set
at (more or
less).

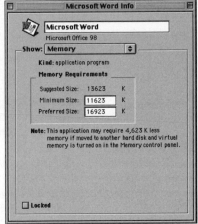

Here's a brief review of what these memory sizes mean:

- ✔ The Suggested Size is the size the manufacturer of the program recommends. In most cases, the Preferred Size should be set to at least this amount. You can't change the Suggested Size.

- ✔ The Minimum Size is the smallest amount of memory the program needs to run. It is usually (but not always) slightly smaller than the Suggested Size.

- ✔ The Preferred Size is the amount of memory the application requests (and gets, as long as that much memory is available when the application is launched). Your Mac doesn't let you set the Preferred Size lower than the Minimum Size.

When you try to open an application, if the available RAM (Largest Unused Block in the About This Computer window) is less than the Preferred Size but more than the Minimum Size, the program launches. But its performance may be degraded, or you may encounter memory-related errors.

In summation

Make sure that you're clear on this theory stuff before you move on to execution. Three things use RAM: System software (and Finder), extensions and control panels, and applications.

You can make more RAM available for your programs by holding down the Shift key at startup, which disables all extensions and control panels.

You can fiddle with the amount of RAM that a program uses in its Get Info box.

Everything else you need to know about memory involves the Memory control panel, which you're about to meet.

The Shift-key-at-startup technique is wonderful, but it's absolutely absolute. Either your control panels and extensions are on or they're off. The Shift key provides no way to turn some off and leave others on. When they're all off, you lose the ability to share files, use desktop printers, use the CD-ROM drive, and much more.

Well, that's not quite true. If you turn off extensions with the Shift key held down, you can still mount a CD-ROM provided that the CD contains an Apple CD-ROM driver. For example, if you drop an OS disc (or the startup disc that came with your Mac) into the drive and start with Extensions off, that disc will mount. And now that the CD-ROM driver has been loaded into OS memory (from the CD-ROM), any subsequent CDs you toss into the drive will mount as well. How's that for a tip!

That's why Apple provides the Extensions Manager control panel. You use it to selectively disable and enable control panels and extensions. As I keep saying, I discuss this dandy tool in Chapter 16, a chapter designed to help you figure out which extensions and control panels you truly need. You can find out how much precious RAM and disk space each control panel and extension uses, and you can also discover how to get rid of the ones that you don't want (both temporarily and permanently).

In other words, Chapter 16 may be the most useful chapter in this book.

Memories Are Made of This: The Memory Control Panel

You configure memory-related functions for your Mac in the Memory control panel, which is in the Control Panels folder. You open the Memory control panel by choosing Apple menu⇨Control Panels⇨Memory.

Here's a look at the Memory control panel's components, which are for the most part unrelated.

Cashing in with the disk cache

The disk *cache* (pronounced "cash") is a portion of RAM set aside to hold frequently used instructions. In theory, if you set a reasonable-size cache, say 5 percent of your total RAM, your Mac should feel like it's running faster. In reality, many people can't tell the difference.

The first important thing to know is that the size of the disk cache is added to the RAM used by the System software. Therefore, memory assigned to the disk cache is not available for programs to use. In Figure 11-1, the System software is using 15.2MB of RAM. The disk cache is set to 4,096K.

If I increase the size of the disk cache to 8,160K (see Figure 11-5) and restart the Mac, the System software balloons to 37.5MB (see Figure 11-6).

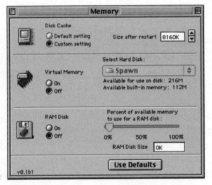

Figure 11-5:
The disk cache is increased to 8,160K. See the results in the next figure.

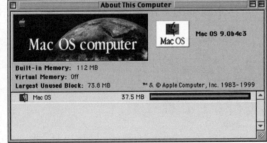

Figure 11-6:
The System software uses 7.7MB more RAM than before ("before" being Figure 11-1).

Those of you who caught the math thing a few pages ago have certainly noticed that the numbers here don't add up correctly. 37.5MB - 29.8MB = 7.7MB, which does not equal 4,064K (the amount I increased the Disk Cache by) as it should.

The vagaries of RAM usage are well known. The amount of RAM that System software uses changes from hour to hour, seemingly at random. I opened About This Computer three times today and got three different numbers, ranging from a low of 24MB to a high of 30MB.

In other words, RAM usage is not a precise science. Take all numbers in this chapter with at least one grain of salt.

How to set your disk cache

If RAM usage is an imprecise science, telling you how to set your disk cache is imprecise science fiction. Bearing that in mind, here's some excellent advice on figuring out the best setting for you.

As I said in the preceding section, some people don't notice the speed improvement provided by a larger disk cache. So first you must determine whether you can tell the difference in speed by cranking the disk cache size way up. Here's how to crank up the disk cache size:

1. **Choose Apple menu➪Control Panels➪Memory.**

   The Memory control panel appears.

2. **Click the Custom Setting option.**

   You see a warning that diddling with the cache size can "severely decrease performance."

3. **Ignore the warning and click the Custom button.**

4. **Click the upward-pointing arrow next to the Size After Reset box until it won't increase any further.**

   Check out Figure 11-7.

Figure 11-7:
Keep clicking the up-arrow.

5. **Click the down-arrow two or three times.**

   This way, you leave enough RAM available to open an application.

6. **Restart your Mac.**

   You now have a huge disk cache, larger than you would actually use in real life. But I want you to exaggerate its effects for this experiment.

7. **When your Mac gets back to the Finder, open the System Folder.**

   Notice how long it takes for the entire window to appear.

8. Close and then reopen the System Folder window.

Again, notice how long it takes the window to appear.

The difference in speed (the System Folder should have opened noticeably faster the second time) is a result of the increased size of the disk cache.

You should also notice a speed improvement when you scroll through documents. Launch your favorite application and scroll around a document for a while.

If you don't notice any speed improvement in the Finder or in your favorite application, return to the Memory control panel, set Size After Restart to its lowest setting (96K or 32K), and be done with it.

If you notice (and like) the speed improvement, you still have a little more work to do. As you may remember, memory assigned to the disk cache is not available for applications. So you want to set the disk cache to the lowest possible number that still feels fast to you.

To lower the disk cache, repeat the preceding steps, lowering the disk cache one click each time. Restart after each change. Then close and reopen the System Folder two times and note the difference in speed the second time. When you begin to notice sluggishness when closing and opening or when scrolling through documents, you've discovered your threshold. Return to the Memory control panel, increase Size After Restart one click, and be done with it.

The old rule about the disk cache is to allow 32K per megabyte of RAM. I've always thought that this suggestion was bunk, as many people can't tell the difference between a 32K disk cache and a 1,024K disk cache. And why should they waste a megabyte of perfectly good RAM? So I've always encouraged people to try the experiment I've just described and see for themselves. That said, I have to admit that the disk cache in Mac OS 9 feels a bit zippier than earlier disk caches. I notice a definite speedup with the disk cache set to 4,096K. Under System 7.1 and earlier versions, the speedup didn't feel as great.

For what it's worth, I'm leaving mine set to the default for my Mac, which is 4 megs (4,096K) for now, and I may even bump it up to 5 or 6 megs. Because I've got oodles of RAM (128MB!), that still leaves me plenty of RAM for applications, so I'm willing to trade a meg or two of RAM for the speedup. Once again, your mileage may vary.

If none of this made sense to you or it seems like too much trouble, click the Default button and be done with it. You can't go wrong using the default settings because Mac OS 9 chooses the optimal default cache size for you based on how much RAM is installed on your Mac.

It's not real, it's virtual (memory)

The truth is that you should have enough real RAM to use your favorite application or applications (if you like to keep more than one program running) comfortably. You should have enough real RAM to open all the documents and programs you need.

You access virtual memory through the Memory control panel, as shown in Figure 11-8. Just click the On option and use the arrows to adjust the total amount of memory you will have after you restart your Mac. (Yes, you have to restart if you want to turn virtual memory on, turn virtual memory off, or change virtual memory settings. Sorry.) In Figure 11-9, after making the appropriate adjustments in the Memory control panel and restarting, my 128MB Mac thinks that it has 200MB.

Figure 11-8:
Making a
128MB Mac
think that it
has 200MB.

Figure 11-9:
After
restarting,
this Mac
acts as if it
has 200MB
of RAM.

Virtual memory works by setting aside space on your hard disk that acts as RAM. It creates a very big, invisible file on your hard disk equal to the amount of virtual memory in use plus all the installed RAM! So if you have a 32MB Mac and want to make it think it has 64MB using virtual memory, you'll have an invisible 64MB file on your hard disk taking up space. For me the cost is even higher — I start out with a 200MB invisible file as soon as I turn virtual memory on.

Many Macs come with Virtual Memory (VM) turned on, which adds 1MB of memory to the real RAM you have installed. If you have enough real RAM to do your work, turn VM off. When you reinstall Mac OS, the installer sometimes turns virtual memory on for you, if it decides that you don't have sufficient real RAM installed. The installer is usually right, so it's probably a good idea to keep things the way they are until you can spring for additional RAM.

So now you know that virtual memory eats up some hard disk space, but it does have some benefits. First, virtual memory lets your Mac think that it has more RAM than it actually does. This additional, almost magical RAM is more effective in allowing you to run several small programs than one large program. Second, turning virtual memory on, even if you only set it to add 1MB of virtual memory, allows many applications to run using less RAM on Macs with PowerPC processors.

Go back and take another look at Figure 11-4. See that little note at the bottom that says "This application may require 4,623K less memory if moved to another hard disk and virtual memory is turned on in the Memory control panel?" It disappears (and Microsoft Word requires about 4MB less RAM to run) with virtual memory turned on. This tip alone makes it worth turning on VM even if you set it to only 1MB.

For what it's worth, programs also require less RAM if you use Connectix RAM Doubler 8, a virtual memory substitute that has the added advantage of not using *any* hard disk space to create the virtual memory effect.

Faster than a speeding bullet: It's a RAM disk

A RAM disk enables you to use part of your installed RAM as a temporary storage device, a virtual disk made of silicon. A RAM disk is much, much faster than any other kind of disk and, if you're using a battery-powered Mac, it's much more energy efficient.

Many Macintoshes include a RAM disk feature. To find out if yours is one of them, open your Memory control panel. If you see RAM disk controls like those shown in Figure 11-10, your Mac has the RAM disk feature.

Figure 11-10:
Macs that
support
RAM disks
have these
controls.

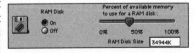

Memory assigned to a RAM disk is not available for opening programs or loading extensions and control panels. So unless you have 64 or more megabytes of RAM, a RAM disk is probably not practical. Even with 64MB, it probably won't be that useful.

RAM disks are wickedly fast while you use them, but they are temporary. When you shut down your Mac (or if the power is interrupted to a non-PowerBook Mac), the contents of a RAM disk are wiped out. In addition, certain kinds of System crashes can erase a RAM disk's contents. The contents of a RAM disk do, however, survive a restart.

Even so, you should never store your only copy of a file on a RAM disk. If you save files on a RAM disk, make sure to copy them to your hard disk every so often — just in case.

Creating a RAM disk

To create a RAM disk, click the On button in the RAM Disk portion of the Memory control panel and drag the slider to choose the percentage of the available memory that you want to use for your RAM disk. Close the control panel and restart your Mac. The new RAM disk appears on your desktop, as shown in Figure 11-11. With the game residing on the RAM disk, I can kick your butt at Myth II any time.

Figure 11-11:
A RAM disk acts like any other, only faster.

Erasing a RAM disk

You can erase the contents of a RAM disk in three ways. One, of course, is to shut down your Mac. You'll see a warning that the contents of the RAM disk will be lost; when you click OK, the contents are gone.

You can also erase a RAM disk by doing one of the following:

- ✔ Selecting the RAM disk's icon and choosing Special⇨Erase Disk
- ✔ Dragging everything on the RAM disk to the Trash and then choosing Special⇨Empty Trash

Resizing or removing a RAM disk

To resize a RAM disk, use the slider in the Memory control panel to choose a new size; then restart your Mac.

The contents of a RAM disk are lost when you resize it, so copy anything important to your hard disk before you resize.

To remove a RAM disk, click the Off button in the Memory control panel and then restart your Mac. It the RAM disk isn't empty, the Off button is disabled.

Good things to try with a RAM disk

Some applications run a lot faster when they're on a RAM disk. Copy your favorite game to a RAM disk and give it a try.

Your Mac runs screamingly fast if your System Folder is on a RAM disk. You need at least 256MB of RAM to create a RAM disk big enough for most System Folders.

Another thing to try is to move your favorite application to the RAM disk and run it from there. Many applications — including Web browsers — run significantly faster from a RAM disk. And storing your Web browser's cache of recently viewed pages on a RAM disk makes pages appear blazingly fast the second time you visit them. Use your browser's preferences to set the cache on your RAM disk.

And there you have it. More than you really need to know about RAM and your Macintosh!

Part III
U 2 Can B A Guru

The 5th Wave   **By Rich Tennant**

IF BOB DYLAN HAD PURSUED A CAREER IN COMPUTERS.

"PUT HIM IN FRONT OF A TERMINAL AND HE'S A GENIUS, BUT OTHER-WISE THE GUY IS SUCH A BROODING, GLOOMY GUS HE'LL NEVER BREAK INTO MANAGEMENT."

In this part . . .

1 discuss tips, tricks, and techniques that make using your Mac easier and more fulfilling. More succinctly, this part is about how things work and how you can make them work better.

After two chapters full of tips and tricks, I crawl through the Control Panels folder and discuss each and every control panel and its recommended settings.

Moving right along, I next delve into automating your Mac using AppleScript, complete with some easy-to-follow info that's guaranteed to get you scripting. More or less.

Next up, in what may be the most useful chapter in the book, I look at every single file installed with Mac OS 9. I tell you who needs the file, how much RAM it uses, how much disk space it uses, and most important of all, how to get rid of it safely if you don't need it.

Then I introduce you to the Web and your Internet tools, including the infamous Web browsers from Netscape and Microsoft.

And finally, you take a tour of Dr. Mac's top troubleshooting tips, for those times when good System software goes bad.

Chapter 12

Sure-Fire, Easy-to-Use, No (or Low)-Cost Timesaving Tips

· ·

In This Chapter

▶ Flying fingers

▶ In living color — or not

▶ Using contextual menus

▶ Getting your Views under control

· ·

Some of what you're about to read has been mentioned somewhere in the first eleven chapters already. But this chapter isn't a blatant attempt at upping my page count. No siree. This chapter is here because, by now, you lust for speed.

If you're normal, after you understand the basics, you wish your Mac worked faster. (You're not alone — all users wish that their Macs worked faster at some time, even those of us with Power Macintosh G3s.) So in this chapter, I cover things that can make your Mac at least seem faster, most of which won't cost you a red cent.

Let Your Fingers Do the Flying

One way to make your Mac faster is to make your fingers faster. Here are a couple of ways.

Use those keyboard shortcuts

The less often you remove your hand from the keyboard to fiddle with the mouse, the less time you waste. Learn those keyboard shortcuts. Memorize them. Make your fingers memorize them. The more keyboard shortcuts you use, the faster you can do what you are doing. Trust me.

Learn to type better

Learning to type faster may be the very best way I know to make your Mac faster. As a Macintosh consultant and trainer, I get to spend a lot of time with beginners. And almost all of them are lousy typists. When they complain that their computer is too slow, I ask them to perform a task for me. Then I perform that same task for them. I can type about 50 words per minute, and I type without looking at the keyboard. I always accomplish the task in less time; if the task involves a lot of typing, I accomplish it in much less time.

Because you're there and I'm here, I can't provide you with as dramatic an illustration. But trust me, typing fast saves you time at your Mac — a lot. And this speed gain isn't just in word processors and spreadsheets. When you're a decent touch typist, you fly when you use those nifty keyboard shortcuts that I mention so frequently.

What? You learned to put two spaces after a period in your high school typing class? Well, you learned wrong, at least if you're going to use a computer. The double space after punctuation is a throwback to the days when typewriters were king and we had no personal computers or printers. Because typewritten text is monospaced (that is, all letters are the same width), a double space after a punctuation mark looked better than a single space.

With the advent of the computer and laser printer, most fonts are no longer monospaced. (Courier and Monaco are monospaced.) Today, on most personal computers, most fonts are spaced proportionally. In other words, some characters are wider than others. The width of a space in a proportionally spaced font is just the right size to use a single space after punctuation. A double space looks unattractive.

End of sermon.

The Mac is not a typewriter

The Macintosh is more of a typesetting machine than a typewriter. So when you use a Macintosh, you should follow the rules of good typography, not the rules of good typewriting. If you want your documents to look truly professional, you need to understand the difference between inch and foot marks (" and ') and typographer's quotation marks (' and ' or " and ") in addition to putting single spaces after punctuation. You also need to know when and how to use a hyphen (-), an en dash (–), and an em dash (—).

In other words, the Mac is not a typewriter. If you want to make your documents look more elegant and professional, get a hold of an excellent book by Robin Williams, *The Mac Is Not a Typewriter* (published by Peachpit Press). It's wonderful and easy to understand, and it covers all the stuff I mention (and much more) in great detail.

Why Living Color May Not Be So Great

Chances are good that your Macintosh has a color monitor (most do). And chances are also good that you keep that monitor set to the maximum number of colors it supports. That may be a mistake.

Monitor settings

Your screen consists of thousands of square dots (more than 300,000 for the average Mac monitor) known as *pixels* (an acronym of sorts for *picture element*). Most 13- or 14-inch monitors display a picture that is 640 pixels wide by 480 pixels high — more than 300,000 pixels on the screen for your Mac to deal with. Larger monitors have more pixels; smaller monitors have fewer.

The number of colors that you choose to display on your monitor has a significant impact on how quickly your screen updates. The more choices your Mac has to make about the color of each pixel, the longer it takes for the screen to update completely so that you can continue your work.

When I say *update,* I'm talking about the amount of time it takes for your screen to paint all the pixels their proper color or colors after opening or closing an icon or a document. For example, when you open a color picture in a graphics application or open a window in the Finder, the screen updates until every element is drawn on-screen in its proper place and in its proper color.

Some people call screen updating *screen redrawing.* It means the same thing: the time you spend waiting for Finder windows to draw themselves completely or the time it takes for documents to appear completely in their windows on-screen. When your screen is updating, you have no choice but to wait for it.

You might sometimes hear this scourge referred to as *refreshing,* but that term is incorrect in this context. Screen refresh rate is a technical term, measured in hertz (Hz), which has to do with the video hardware. Even so, people use the three words — update, redraw, and refresh — more or less interchangeably.

How quickly your screen updates depends on a few things — mostly CPU speed, hard disk speed, and video circuitry (built-in or on a video card).

You shouldn't find it surprising that much of what's in the rest of this chapter is about making your screen update faster no matter what CPU, hard disk, or video gear you have.

I admit that the faster your Mac is, the less difference the techniques in this chapter will make to your overall performance. If you have a Mac with a G3 chip, try my suggestions out for a while and see whether you think they're worth it. Because your Mac has relatively high performance, screen updating is relatively speedy, even with some of the options mentioned in this chapter turned on. You be the judge.

Depending on your video card or built-in video hardware, you can choose from black and white, 4 colors, 16 colors, 256 colors, thousands of colors, or millions of colors.

You choose the number of colors that you want your screen to display in the Monitors control panel, which is shown in Figure 12-1.

Figure 12-1: The Monitors control panel lets you choose the number of colors you want to see on-screen.

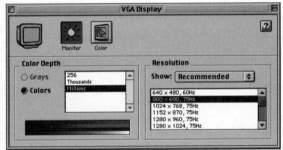

The Power Macintosh G3 has a video card that can display millions, thousands, or 256 colors at once on a 20-inch monitor.

Most Macs today can display a maximum of millions of colors on a 14-inch monitor using built-in video circuitry. And many of these Macintosh models can be upgraded to display thousands or millions of colors on larger monitors by adding an inexpensive VRAM (video RAM) chip.

If you want more colors than your Mac model supports (even with additional VRAM), or you want to use a larger monitor, you may need to purchase a video card that supports that combination of colors and size. Video cards range from a low of a couple of hundred dollars to several thousand dollars. For the big bucks, you can get a super-fast, accelerated video card capable of powering a 21-inch monitor set to display millions of colors with bells and whistles such as virtual desktops, hardware zoom and pan, and resolution switching.

Of course none of this matters if you have an iBook or an iMac, which don't support the use of an external monitor.

If you choose the Black & White option, each pixel on the screen has only two options: to be black or white. If you choose 256 colors, each pixel on-screen can be any of 256 possible colors. If you choose millions of colors, each pixel on-screen can be any one of millions of possible colors. Unfortunately, not all Macs (mine included) offer Black & White as an option these days.

As you might expect, the more choices each pixel has, the more processing time your Mac requires to update the screen. So the more colors you choose in the Monitors control panel, the more sluggish your Mac feels. Scrolling in many programs is much faster if you choose the Black & White option. And in some programs, 256 colors is faster than thousands or millions of colors.

So here's my advice: Unless your application requires color, set your monitor to Black & White (if Black & White is even offered) for maximum performance. When you're using your word processor or spreadsheet, you probably don't need color anyway. Why make your Mac slower if you don't have to?

Use 1-bit color for speed and 8-bit color for games. Use millions of colors only if you need them (for Photoshop, PageMaker, and so on).

In computerese, the number of colors that your monitor displays is often referred to as *bit depth* (or sometimes pixel depth). In a nutshell, *bit* is short for binary digit, the smallest unit of information that the computer can understand. The bit depth describes how many bits of information can be sent to each pixel.

Here are the English translations for the most common bit depths:

- 1 bit means black and white
- 8 bit means 256 colors
- 16 bit means thousands of colors
- 24 bit means millions of colors

Resolution? It's not just for New Year's anymore

Another setting you can change to improve performance is the resolution of your monitor. Most modern monitors and video cards (or onboard video circuitry, depending upon your Mac model) are capable of displaying multiple resolutions on your monitor. You choose these resolutions in the Monitors control panel.

You can also change resolutions using the Resolution module in your control strip.

So here's the deal: The lower the numbers in your resolution, the faster your screen refreshes. 640 x 480 is faster than 832 x 624; 832 x 624 is faster than 1,024 x 768; and so on. That's because, as I mention earlier, if there are fewer pixels to refresh, they refresh faster.

On the other hand, the speed difference between resolutions these days is relatively minimal. In fact, I can hardly tell the difference between one and the other. So mostly you should choose a resolution based on your preference rather than which one you think might be faster. That said, if your Mac seems slow at 1,024 x 768, try a lower resolution and see whether it feels faster.

Contextual menus: They're great in context

While we're on the topic of speed and shortcuts, don't forget about those delightful contextual menus. Just hold down the Control key and click any item in the Finder.

My personal fave is the Move To Trash shortcut. That's good. And it has a keyboard shortcut worth memorizing: ⌘+Delete. That's even better.

A Mac with a view — and preferences, too

The View Options and Appearance windows (shown in Figure 12-2 and accessed via View⇨View Options and Apple Menu⇨Control Panels⇨ Appearance) are other places where your choices affect how quickly your screen updates in the Finder.

The View Options window, like my old friend the contextual menu, is . . . well . . . contextual. Depending on what is active when you choose it from the View menu, you see one of two similar versions: folders in icon or button view or the desktop (top left in Figure 12-2) and folders in list view (top right in Figure 12-2).

Geneva: It's not just a city in Switzerland anymore

Let's start with the one speed improvement you can make in the Appearance window (Apple Menu⇨Control Panels⇨Appearance). Using the Geneva font in the Finder is slightly faster than using most other fonts because Geneva is one of the fonts that your Macintosh stores in its ROM (read-only memory).

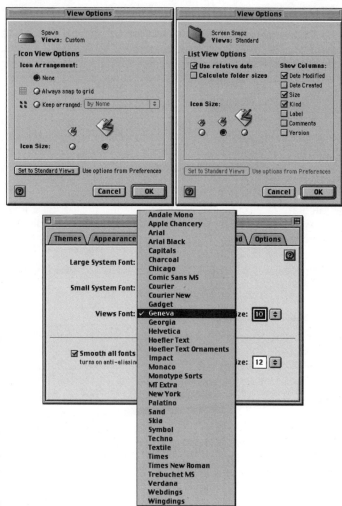

Figure 12-2:
Your choices in the View Options and Appearance windows can make your Mac feel faster.

One thing's for sure: If you select a third-party PostScript font in an uninstalled size, it will definitely be slower than Geneva 9. And it will look uglier.

Other fonts included in your Mac's ROM include Charcoal and Chicago. But both are ugly as a Finder view font, in my humble opinion.

When bigger isn't better

The smaller the icon, the faster the screen updates. In the View Options windows, the tiny icon on the left is the fastest; the big, horsey-looking icon on the right is the slowest. (In list view, the one in the middle is, of course, the middle size.)

It doesn't pay to calculate folder sizes

I recommend that you deactivate Calculate folder sizes (that is, uncheck, or clear, its check box) to make the screen redraw faster in the Finder. At least to me, the screen feels as if it redraws faster with this feature turned off. This feature is offered only for windows that sport one of the list views, for obvious reasons.

The Finder is kind of smart about the Calculate folder sizes option. If you try to do anything in the Finder — make a menu selection, open an icon, move a window, and so on — while folder sizes are calculating, the Finder interrupts the calculation and lets you complete your task before it resumes calculating. So, in theory, you should never notice a delay when Calculate folder sizes is on.

Try the Calculate folder sizes option both on and off. I don't know about you, but I find any noticeable delay unacceptable, and I notice a delay when it's turned on, even on very fast Macs. Maybe this feature is just annoying and not actually slowing things down, but I can't stand having it on. If I want to know how big a folder is, I select it and select the Get Info command from the File menu (⌘+I).

Getting ahead-er and other stuff

The Show Columns check boxes in the View Options window for list views — Date Modified, Date Created, Size, Kind, Label, Comments, and Version — have a slight impact on screen update speed when you open a Finder window in list view. The fewer items you have checked, the fewer items the Finder has to draw. As a result, the Finder updates windows faster.

The impact of these seven items on screen updating is pretty small, so your choice should be made based on what information you want to see in Finder windows, not on whether choosing them slows down your Mac. Play around with these options if you like, but unless your Mac is very slow, you probably won't notice much difference between on and off.

If you don't need it, turn it off or toss it out

I devote an entire chapter (Chapter 16) to showing you how to turn off or eliminate Mac OS 9 features that you don't need or want. Read it carefully. Features such as AppleTalk, file sharing, and QuickDraw 3D use prodigious amounts of memory and can also slow down your Mac's CPU. If you don't need 'em, don't let 'em clog up your Mac. Read Chapter 16 carefully and then fine-tune your Mac for the best performance.

What Else Can I Do?

If you've tried every trick in the book (or at least in this chapter) and still think that your Mac is too slow, what can you do? Here are four suggestions:

- ✔ **Get a new, faster model or upgrade yours.** Apple keeps putting out faster and faster Macs at lower and lower prices. From time to time, Apple and other venders offer reasonably priced upgrades that can transform your older, slower Mac into a speedy new one.

- ✔ **Get a G3 or G4 accelerator.** But remember this: An accelerated G3 or G4 Mac may not run the next generation of Mac OS, called "Mac OS X." Apple has pretty much said this version of the OS will run only on Apple-branded G3 and G4 systems without accelerator cards. So if you want to be with the Mac OS X program, an accelerator card (often referred to as a CPU upgrade) is a bad idea.

- ✔ **Get an accelerated graphics card.** Rather than attempting to accelerate your CPU, an accelerated graphics card is designed to speed up one thing: the screen update rate. Accelerated graphics cards work, blasting pixels onto your screen at amazing speeds. They're extremely popular with graphic arts professionals who would otherwise suffer agonizingly slow screen redraws when working with 24-bit graphics.

- ✔ **Get a new hard disk.** Depending on the speed of your Mac, a faster disk may provide a substantial speedup. And if you really crave speed, get a SCSI accelerator and set up a RAID (Redundant Array of Inexpensive Disks) system, which stripes your data onto two fast hard drives at once, literally doubling the speed of data access. Or if you have a new blue-and-white G3 or PowerBook with FireWire, try a FireWire hard disk.

Chapter 13

Advanced Techniques for Beginners

In This Chapter

▶ Modifying your Apple menu

▶ Using startup items

▶ Tweaking the Control Strip

1 n Chapter 12, I show you how to make your Mac faster. In this chapter, I show you ways to make it better. Indeed, if you haven't guessed already, this chapter is about ways to make your Mac easier to use.

Apple Menu

A customized Apple menu is an absolute must in my book. It's the fastest, easiest, most happening way to manage your Mac. If you don't put your Apple menu to work for you, you're missing out on one of the best things in the Mac OS.

Your Mac sorts the items in your Apple menu alphabetically, so they appear in alphabetical order in the Apple menu. If you understand how the Macintosh sorts items in a list, you can use this knowledge to your advantage.

Remember, everything in your Apple Menu Items folder appears in your Apple menu.

If you want an item to appear at the top of the Apple menu, precede its name with a number (or a space).

In Figure 13-1, I forced the first four items on the menu to be Spawn (an alias of my hard disk), Documents (an alias of my Documents folder), Desk Accessories (which I create in Chapter 7), and Control Panels by preceding each one's name with a number. Because the Macintosh sorting algorithm

sorts numbers before letters, these items now appear before the first alphabetical entry (Apps) in numerical order.

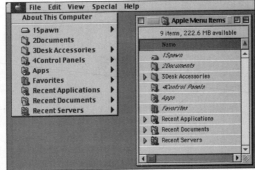

Figure 13-1:
Controlling
the order of
items in the
Apple menu
with
numbers.

Notice that I chop the word *alias* off the end of my aliases. This is strictly a
personal preference. I feel that having that extra five letters tacked onto a
file's name is unsightly.

Space cowboy

A second, slightly prettier way to accomplish the same sort is to precede the
item names with one or more spaces instead of numbers, as I demonstrate in
Figure 13-2.

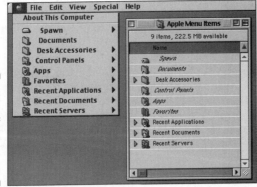

Figure 13-2:
Controlling
the order of
items in the
Apple menu
with spaces.

In Figure 13-2, Spawn has four spaces before its name, Documents has three
spaces before its name, Desk Accessories has two spaces before its name,
and Control Panels has a single space before its name.

Divide and conquer

You can create dividers in your Apple menu using the same principle. Suppose I want a dividing line after Control Panels. I just use the principles of Macintosh sorting to create a divider line of dashes using an empty folder. (See Figure 13-3.)

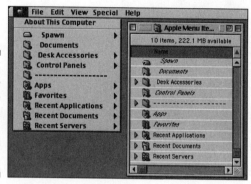

Figure 13-3: An empty folder becomes a divider in the Apple menu.

The divider appears between Control Panels and Apps because hyphens (the empty folder's name) are sorted after spaces but before letters (or numbers).

Instead of using an empty folder for a divider, make an alias of the Clipboard in your System Folder and use it. Using Clipboard aliases makes dividers at least somewhat useful because you can choose one instead of using the Finder's Show Clipboard command. Just create an alias of the Clipboard, rename it - - - - - -, and toss it in your Apple Menu Items folder.

To force a specific sorting order, you may use plenty of interesting characters on your Mac keyboard instead of spaces. The bullet (•, which you create by typing Option+8) sorts after the Z, so items with names preceded by a bullet sort at the bottom of the list after items starting with Z, as shown in Figure 13-4.

Notice in Figure 13-4 that all folder aliases in the Apple menu (except the Documents folder, which happens to be empty) have submenus. This feature is what makes all my organizational tips so great. You can organize your Apple menu so that you can quickly get to any file on your hard disk.

One thing to note is that you can't change the names of the Recent Applications or Recent Documents folders or move them from the Apple Menu Items folder. If you change either one, they'll stop working — and your Mac will create new Recent Applications and Recent Documents folders and stash them in the Apple Menu Items folder for you.

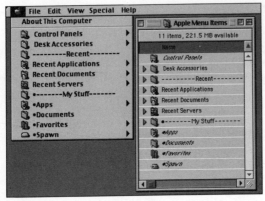

Figure 13-4:
You can
even use
unusual
characters
to reorder
your Apple
menu.

All these sorting and organizing tricks are easy after you get the hang of the way the Mac sorts items in folders. And the principles you discover here work in any window.

I use my sorting tricks in most of my folders. In Figure 13-5, I force the most frequently used item (Outgoing Files) to the top of the list by preceding its name with a space, and I force less important items (Archived Projects and On Hold Projects) to the bottom by preceding their names with a grave accent (`).

Figure 13-5:
Use a space
or a grave
accent
before a
file's name
to force it to
the top or
bottom of
the list,
respectively.

When you press the tilde key (usually found in the upper-left corner of the keyboard), your Mac types a grave accent (`) if the Shift key isn't down; it types a tilde (~) if the Shift key is held down. The tilde sorts after the Z in the Macintosh sorting scheme. (To be perfectly precise, the tilde sorts after the grave accent, which sorts after the Z.) Figure 13-6 shows other characters that sort after the tilde; these include ™ (Option+2) and • (Option+8). But the accent/tilde is handy, being right there in the corner of my keyboard.

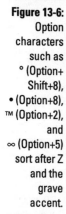

Figure 13-6:
Option
characters
such as
° (Option+
Shift+8),
• (Option+8),
™ (Option+2),
and
∞ (Option+5)
sort after Z
and the
grave
accent.

Rather than have me tell you about file sorting, why don't you give it a try for yourself? Go to your Mac right now (unless you've been there all along) and try all the tips you just discovered.

If the stuff you've read so far in this chapter is not making sense or not working for you, do the following:

1. **Choose View⇨As List.**

2. **Choose View⇨Sort List⇨By Name.**

These sorting tips work only in windows viewed as lists and sorted by name.

If you're in the list view but it's not sorted by name, merely click the word *Name* under the window's title bar.

Start Up Your Mornings Right

This section presents a pair of techniques for making your Mac start up better. The Startup Items folder tip is the most useful, but the other one, which closes all open windows automatically at startup, can be convenient as well. Both techniques are worth knowing.

Don't overlook the convenience of the Startup Items folder in your System Folder. Everything in this special folder launches automatically at startup.

Think about that for a second. What's the first thing you do after you turn on your Mac and the desktop appears? If your answer begins with the word

Open or *Launch,* you can save yourself some effort by putting an alias of the launched or opened item in the Startup Items folder. It then launches automatically at startup.

If you work with a single database or spreadsheet file every day, why not put an alias of it in the Startup Items folder? Then when you turn on your Mac, that document automatically appears on the screen. Or if the first thing you do each morning is check your e-mail, put an alias of your e-mail program in the Startup Items folder.

You can even put a sound in the Startup Items folder. Thereafter, that sound plays as the Finder appears. For this trick to work, the sound must be stored in the System 7 sound format. You can tell if a sound is in this common format by opening the sound file. If the sound is a System 7 sound, you'll hear it play when you double-click it. Other sound file formats (such as AIFF, WAV, and so on) will open the QuickTime Player, do nothing, or display an "application can't be found" error message when you open them.

Most sounds floating around Mac circles these days are in the System 7 format.

The Stickies feature is neat to have around all the time. If you put an alias of Stickies in the Startup Items folder, your sticky memos will always be available, as shown in Figure 13-7.

Figure 13-7:
Now
Stickies
launches
automati-
cally.

Stickies knows that you're likely to want to use it all the time, so it has a preference setting that not only puts an alias of it in the Startup Items folder, but also makes sure that it launches into the background, making the Finder the active application at startup.

To use this feature, launch Stickies, choose Edit⇨Preferences, and check both the Launch at System Startup and In the Background check boxes, as shown in Figure 13-8.

Figure 13-8:
Select the
last two
options.

Not all programs are as considerate as Stickies; the items in the Startup Items folder launch alphabetically, using the same Macintosh sorting order that I talk about in the preceding section. And under ordinary circumstances, the last item to launch would be the active application at the end of the startup sequence.

Stickies can launch itself and then make the Finder the active application.

So if you want the Finder to be the active application at startup and you have several items in your Startup Items folder, just make sure that Stickies loads last and that you've checked the In the Background check box in the Stickies preferences.

In other words, precede Stickies' name with a few Zs (or a tilde or a bullet) to make it the last item in the list when you view the Startup Items window by name.

Control Strip Poker

One relatively new feature that can save you time and effort is the Control Strip, which (if it's turned on in the Control Strip control panel) appears somewhere on your screen.

With the Control Strip, you can adjust your Mac's speaker volume, change the bit depth and resolution of your monitor, select a printer, and turn file sharing and AppleTalk on and off, all without visiting a control panel or the Chooser. Figure 13-9 shows the Control Strip with its collection of Apple-supplied modules as it appears on your desktop. Just click one to see its menu.

Figure 13-9:
The full complement of the Apple-supplied Control Strip.

That's not exactly true. Figure 13-9 shows the full complement for a desktop Mac. If you have a PowerBook or an iBook, you may also have Battery Monitor, Energy Settings, HD Spin Down, Media Bay, TV Mirroring, and Video Mirroring control strip modules.

You can find out more about the Control Strip in Chapter 14, but for now, here are a few things you should know. Control Strip modules live in a folder in your System Folder named (what else?) Control Strip Modules. If a module is in this folder at startup, it appears in your Control Strip on-screen.

Apple provides 18 Control Strip items. If you don't want or need some of them, you can delete them (that is, trash 'em) and make your Control Strip even shorter and more efficient. But the Control Strips are handy if you need to do the things they do.

Your mileage may vary. Not every Mac gets all the Control Strip items. Although Apple provides at least 18 different Control Strip modules, some are meant for PowerBooks and aren't installed on desktop machines.

Many freeware and shareware Control Strip modules are available, and some commercial programs include Control Strip modules. For example, my shareware bookmark program, URL Manager Pro, includes a module that lets me perform a number of bookmark-related actions right from my Control Strip. And the popular commercial antivirus program, Virex, has a Control Strip module that lets you scan files for viruses right from the Control Strip. And so on.

Chapter 14

Control Tweaks

. . . .

In This Chapter

▶ Instructions on tweaking every single control panel

▶ Lots of pictures

. . . .

*T*he Control Panels folder contains (what else?) your control panels. What exactly are control panels? They're usually miniprograms that control a single aspect of your Mac's operation.

I talk about some control panels (such as Memory and File Sharing) in detail in other chapters. In this chapter, I go through the 33 control panels (found in a typical installation) in alphabetical order, describing and suggesting settings for every one.

In Chapter 16 I continue this discussion with a full disclosure of how much memory and disk space each control panel uses and how to remove or temporarily disable ones that you don't need. I even explain why you might want to do this stuff.

I include no-brainer settings at the end of many sections for those of you who just want to know how to set the thing and don't care what it does or why. These no-brainer settings are not the gospel, but they're a good place to start. (You can always come back and change them later after you figure out what they are and what they do.)

If your Mac is working the way you expect it to right this second, I implore you to take a moment to note the current settings of any control panel before you change anything. Nothing is more frustrating than changing something and then being unable to change it back to the way it was. So before you change any control panel settings, either write down the current settings or make a screen shot of them so that you can set things straight should the change not suit you. (⌘+Shift+3 captures everything on your screen and saves it as a PICT file at root level on your startup disk. You can open the files — named Picture 1, Picture 2, and so on — using SimpleText.)

Appearance

Mac OS 9's Appearance control panel (see Figure 14-1) replaces the old Color, Windowshade, and Desktop Pictures control panels and adds a few twists, including a first-ever opportunity to change the entire look and feel of your Mac using slick new themes.

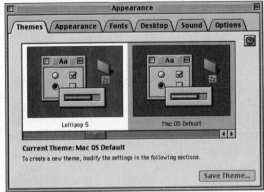

Figure 14-1:
The Mac OS Default Theme in all its glory.

The Appearance control panel window has six tabs: Themes, Appearance, Fonts, Desktop, Sound, and Options. Each governs a particular aspect of how your Mac looks and feels. I cover each in turn. But first, you need to understand what a theme is.

A *theme* is the summation of all the settings you can choose in the Appearance control panel. So in effect, a theme is how your Mac looks and feels. Among the items in each theme that can be customized are the menu font, the Finder font, the desktop background, and sounds.

When you have all six Appearance tabs set just the way you like them, click the Themes tab and click the Save Theme button. All your Appearance settings are saved as a theme; you then have the opportunity to name your new theme whatever you like.

Themes

Not much to it. You choose the theme that you like best by clicking it in the Themes tab of the Appearance control panel.

Appearance

Here you can choose specific aspects of how your Mac looks and feels.

To wit:

- ✔ The Appearance pop-up menu lets you choose from different appearances. But Apple, in their infinite wisdom, provides only one — Apple Platinum. Other appearances may be available (try the Internet) but are not sanctioned by Apple.

- ✔ The Highlight Color pop-up menu lets you choose the color that text turns when you select it in a document or in an icon's name in the Finder.

- ✔ The Variation pop-up menu lets you choose the color that menu items turn when you select them and also the color of scroll boxes in windows.

Fonts

This is where you choose the fonts your Mac uses in several different places. See Figure 14-2.

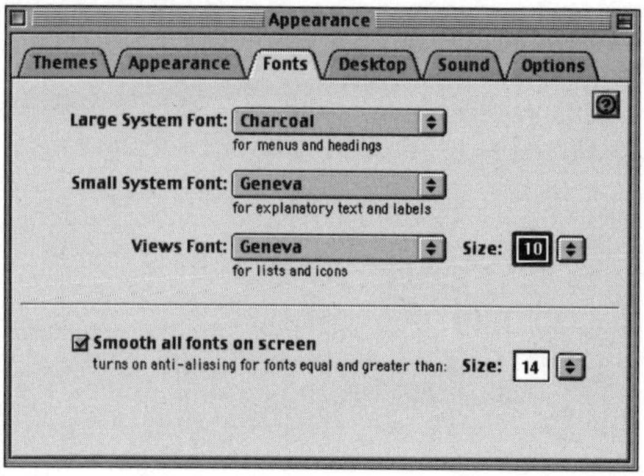

Figure 14-2:
Choose the
fonts you
see in the
Finder and
turn font
smoothing
on or off.

The Large System Font pop-up menu governs the font used in all menus and headings (such as the tabs in the Appearance window).

The Small System Font pop-up menu governs the font used in explanatory text and labels.

The Views Font pop-up menu governs the font used in lists and icons in the Finder. Unlike the other two font menus on this tab, you can choose the size of the Views font.

I like to use 10-point type in my Finder views. You can see more stuff in each window that way. If you have good eyes, you might even try 9 point.

Finally, you have a check box called Smooth All Fonts On Screen and a pop-up menu to select a minimum size for smoothing, or anti-aliasing.

Turning on font smoothing may make your Mac feel sluggish. Leave it turned off unless you really like its effect. And if you do turn it on, smooth sizes only 18 and above for minimal impact on your Mac's performance.

Desktop

The Desktop tab is where you choose a desktop pattern or picture. For background patterns, merely choose one from the list. To have a picture as your desktop background, click the Place Picture button and choose a picture in PICT, JPEG, or GIF format. When the picture or pattern you like best is shown in the preview on the left side of the window, click the Set Desktop button.

You can also drag any appropriate picture (and by *appropriate,* I mean PICT, JPEG, or GIF, not the picture's subject matter) onto the little screen on the right side of the window (the one showing the current pattern or picture), and then click the Set Desktop button. Or (and this is one of my favorite tricks), you can drag a folder full of appropriate pictures onto the little screen and a picture from that folder will be chosen at random to be your desktop every time you restart your Mac.

The pop-up Position menu controls how pictures are displayed: tiled, centered, scaled, filling the screen, or positioned automatically.

Sound

The Sound tab lets you select different sound effects for Finder events such as opening menus, choosing items, dragging, and resizing. Check out Figure 14-3.

Options

The Options tab controls two aspects of the way windows appear on your Mac. Clicking the Smart Scrolling check box makes scroll arrows in windows double-sided and varies the size of the scroll box depending on how much of the window contents are hidden.

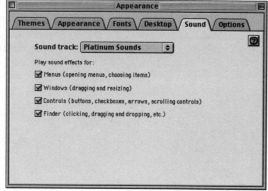

Figure 14-3:
First choose
a sound
track, and
then choose
which
sounds you
want
turned on.

Clicking the check box called Double-Click Title Bar to Collapse Windows
makes you able to double-click the title bar of any window to roll it up, the
same as if you clicked its Windowshade box (in the upper-right corner of
most windows, to the right of the Grow box).

Appearance no-brainer setting. Choose a theme in the Themes tab and then
close the Appearance control panel and be done with it.

Don't forget, the no-brainer settings are merely suggestions. For example, if
you choose a theme that has sounds attached to it and you discover you hate
them, by all means turn them off in the Sound tab.

Apple Menu Options

The Apple Menu Options control panel has two functions:

- It turns submenus on or off.
- It lets you specify how many recent documents, applications, and
  servers your Mac should track.

The first function controls whether or not folders (and aliases of folders as
well as disks) in the Apple menu display their contents when you highlight
them. Put another way, the Submenus on/off switch (actually, a pair of radio
buttons) turns the little triangles on and off. It works while the control panel
is open, so try each choice and then pull down the Apple menu to see the
results.

The second function requires that you click to check the Remember Recently Used Items check box. When you do so, your Mac remembers the specified number of documents, applications, and servers for you. You can find the remembered items in the similarly named folders in the Apple menu. (See Figure 14-4.)

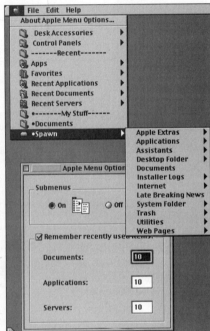

Figure 14-4:
The Apple
Menu
Options
control
panel and
its two
offspring:
submenus in
the Apple
menu and
the Recent
Items
folders in
the middle
of my Apple
menu.

The Mac remembers these items by creating aliases and putting them in the appropriate Recent Items folder. All three Recent Items folders are in the Apple Menu Items folder.

The Mac uses FIFO (first in, first out) to limit the number of items in each folder according to your choices in the Apple Menu Options control panel. Suppose you set the number of documents to 20. When you open document 21, document 1 is forgotten. More long-windedly, when you open document 21, your Mac creates an alias for document 21. It then deletes the alias for document 1 so that there are again only 20 items in the folder, as you requested.

All this stuff is accomplished invisibly, without your knowledge or intervention.

Apple Menu Options no-brainer settings. Submenus: On. Documents: 15. Applications: 15. Servers: 0 (unless, of course, you're connected to a server, in which case it's your call).

AppleTalk

The AppleTalk control panel (see Figure 14-5) lets you choose how and where to network your Mac or Mac compatible. Its main function is to let you select ports — Printer, Modem, Ethernet (if you have it; I do), Infrared Port (IrDA, if you have it; I don't), or Remote Only — for dial-in connections. For more information, check out Chapter 10.

Figure 14-5:
Choose your
network
connections
here.

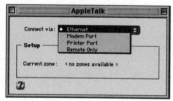

But wait, there's more! You can choose Edit⇨User Mode, promote yourself to Administration level, and then password-protect your network settings and much more. If you do that, you'll have access to an Options button that lets you turn AppleTalk on and off. (Big deal. You can turn AppleTalk on and off also in the Chooser desk accessory.)

Or choose File⇨Get Info (⌘+I) to find out more about your Mac and its addresses and software version numbers, which may someday come in handy.

Finally, choosing File⇨Configurations (⌘+K) lets you create, rename, import, or export your specific configurations.

Most of you will probably use this control panel once and then forget about it forever.

At least now you can say you know what it is and what it does. Don't forget that Mac OS Help is only a keystroke (that would be ⌘+?) away.

ColorSync

ColorSync is a color-matching technology that ensures color consistency between screen representation and color output. It is of no importance unless you are also using the ColorSync color-matching system on your printing devices and scanners.

I thought not.

So this control panel's settings are irrelevant. Nothing good whatsoever will happen if you change them.

ColorSync no-brainer setting. Don't touch it.

Control Strip

You can show or hide the Control Strip by choosing the appropriate option in the Control Strip control panel.

Use the Control Strip's built-in hide and show feature (demonstrated in Figure 14-6) to collapse and expand the strip on-screen. Click the little nub at the bottom of Figure 14-6 to expand it again.

Figure 14-6:
Click either
end of the
Control Strip
(circled, top)
to collapse
it to a nub
(bottom).

Hold down the Option key and click the roughly triangular nub at the end of the strip to move it around your screen. (***Note:*** Your Control Strip must be touching either the left or right side of the screen. Them's the rules.)

The default keyboard shortcut to hide the Control Strip completely or bring it back if it's hidden is ⌘+Control+S. You can change this shortcut to any key combination you like by clicking the Define Hot Key button. (This trick won't work if you haven't first clicked the Hot Key to Show/Hide radio button in the Control Strip control panel.)

Control Strip no-brainer setting. Click the Show Control Strip option.

Date & Time

The Date & Time control panel lets you configure your Mac's internal clock, which many programs use, and configure the menu bar clock. See Figure 14-7.

Figure 14-7:
Set your
Mac's clock
and the
menu bar
clock here.

To set the date or time

Click the number that you want to change in the Current Date or Current Time field. The number is highlighted when you click it, and a pair of arrows appears. Increase the selected number by clicking the up arrow; decrease it by clicking the down arrow. You can also use the arrow keys on the keyboard to increase or decrease the number. Or you can type a new number right over the selected number.

Use the Tab key to move from number to number. Month, day, year, hour, minute, second, and AM/PM are selected in sequence when you press the Tab key. If you want to move backward through the sequence, press Shift+Tab. As long as you hold the Shift key down, you'll cycle through the numbers in reverse order as you press Tab.

Time and date formats

You see your choices in the Date or Time Formats dialog boxes anyplace your Mac displays the date and time: in the menu bar, in programs that date- or time-stamp documents, in the Finder (creation and modification dates), and so on.

To change formats, click the appropriate button. The Date Formats dialog box, which is shown in Figure 14-8, lets you change the punctuation marks in the long date and the dividers in the short date.

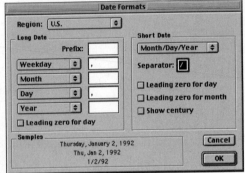

Figure 14-8:
Apple
thinks of
everything,
doesn't it?

You can change the display order of both long and short dates. Use the Weekday, Month, Day, and Year pop-up menus to change the order of the long date; click the Month/Day/Year pop-up menu to choose a different order for the short date.

The Time Formats dialog box lets you choose a 14-hour or 24-hour clock and a bunch of other stuff, as Figure 14-9 shows.

Figure 14-9:
The Time
Formats
dialog box,
which
doesn't
need any
changing.

The rest of it

The Daylight Savings Time check box sets the clock forward one hour (checked) or backward one hour (unchecked).

The Set Time Zone button lets you choose your time zone from a scrolling list.

Type the first letter of a big city near you to scroll to that city's name in the list. Is this thrilling or what?

The Use a Network Time Server check box and Server Options button let you synchronize your Mac's clock to a super-accurate time server on the Internet. This function requires a working Internet connection.

I love this new feature. I'm anal about this type of thing and love having my clock 100-percent accurate. I used to use SetClock (freeware for modems) or Vremya (freeware for TCP/IP connections) to do the same thing, but now I don't have to, thanks to Apple's foresight.

Finally, the Menu Bar Clock On and Off radio buttons and associated Clock Options button let you do all kinds of fun stuff with your menu bar clock, as shown in Figure 14-10. You can set the clock to chime on the hour or quarter-hour, and you can select custom fonts and colors.

Figure 14-10: If you're a tweak freak, you'll have a field day with all the options for the menu bar clock.

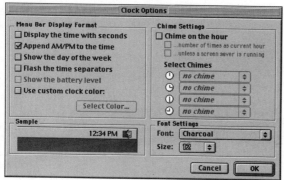

Apple's menu bar clock is based on Steve Christensen's popular freeware menu bar clock, SuperClock, which many Mac users loved and revered long before Apple began including it back in System 7.5.

Dial Assist

No cop-out, but I cover this little doohickey in clear and loving detail in Chapter 10. I don't want to waste trees, okay?

Energy Saver

Almost all recent Mac models (and the no-longer-sold clones) are said to be Energy Star compliant — they can turn themselves off at a specific time or after a specified idle period. If your Mac supports this feature, the Energy Saver control panel is installed when you install Mac OS 9. (If your Mac doesn't support this control panel but it was somehow installed and you try to open it, you'll see an error message haughtily informing you that your Mac can't use it. No problemo. Trash the dastardly Energy Saver control panel and be done with it.)

In the top part of the dialog box, you can choose to have your computer go to sleep (a low-power mode) or shut down automatically after so many minutes of idle time (kind of like a killer screen saver).

 The first time you restart your Mac after installing Mac OS 9, a helpful dialog box tells you that you now have Energy Saver and asks whether you would like to configure it now. Nice, eh?

To turn this feature on, move the slider until the appropriate time appears beneath it. To turn it off, slide the slider to Never. Figure 14-11 shows this little gadget.

Figure 14-11:
To set the idle time before your Mac goes to sleep, or shuts down, click the slider and drag.

Energy Saver
Sleep Setup   Schedule
Put the system to sleep whenever it's inactive for
☐ Shut down instead of sleeping.
30 min   40   50   60   Never
Sleep is a low-power mode. Waking up from sleep is faster than restarting.   **Show Details**

Click the Show Details button and you'll see two additional sliders to control your display and hard disk sleep patterns separately.

And if you click the Scheduled Startup and Shutdown button at the top of the Energy Saver window, you can choose to have your Mac start up or shut down once at a specific time, or you can set up a recurring shutdown (for example, shut down every day at 10:29 P.M., just in time for Letterman — for those of us in the central time zone).

If you're not around when one of these shutdowns occurs and you have unsaved work in any application, you'll see a dialog box asking whether you want to save your changes. The Mac won't shut down until you click a button in this dialog box. In fact, if you click the Cancel button in this dialog box, the shutdown is canceled along with the Save dialog box.

One last thing: To wake up your Mac from its sleep, merely move the mouse or press any key on the keyboard.

Energy Saver no-brainer setting. Drag the slider to 30 or 45 minutes for sleep (not shutdown); then remember to turn off your Mac manually when you're not going to need it for a while.

Extensions Manager

Extensions Manager is another program that has been around for years as freeware. It made its first appearance as an Apple product in System 7.5 and was overhauled extensively for Mac OS 7.6. Extensions Manager lets you turn extensions, control panels, startup items, and shutdown items on and off easily.

I provide a longer, more technical discussion of why you need Extensions Manager, along with some tips, in Chapter 16.

Extensions and control panels load into memory if they're in the Extensions or Control Panels folder at startup. Without Extensions Manager (or one of its third-party counterparts, such as Casady & Greene's excellent and highly recommended Conflict Catcher 8), you would have to move an extension or control panel out of its special folder manually and then restart your Mac to disable it — which, as you might guess, isn't much fun.

You still have to restart your Mac, but you can use Extensions Manager to turn individual control panels and extensions on and off without moving them manually.

You can work with Extensions Manager in the Finder by opening its icon or choosing Apple menu⇨Control Panels⇨Extensions Manager. Or you can work with it at startup, before any control panels or extensions load.

To open Extensions Manager at startup, hold down the spacebar on your keyboard until the Extensions Manager window appears, as shown in Figure 14-12.

Figure 14-12:
The
Extensions
Manager
window lets
you turn
control
panels,
extensions,
startup
items, and
shutdown
items off
and on at
will (at
startup).

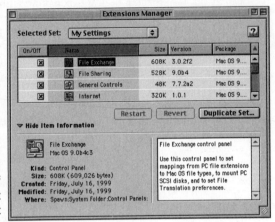

Regardless of which way you open the Extensions Manager, you choose which items you want to turn on or off by clicking the box before their name. (An X means the item is turned on.) Your choices remain in effect until you change them again in the Extensions Manager window.

You can create sets, or groups of extensions and control panels that you want to use simultaneously. To create a set, click items in the list until the ones that you want turned on have Xs and the ones that you want turned off don't. When everything is just the way you like it, choose File⇨New Set. You'll be asked to name the set. After you do, the set appears in the Sets menu as a custom set along with the preinstalled sets — Mac OS All and Mac OS Base. Sets can be quite convenient, as I explain in Chapter 16.

When you finish making your selections or creating sets, close the Extensions Manager window. If you used the spacebar to open Extensions Manager at startup, your Mac will start up with only the Xed items loaded; if you're in the Finder, click the Extensions Manager's Restart button for your selections to take effect.

The Mac OS Base set turns on only the most essential control panels and extensions, turning off memory hogs such as QuickDraw 3D. (See Chapter 16 for details.) Using it may regain some of your precious RAM for other purposes.

You can also turn on or off the entire Extensions, Control Panels, Startup Items, and Shutdown Items folders by clicking the On/Off box next to their names. In other words, turning off the Control Panels folder in Extensions Manager turns off all your control panels at once. You'll find Duplicate Set, Delete Set, and Rename Set commands in the File menu. They do what they sound like they do.

Finally, if you click an item in the Extensions Manager window (File Exchange is selected in Figure 14-12), some information about it will appear in a box in the lower-right corner of the window when you click the triangle below the list of extensions. Although Chapter 16 does a more thorough job of explaining this stuff, the little box in the corner will do in a pinch if your copy of *Mac OS 9 For Dummies* isn't handy.

File Exchange

The File Exchange control panel combines the features of two Mac OS 8 control panels, PC Exchange and Mac OS Easy Open.

PC Exchange tab

The PC Exchange tab of the File Exchange control panel manages which Macintosh program launches when you open documents created on that other kind of computer that runs those other operating systems, MS-DOS or Windows. (See Figure 14-13.)

Figure 14-13:
If I open a
DOS or
Windows
document
with the aif
suffix, PC
Exchange
tells
QuickTime
Player to
launch and
open the
document.

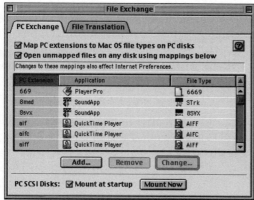

Apple throws in this application assignment — .aif documents open in QuickTime Player — for free. If you would prefer to read DOS files in a program other than QuickTime Player, click the application assignment to select it, click the Change button, and then choose a new application.

In the Change dialog box, you can change the three-letter suffix, the application program that you want to use to open that type of document, and the type of document.

If you click the Document Type pop-up menu and nothing happens, the type is set already for that document and you can't change it.

To remove an application assignment, select it by clicking and then click the Remove button.

Double-clicking an application assignment opens the dialog box, just as selecting it and then clicking the Change button does.

The Add button in the PC Exchange control panel brings up the same dialog box as the Change button. To create a new application assignment, make your choices in the dialog box and then click OK.

Finally, click the Mount at Startup check box to tell PC Exchange that you want it to work on other SCSI devices such as external hard drives or Zip, Jaz, Orb, or SyQuest drives. If you insert such a disk and it doesn't mount automatically, you can click the Mount Now button.

File Translation tab

The File Translation tab governs the functions that used to be called Mac OS Easy Open (MEO), the enabling technology that lets you choose another application to open a document when you don't have the actual application that created it. If you try to open a document and don't have the application that created it on your hard disk, you see a dialog box that enables you to choose a different application to open that document.

If the Translate Documents Automatically check box isn't checked or if the File Exchange control panel is disabled or deleted, you see not the dialog box but an error message telling you that an application couldn't be found for this document.

The four check boxes in this tab of the File Exchange control panel manage how the translation dialog box works, as shown in Figure 14-14.

If you check the Translate Documents Automatically check box, the entire process occurs automatically. If you don't have the application available, your Mac will choose another one for you without any intervention on your part.

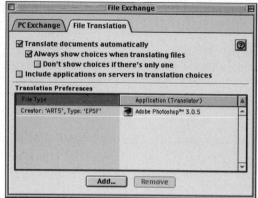

Figure 14-14:
The File
Translation
tab of the
File
Exchange
control
panel.

If you check Always Show Choices When Translating Files check box, you must confirm your translation preference every time you open a document. In other words, if this item is checked, you see the "choose an application" dialog box every time you open a file and don't have the program that created it. If you uncheck this option, the second time (and every time thereafter) that you open a document of the same type, the translator automatically launches into the alternate program you selected the first time.

If you check the Don't Show Choices If There's Only One check box, you won't see the "choose an application" dialog box if only one program on your hard disk can open the file.

If you check the Include Applications on Servers in Translation Choices option, your Mac will look on all network volumes currently mounted for an application that can open the document.

If you don't have a high-speed network (such as Ethernet or token ring), launching a remote program can take a long, long time. You may want to consider leaving this option off unless you really, really need it.

The Add button lets you link specific types of documents to a particular application manually.

The Remove button deletes the selected link.

File Exchange no-brainer settings. PC Exchange tab: Check all three check boxes. File Translation tab: Check Translate Documents Automatically and Don't Show Choices If There's Only One. Uncheck Always Show Choices When Translating Files and Include Applications on Servers in Translation choices.

File Sharing

The File Sharing control panel combines the features of two older control panels, File Sharing Monitor and Sharing Setup. This is where you turn File Sharing on and off and find out which items on your local disk are currently being shared, how much network activity there is, and who is currently connected to your hard disk.

I won't waste any more of your time with this one; I cover it in great detail in Chapter 8.

General Controls

The General Controls control panel is the big fellow, the granddaddy of all control panels. Figure 14-15 doesn't do it justice.

Figure 14-15:
The General
Controls
control
panel is like
six control
panels
in one.

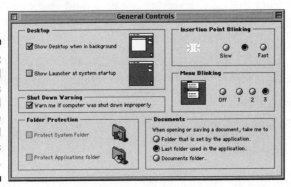

General Controls manages a whopping six options.

Desktop options

The Show Desktop When in Background check box determines whether the Finder shows through in the background when you have another application open. Unchecking this option makes Finder windows and icons disappear when other programs are active, which means that the only way to switch to the Finder is to choose it from the Application menu. In other words, if you click outside a word processor window, you don't pop into the Finder.

Checking the Show Desktop When in Background option makes it more convenient to return to the Finder from other programs by clicking the desktop or a Finder window, but this feature may be more confusing for beginners.

The Show Launcher at System Startup check box governs whether the Launcher is active. I rant about Launcher in Chapter 8, so I won't bore you with my vitriol. Suffice it to say that I don't find it very useful, but beginners might.

Shut Down Warning

If you select the check box in the Shut Down Warning area, you'll see a warning like the one in Figure 1-1 (see Chapter 1) when you restart your computer after a crash, a freeze, a power interruption, or an improper shutdown.

Folder Protection

If you check the Folder Protection check boxes, you can't rename or delete items in those folders (System or Applications or both).

Insertion Point Blinking

The Insertion Point Blinking option sets the speed at which the text insertion point (a flashing vertical line) blinks in documents. Your choices are Slow, Medium, or Fast. I like Medium or Fast because I find it easiest to see the cursor that way. Your mileage may vary.

Menu Blinking

The Menu Blinking option controls whether or not menu items flash when you select them, and if they flash, how many times.

Off is the fastest setting.

Documents

The set of options for Documents determines what folder will be active in Open and Save dialog boxes:

- ✔ **Folder that is set by the application:** This option displays the Open or Save dialog box ready to save or open files in the folder that contains the program you're using or whatever folder that program ordinarily defaults to, often the last folder you opened a file from or saved a file to. So if you're using AppleWorks and you choose File➪Save or File➪Open, the list of files you see in the Open or Save dialog box are the contents of the AppleWorks folder or perhaps the last folder you saved a file into.

- ✔ **Last folder used in the application:** This option displays the Open or Save dialog box ready to save or open a file in the last folder you saved to or opened a document from. In other words, your Mac remembers for you. Many programs do this automatically. Clicking this setting makes sure every application does it.

- ✔ **Documents folder:** This option displays the Open or Save dialog box ready to save or open a document in the Documents folder.

General Controls no-brainer settings for beginners. Show Desktop When in Background: Off. Show Launcher at System Startup: On. Shut Down Warning: On. Folder Protection: On for both. Insertion Point Blinking: Fast. Menu Blinking: 3 times. Documents: Documents folder.

General Controls no-brainer settings for more advanced users. Show Desktop When in Background: On. Show Launcher at System Startup: Off. Shut Down Warning: Your call. Folder Protection: Off for both. Insertion Point Blinking: Fast. Menu Blinking: Off. Documents: Last folder used.

Internet

I cover the Internet control panel in full and loving detail in Chapter 17, so I won't waste trees on it here.

Keyboard

The Keyboard control panel modifies how your keyboard responds to your keystrokes. It's shown in Figure 14-16.

The Keyboard Layouts section allows you to choose a different keyboard layout for languages other than United States English.

The Key Repeat Rate sets how fast a key will repeat when you hold it down. This feature comes into play, for example, when you hold down the dash key to make a line or the * key to make a divider.

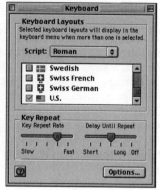

Figure 14-16:
The
Keyboard
control
panel
governs
how your
keyboard
responds.

The Delay Until Repeat option sets how long you have to hold down a key before it starts repeating.

Because changes to the Keyboard control panel take place immediately, you can open it and a word processor and experiment with its settings until you are comfortable.

Do not under any circumstances click the Options button unless you have good reason to use foreign keyboard layouts on occasion. The ⌘+Option+spacebar keyboard shortcut, when turned on, can cause unpredictable behavior if you later forget you've turned it on. Use this thingy with caution, especially if you use Photoshop (which uses ⌘+Option+spacebar as the shortcut for Zoom Out).

Keyboard no-brainer settings. Look at Figure 14-16. Duplicate its settings. If you live somewhere other than the United States and see a familiar sounding keyboard layout in the scrolling part of the window, select it.

Keychain Access

With the new Keychain Access control panel, you can organize passwords and encryption keys — codes that let you connect to secure computers or Internet sites — under one nifty little place, the Keychain. Enter a master password for your keychain, and get access to all the other passwords and keys you use to connect to encrypted stuff. If, like most people, you don't connect to encrypted stuff, you don't need the keychain. Consult Mac OS Help for more info about the keychain if you need it.

Launcher

Launcher is Apple's cheesy little file launcher. It lets you open items in its window with a single click, which saves you the trouble of rummaging through folders. The Launcher window's buttons reflect the contents of the Launcher Items folder in your System Folder.

To add an item to Launcher, drag it onto the Launcher window. This action automatically creates an alias for that item in the Launcher Items folder. To delete an item from Launcher, hold down Option and drag the item from the Launcher window to the Trash.

Whatever is in the Launcher Items folder appears as a button in the Launcher window. Single-clicking the button opens the item, which can be a file, a folder, a document, a control panel, or (better idea) an alias of a file, a folder, a document, or a control panel.

If you want Launcher to start up automatically, an option for that very thing is in the General Controls control panel.

If you like Launcher, read up on how to make it better in Chapter 8.

Launcher is even less necessary now that the Finder has single-click buttons in any window. Why they don't retire this old hag is a mystery to me.

Memory

See Chapter 11, which covers the Memory control panel and nothing else.

Memory no-brainer setting. Click the Use Defaults button and be done with it.

Modem

The Modem control panel, which is shown in Figure 14-17, lets you choose which port your modem is connected to, as well as sound and dialing options (available only for internal modems, alas).

Figure 14-17:
The Modem
control
panel
doesn't do
much,
does it?

Monitors

In the Monitors control panel, you control your Mac's monitor options. Old-timers may remember that this control panel used to be called Monitors & Sound, and before that, it was just Monitors. Oh well. Everything old is new again, I suppose.

Click the Monitor button at the top of the window. You can now select either Grays or Colors; if you select Colors, you also need to select the number of colors in the Color Depth scrolling list. If your monitor and video card support what is known as MultiSync, you can also change resolutions, as shown in Figure 14-18. Finally, some monitors let you adjust their brightness and gamma settings. If your monitor supports these features, you'll see brightness (not shown in Figure 14-18) and gamma (also not shown) controls in this window. If you have these features, adjust them the way that looks best to your eyes.

Figure 14-18:
The Monitor
control
panel with
the Monitor
button at the
top
selected.

Mouse

The Mouse control panel, shown in Figure 14-19, sets the mouse-tracking and double-click speeds.

Figure 14-19:
The Mouse control panel, where speed is king.

The Mouse Tracking setting governs the relationship between hand movement of the mouse and cursor movement on the screen. Fast mouse-tracking settings send the cursor squirting across the screen with a mere flick of the wrist; slow mouse-tracking settings make the cursor crawl across in seemingly slow motion, even when your hand is flying. Set it as fast as you can stand it. I like the fastest speed. Try it. You might like it.

The Double-Click Speed setting determines how close together two clicks must be for the Mac to interpret them as a double-click and not two separate clicks. The leftmost button is the slow setting. It lets you double-click at an almost leisurely pace. The rightmost is the fast setting (which I prefer). The middle button represents a double-click speed somewhere in the middle.

Changes in the Mouse control panel take place immediately, so you should definitely play around a little and see what settings feel best for you.

Mouse no-brainer settings. Mouse Tracking: Moderately fast to fast. Double-Click Speed: Middle setting.

Multiple Users

Mac OS 9 is the first version of Mac OS to give you an easy way to share your Mac with several people, giving everyone his or her own folder, and allowing you, Mom, and Dad to control access to some applications, disks, or other goodies on the family Mac.

It works like this: You create a user profile for each person who will be working on your Mac and assign a password. At startup, the Mac asks who will be using it, and grants entry based on the password you've set.

When you open the Multiple Users control panel, you'll find one user — the name you entered in the File Sharing control panel — already created. That user has full access to everything on your Mac. Follow these steps:

1. **Click the New User button to add a second user.**

   Because Multiple Users is off right now, you'll get a dialog box reminding you that the settings you're about to create won't take effect until you turn Multiple Users on.

   Figure 14-20 shows the Edit New User window. I'm creating a user profile for my seven-year-old son, Jacob.

Figure 14-20: Choose applications you want your new user to be able to use by clicking the check boxes next to them.

2. **Click the Limited button, and then click the triangle to the right of the Show pop-up menu. Make your selections.**

   Jacob uses only a few applications, so I'll check those he needs and leave the rest unchecked.

3. **Click the User Info tab.**

4. **If you want to attach an icon or picture to this user, choose one from the list by clicking the up and down arrows, or drag a picture into the window.**

   Leave the other options alone, but check Access by Others to User's Documents if you want the rest of the family to be able to work with this user's files. I'll do that for Jacob, and leave the Read Only option selected.

5. **Click the Privileges tab.**

The Privileges tab, which is shown in Figure 14-21, lets you restrict access to CD-ROMs and other removable media, network items, and printers. I'll give Jacob full access to the CD-ROM drive. I could click the List for Restricted Users button to create a list of CDs that Jacob can use, but I'll leave access unlimited for now. If I click the Other Removable Media check box, Jacob won't be able to use Zip disks or floppies. We have several printers. Jacob uses the HP LaserJet 4ML, so I'll give him permission to print, and select that printer. I'll unselect Chooser and Network Browser, just to keep things simple, and I'll leave the rest of the options alone.

Figure 14-21:
The Privileges tab lets you choose whether the user can print, use CDs and other media, and connect to a network.

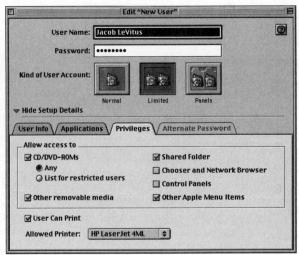

6. **Close the window to save your options.**

7. **Click On to activate Multiple Users.**

8. **Create more users, or restart the Mac.**

When you restart, you see a list of users. Click the one you want, and type the password. If you log on as a limited user, like Jacob, you see a shared folder on the desktop. Everything else will look normal, but you won't be able to launch applications or use other options that have been restricted in the Multiple Users control panel.

The Options button

Click the Options button, then click the Login tab to:

- ✔ Create a customized login message
- ✔ Enable voice verification of password (way cool!)
- ✔ Select a microphone
- ✔ Choose to log the user out or lock the screen after a specified amount of idle time

Click the CD/DVD-ROM Access tab to specify content restrictions for specific CD/DVD discs on a file-by-file basis.

Click the Other tab to enable a Guest User Account, notify you when new programs are installed, choose whether users have to type their name at login or choose it from a list, and choose whether this computer is on a network or not.

For more information on any of these features, see Mac Help.

Numbers

You use the Numbers control panel to change the decimal and thousands separators (the period and comma in, for example, $1,000,000.00) as well as the symbol used to denote currency ($ in the United States, £ in England, and so on).

You could go through your entire life without ever needing to open the Numbers control panel.

QuickTime Settings

The QuickTime Settings control panel is a no-brainer. It's probably already configured properly, in which case, leave it alone. Just check to make sure it's set as follows.

First choose AutoPlay from the pop-up menu if it's not already selected; then uncheck both check boxes — Enable Audio CD AutoPlay and Enable CD-ROM AutoPlay. Although these settings enable your Mac to automatically start playing all audio CDs and some CD-ROM titles, they also allow a nasty virus/worm called Autostart 9805 to infect your hard disk.

This topic brings up the bigger question of "Do I need an antivirus program?" The answer is, "You do if you're at risk." How do you know if you're at risk? You're at risk if you

✔ Download files from the Internet

✔ Receive e-mail with attachments

✔ Are on a network and share files with others

✔ Use floppy disks that have been inserted in anyone else's Mac

Those are the ways viruses spread, so if any or all of the preceding apply to you, you would be well served to run an antivirus program, such as Dr. Solomon's Virex or Symantec's Norton Anti-Virus for Macintosh.

Now choose Connection Speed from the pop-up menu and select the speed of your Internet connection by clicking the appropriate option.

Ignore the Media Keys item. It says "Media keys authorize your access to secured media files." I still haven't figured out what it means. I guess if someone sends you a secured media file (or you download one), you can figure it out then. So far I've never seen one.

Now choose Music from the pop-up menu and make sure that QuickTime Music Synthesizer is selected.

Now choose QuickTime Exchange from the pop-up menu and click the Enable QuickTime Exchange check box so you can play files created on non-Mac computers.

Finally, if you want to purchase QuickTime Pro, choose Registration from the pop-up menu and click the Register Online button. If you choose to upgrade to QuickTime Pro, you'll be able to

✔ Play back full-screen, broadcast-quality video (assuming your Mac is powerful enough).

✔ View high-quality streaming media in leading Internet browsers.

✔ Access more than 85 percent of the multimedia content on the Web with one package.

✔ Play more than 30 different audio and video file formats — on and off the Internet.

✔ Edit and manipulate both existing and newly created movies and audio.

✔ Export movies using the best compression technology available.

✔ Save audio and movie files for later use through a convenient pop-up menu.

- ✔ View all the most popular Internet media formats with a single browser plug-in.

- ✔ Resize movies to a variety of window sizes.

- ✔ Copy and paste content from any supported format to create a new QuickTime movie.

- ✔ Prepare and compress content for streaming delivery from any Mac OS or Windows-based Web server.

- ✔ View images, including JPEG, BMP, and PNG formats, from a wide variety of sources.

- ✔ Enhance movies and still pictures with filters for sharpening, color tinting, embossing, and more.

- ✔ Save in the exciting new DV camcorder format for high-quality consumer video.

- ✔ Create slide shows from any number of picture sources that play in any QuickTime application.

All for just $29.99 with a 30-day, money-back guarantee. There's no new software to install — just unlock the extended features of QuickTime 4, and you're ready to rock. I say it's worth every penny.

That'll do it. Close it and forget it.

Remote Access

See Chapter 10 for the gory details on the Remote Access control panel. I won't waste trees on it.

Software Update

The Software Update control panel is not too complicated. Click the Software Update button and your Mac will look for updated versions of your system software by connecting to Apple's Web site. You can look for updates manually, or have the update application look for new software on a schedule you set. Click Update Software Automatically and then click the Set Schedule button.

Sound

In the Sound control panel, you control the way the Mac plays and records sound.

Alert Sounds (beep sounds)

When you open the Sound control panel, you see the Alert Sounds option, as shown in Figure 14-22. Now you can choose your Mac's System Alert sound, also known as its beep sound. The Alert Volume slider controls System Alert (that is, beep) volume.

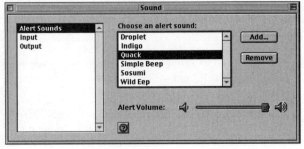

Figure 14-22:
The Sound control panel's Alert Sounds panel.

If you have a microphone that works with your Mac or have sounds you've downloaded or traded with others, you can add additional sounds by dragging any sound file onto the System Folder icon. The OS automatically puts them in the proper place for you when you drag them onto the closed System Folder icon. The sound files must be in the System 7 sound format for this to work.

Don't believe me? Here's how to record your own sound (microphone required, of course):

1. **In the Alert Sounds panel, click the Add button.**

   A recording dialog box appears, as shown in Figure 14-23.

Figure 14-23:
The record-your-own-sound dialog box.

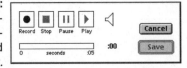

2. **Click the Record button.**

3. **Make your noise or sound.**

4. **Click the Stop button.**

5. **Name the sound.**

Bingo. That's it. Your new sound appears in the list of sounds. Select it now as your beep sound if you like. See. Told you it was a piece of cake (as long as you have the microphone).

Input

The Input window lets you choose from External microphone, CD, Modem, or none using the Input Source pop-up menu, Whatever you choose will be heard through your Mac speakers.

Output

If you have speakers connected to your Mac, use the Output window to choose them and to adjust their volume. If you don't have speakers, the volume slider changes the volume of your Mac's built-in speaker. The Volume Mute check box turns off your Mac's internal speaker.

Speech

Choose Voice from the Options pop-up menu (see Figure 14-24) to select the voice your Mac will use for speech-to-text applications. Now choose a voice from the 25 wild and wacky selections in the Voice pop-up menu. To check out your handiwork, click the speaker icon. Each voice says something different. My favorite is Fred, who says, "I sure like being inside this fancy computer." If you think that's fun, try this: Launch SimpleText, type a few words, and then choose Sound⇨Speak All (⌘+J). Cute, eh?

For a really good time, choose Talking Alerts from the Options pop-up menu and click both check boxes (as shown in Figure 14-25). From the Speak the Phrase pop-up menu, select the Random from the List option, and then close the Speech control panel. The next time a program displays an alert box on the screen ("Save changes to the document 'untitled' before closing?"), your favorite voice will speak it for you.

Figure 14-24:
The Speech control panel — choose from 25 wild and wacky voices and make them talk slower or faster.

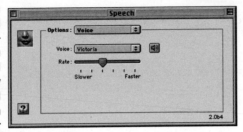

Figure 14-25:
Set yours like mine, and your Mac will squeak alerts at you.

Here's my guess: You'll leave it turned on for maybe a week — or less.

Startup Disk

With the Startup Disk control panel, you choose which hard disk or hard disk volume (if you've partitioned your hard disk) should act as the startup disk when more than one drive with a System Folder is connected to the Mac. (See Figure 14-26.)

Figure 14-26:
This Mac has three hard disks attached. Spawn is selected, so it's the startup disk.

TCP/IP

Sorry to disappoint again, but you have to read Chapter 17 if you want to know about TCP/IP, the alphabet soup control panel.

Text

Text is a control panel you'll never need. Unless, of course, you have a version of Mac OS 9 other than the United States version. If you use more than one language on your Macintosh, you can choose between them in the Text control panel, which is shown in Figure 14-27.

Figure 14-27: You'll probably never need to touch the Text control panel, but here's what it looks like.

Web Sharing

I hate to sound like a broken record again, but you'll discover more than you can stand about the Web Sharing control panel in Chapter 17. Leave it turned off for now.

Chapter 15

How to Write an AppleScript in 21 Minutes

*(T*he chapter title is a takeoff on Viki King's wonderful book about that other kind of script writing, *How to Write a Movie in 21 Days.*)

AppleScript is like a tape recorder for your Mac. It can record and play back things that you do, such as opening an application or clicking a button.

Describing AppleScript to a Mac beginner is a bit like three blind men describing an elephant. One man might describe it as the Macintosh's built-in automation tool. Another might describe it as an interesting, but often over-looked, piece of enabling technology. The third might liken it to a cassette recorder, recording and playing back your actions at the keyboard. A fourth (if there were a fourth in the story) would assure you that it looked like com-puter code written in a high-level language.

They would all be correct. AppleScript is the Mac's built-in automation tool. It is a little known (at least up to now) enabling technology. It is like a cassette recorder (for programs that support AppleScript recording). And scripts do look like computer programs (which could be because they *are* computer programs).

I call AppleScript a time and effort enhancer. AppleScript, if you just spend the time and effort it takes to understand it, will save you oodles of time and effort.

Therein lies the rub. This stuff isn't simple. There's no way in heaven I'm going to teach you how to use AppleScript in the next few pages. Entire books have been written on the topic, for gosh sake!

And don't kid yourself. AppleScript is complicated and will take some effort to master. So rather than try to teach you how to use it, I try to show you what AppleScript can do for you, and I get you to the point where you can write a simple script of your own, all in about 21 minutes.

What the Heck Is an AppleScript, Anyway?

In the broadest sense, AppleScript is an enabling technology that lets you record and play back complex sequences of Macintosh events occurring in the Finder, in programs, or in any combination of the Finder and programs. In a narrower sense, AppleScript now makes it possible to automate multistep sequences, such as changing the bit depth of your monitor. What used to take at least three steps . . .

1. Open the Monitors control panel.
2. Click a number of colors.
3. Close the Monitors control panel.

. . . can now be performed instantly and effortlessly with one script. This feature may not sound like much, but it can sure save you time and effort. The more often you perform a task each day, the more you should consider automating it (if, of course, it can be automated — not all tasks can be automated, as you soon see).

The AppleScript components are installed automatically when you install Mac OS 9. (I discuss the components one by one after a brief rant.)

AppleScript has been around for a few years, but before System 7.5 it wasn't included in Apple System software releases. Instead, it came in separate Scripter and Developer packages at additional cost. So it never really caught on with the masses.

In the meantime, many forward-thinking developers have incorporated AppleScript support into their programs. Better still, that number is growing faster now that AppleScript is part of the System software.

Power users have been clamoring for this stuff for years. It's finally here, and it's only going to get better and more powerful as time goes on and more people get copies for free.

If you want to master your Macintosh, I encourage you to become familiar with at least a bit of basic scripting. This chapter is a start, but your investment of time spent finding out about AppleScript will be repaid tenfold in the time you save performing your daily tasks. And at the very least, some of the canned scripts that Apple provides — such as the one that turns file sharing on and off or the one that adds an item's alias to your Apple menu — can save you time and effort every day.

The Script Editor requires at least 1,000K free memory (Largest Unused Block in the About this Computer dialog box). If you don't have enough memory to use it, quit all open applications and try again. If that doesn't do it, open the Extensions Manager control panel, select the Mac OS 9 Base option from the pop-up menu, and then restart your Mac. (Don't forget to switch back to your normal Extensions Manager set later.)

What the Mac OS Installer Installs and Where It Installs It

Mac OS 9 includes a bevy of AppleScript-related items in various places on your hard disk. Some are essential to AppleScript's operation; the rest are merely convenient. Before you read about how to use them, here are your tools.

The AppleScriptLib and AppleScript extensions

The AppleScriptLib and AppleScript extensions are installed in the Extensions folder (in the System Folder). They are the engine that make AppleScript work. If they're not in the Extensions folder at startup, AppleScript won't work. They require no care or maintenance.

The Scripting Additions folder

The Scripting Additions folder, which is in the System Folder, contains add-on parts of the AppleScript system. AppleScript is modular, so you can add new commands to AppleScript by merely dropping a new item into the Scripting Additions folder. Leave it be.

The AppleScript folder

The AppleScript folder is in the Apple Extras folder. It consists of a SimpleText document called "About AppleScript," the AppleScript Guide, and the Script editor:

✔ About AppleScript is a "read me" file. It's not as light and breezy as this chapter but is probably still worth reading. Check it out.

✔ AppleScript Guide provides fodder for Mac OS Help. Without it, Mac OS Help won't be able to help you with AppleScript.

✔ Script Editor is the program with which you edit scripts. Duh. You can play with it in a minute.

But wait, there's more

If you want to use AppleScript with programs other than Mac OS 9 (much but not all of which is scriptable), they have to be AppleScript enabled, which means that they have to be adapted by their developers to work with AppleScript. Three levels of AppleScript support are found in applications: scriptability, recordability, and attachability. Programs can support one, two, or all three levels.

Unfortunately, there is no easy way of telling whether a program is AppleScript enabled at all, much less if it's recordable or attachable. For what it's worth, the Finder supports all three levels.

Following are brief descriptions of the three levels of AppleScript support that you may find in third-party programs.

Scriptable programs

Scriptable means that the program can follow instructions sent by AppleScript scripts. Scriptable apps are the most common kind. If a program proclaims that it supports AppleScript, it's at this level at least.

Unfortunately, it's up to the developer to decide how much of the program is actually scriptable, so some programs are more scriptable than others. Microsoft Excel, FileMaker Pro, and CorelDRAW 8 are a few scriptable programs I know of.

Recordable programs

Recordable programs go scriptable programs one better. *Recordable* means that you can record your actions in the program and automatically create an AppleScript script for future playback based on what you did within the program. Few programs are recordable yet.

Attachable programs

Attachable programs are even rarer than recordable ones. *Attachable* means that the program lets you attach a script to an item or an element in a document, such as a cell in a spreadsheet, a button in a database, or a rectangle in a drawing. The Finder is attachable because you can attach a script to an icon.

What it all means

At this point, you should know at least this much:

- ✔ AppleScript is a type of recording and playback mechanism for repetitive tasks on your Mac.
- ✔ Some programs, most notably the Mac OS 9 Finder, can be scripted to do some things under script control.
- ✔ A few programs can record and attach scripts.

Notice I didn't say *understand* up there, I said *know*. To develop true understanding would require far more pages than I have. But I had to mention this stuff so that when you try to use a script with a nonscriptable (or nonrecordable or nonattachable) program, you have at least a vague idea of why it's not working.

Writing a Simple Script

I agonized for a long time over this section. I wanted to teach you something useful, but it had to be easy enough to show in just a few pages.

I've realized that I can't do it. If a script is useful, it's going to require more explaining than I have space for. So instead, I'm going to show how to write a script that's totally dumb but fun to watch.

If you want to see smart scripts, open any of the ones in the Finder Action Scripts folder (inside the Scripts folder, which you'll find in the System folder) and examine it closely.

So here's how to write a dumb (but somewhat informative) little script:

1. **Launch the Script Editor application.**

   A new, untitled script appears on the screen.

2. **In the description field at the top of the document window, type** My first stupid script.

3. **Click the Record button.**

   After a brief pause, your screen should look more or less like Figure 15-1. Notice the tiny image of a cassette tape where the Apple menu's Apple logo used to be. It flashes to let you know that you're recording.

4. **Make the Finder active by clicking the desktop or any open windows or by choosing Finder in the Application menu.**

Figure 15-1:
Ready to
record a
script.

5. **Close all open windows.**

   Choose File⇨Close All or use the keyboard shortcut ⌘+Option+W. If you
   have no open windows on your screen, ignore this step.

6. **Create a new folder on the desktop.**

   To do so, choose File⇨New Folder or press ⌘+N.

7. **Open the new, untitled folder and then click its title bar and drag it to
   a new location.**

   The farther you drag it, the better.

8. **Click the zoom box of the untitled folder window. Click it again.**

   The zoom box is the first of the two boxes on the far right side of the
   title bar.

9. **Drag the folder to another new location.**

10. **Return to the Script Editor application and click the Stop button.**

That's it! You've written your first script. It should look something like
Figure 15-2. Don't save it yet. (As you can see in the next section, you have
choices to make about how to save your script.)

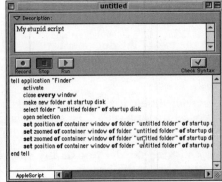

Figure 15-2:
Your first
script.

To see how your script works, click the Run button. Watch closely, because it happens fast. If you blinked and missed it, run the script again. It switches to the Finder, closes all open windows, creates a new folder, moves it, grows it, grows it again, and then moves it again.

I'm fudging a little when I say that you wrote a script. Actually, you recorded a script. If you had written it, you would have typed all the stuff between "tell application Finder" and "end tell" from memory, without performing the actions.

In fact, the most effective way to use AppleScript is with a combination of recording and writing. First record your actions, then analyze the script, and then try to figure out ways to perform each action more efficiently by typing different commands and trying them. To reach this level of scripting mastery, you'll need to know a lot more about the AppleScript language than this chapter can show you.

Okay. You can return to the Finder and trash those untitled folders (one was created each time you ran the script).

So that's how to record a script.

You should know one more thing — unfortunately, many control panels are not scriptable.

If a Script Is Any Good, It Should Be Saved

You may save a script in three ways. If you choose Save or Save As from the File menu in the Script Editor, a pop-up menu in the Save dialog box gives you your choices, as shown in Figure 15-3.

Figure 15-3:
So many
ways to
save a
script.

Here's a rundown of what those Save options do:

✔ The text option creates a text file of your script. This script can be opened in any text editor for editing or reopened by Script Editor.

✔ The compiled script option creates a Script Editor file. You can open, run, or modify the file with the Script Editor program.

✔ The classic applet option creates a self-running script that executes when you open its icon. (See Figure 15-4.)

✔ The Mac OS X applet option saves your script for use with Apple's new server operating system, Mac OS X.

✔ The stationery option lets you save the script as a template for others you plan to build.

Figure 15-4:
If you save
your script
as an
application,
you have
even more
choices to
make.

If the Never Show Startup Screen check box is unchecked in the Save dialog box, your script displays a startup screen with a Run button before it executes, as shown in Figure 15-5.

If you check the Stay Open check box, the script application remains open until you quit it. Scripts saved with this option usually look for something to happen and then perform an action.

Run Only means the saved file can't be edited. You would use the Save As Run Only command (in the File menu) if you had a spiffy script that you didn't want others to see or modify. Anyway, a Run Only script can never be modified. If you choose Save As Run Only instead of Save or Save As, the resulting file will be a Run Only applet or compiled script (you can't save a Run Only text file).

Figure 15-5:
You can eliminate this startup screen by checking the Never Show Startup Screen option in the Save dialog box, as shown in Figure 15-4.

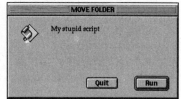

Chapter 16

What Can Stay and What Can Go

*I*n this chapter, which is by far the most useful one in the book, I go through the entire System Folder, one item at a time. I show you how much RAM each item uses, how much disk space it occupies, and what (if any) side effects will occur if you delete or disable it.

There are no substitutes for RAM or hard disk space. But no matter how much you have, there will come a day when you need more of one or the other or both.

My advice: Plenty of real RAM and hard disk space are very good things to have.

Reclamation Theory

RAM and hard disks are expensive. Therefore, I created this chapter — a first, I believe, in System software book history — dedicated to telling you how to get rid of the dead weight among the 110 or so megabytes of files (assuming a full install of Mac OS 9 and all its optional bells and whistles) in your System Folder.

Let's face it: Mac OS 9 puts a lot of files on your hard disk even if you don't choose one of the optional installations. If you do install all the options, Mac OS 9 installs a whopping 1,000+ files and folders, give or take a few. Not everyone needs every single one of these files; many can be deleted to free up (reclaim) hard disk space.

And another thing: Many control panels and extensions load into RAM at startup. So they not only take up disk space, but can also use up your valuable RAM.

If you want my advice about trashing stuff in your System Folder, here it is: Don't trash anything unless you're desperately short of hard disk space. Desperately short! And as far as RAM goes, it's a much better idea to disable items you don't need by using Extensions Manager than to permanently delete them.

I'll go through the System Folder and see what each item costs you in terms of RAM and disk space and what, if any, repercussions you'll feel if you trash or disable the item.

This chapter lists every item that Install Mac OS 9 installs by default, which means it doesn't include such custom installation options as Multilingual Internet Access. For further info on custom options, see Appendix B.

Life after Death: The Truth about Restoring Deleted Files

Before I can show you how to save RAM and disk space, I need to briefly cover a couple of important topics: backing up and reinstalling.

Back up first

If you don't have a backup and you don't have a Mac OS 9 CD-ROM, DO NOT DELETE ANY FILES! I repeat: If you don't have a backup and a Mac OS 9 CD, DON'T TRASH ANYTHING.

Other benefits of a lean, mean System Folder

Here are a bunch of other benefits to keeping your System Folder lean and mean:

- The Apple menu submenu for the Control Panels folder will be shorter.

- The Control Panels folder will contain fewer items and thus be easier to manage.

- The Chooser will be less cluttered after you get rid of printer drivers you'll never need.

- Your Mac might start up and run faster if you don't load unneeded extensions and control panels.

That said, if you're faithful about making backups, you can delete files with relative impunity. If you decide you miss them, restore them from your backup or reinstall Mac OS 9 from the CD.

Beware if you have only one backup set of disks or cartridges. Your backup software might keep a mirror image of your hard disk on the backup media. In other words, when you delete a file from your hard disk, the backup software might delete it from the backup disk(s). Read your backup software manual carefully.

Install Mac OS 9: Restorer of lost items

You can restore any System software file you delete if you have a Mac OS 9 CD-ROM. The degree of difficulty you encounter (and the amount of time it takes you) depends on what you need to restore.

To reinstall any extensions or control panels you delete, just run Install Mac OS 9 (see Appendix A) and reinstall anything and everything in one fell swoop.

You can install certain other Mac OS functions, such as Mac OS Runtime for Java and QuickDraw 3D, individually. Click the Customize button in Install Mac OS 9 to see what's what.

Anyway, that's all you need to know at this time. It's okay to trash any piece of Mac OS 9 as long as you have the Mac OS 9 CD-ROM. That way, you can reinstall whatever you trashed if you discover later that you need or want it.

If you have a Zip, Jaz, Orb, CD-RW, or optical disk drive, consider performing a full install on a cartridge or a disc and setting it aside for a rainy day. That way, if you delete something and later want it back, you can just drag it over rather than performing a complete reinstallation. Or once you're certain that your System Folder is working just right, copy it to a cartridge or CD-R or CD-RW just in case.

What, Exactly, Are Extensions and Control Panels?

Control panels and extensions appear first and second in the chapter because they make the most difference in reclaiming disk space and RAM. (I cover the rest of the System Folder later in the chapter.)

Extensions and control panels are a type of System software file with a special property: If they are not in the Control Panels or Extensions folder at startup, they do not load and will not function. (Or at least most won't. A few control panels can be used even if they aren't in the Control Panels folder at startup.)

Apple isn't the only one to make extensions and control panels. Many popular third-party programs, including famous names such as After Dark, QuicKeys, RAM Doubler, and Speed Doubler are extensions or control panels.

Most extensions and control panels grab a certain amount of RAM when they load at startup. If you choose Apple Menu⇨About This Computer right now, you can see how much RAM they're using by looking at the bar for your System software, which includes the RAM used by all loaded extensions and control panels.

Disabling 'em all with the Shift key

You can disable all control panels and extensions by holding down the Shift key during startup until you see the "Extensions Off" message appear beneath the "Welcome to Mac OS" greeting. That's what I did in Figure 16-1. So my naked System software uses 15MB of RAM, leaving me 96.8MB available for running applications (the Largest Unused Block in Figure 16-1) on this Mac, which has 112MB of RAM installed.

Figure 16-1:
No
extensions
or control
panels
loaded =
15MB used
by my
System
software.

Sharp-eyed readers will notice that there's .2 megabyte of RAM missing in Figure 16-1 (112 − 96.8 = 15.2, not 15). That's the result of something called memory fragmentation. In simple terms, when you quit some programs, they don't release all the RAM they used. You have two solutions: Restart your Mac or buy so much RAM that the little bits you lose to memory fragmentation won't bother you.

Having lots of RAM is way cool. I never get "not enough memory to open the program" messages anymore — even with seven programs open at the same time.

Discriminating disabling with Extensions Manager

When I use the Extensions Manager control panel to turn on all the Mac OS 9 extensions and control panels (by choosing Mac OS 9 All from the Selected Set pop-up menu), the System software uses 28MB of RAM, leaving me less RAM for programs (the Largest Unused Block in Figure 16-2). Note that RAM used by System software includes RAM grabbed at startup by extensions and control panels such as QuickDraw 3D and QuickTime.

Figure 16-2:
With all the extensions and control panels turned on, the System software eats up more RAM.

In the bad old days, disabling extensions and control panels was a messy affair that entailed manually moving them out of the Extensions or Control Panels folder and rebooting. It wasn't long before a wide variety of third-party extension and control panel managers appeared on the market. Before System 7.5, almost everyone I know used one.

Here's an example of why you might want to turn off some items as well: You can reclaim a whopping half a megabyte of RAM by simply disabling the ColorSync extension (which you probably don't need). That's what this chapter is about and why I feel it might be the most important part of this book.

In the rest of the chapter, when I say how much RAM you save by disabling an extension or a control panel, I mean that's how much RAM you save by turning it off (that is, unchecking it) in the Extensions Manager control panel. (You also save that amount of RAM if you delete the file totally.)

The disk space measurement for each file is the size shown in list view in the Finder. The Power Macintosh G3 I use has a 4GB hard disk. If you have a larger disk, the files might occupy slightly more space on your disk than the numbers shown in this chapter because of file allocation blocks, which are complicated and not important.

In other words, your mileage may vary — and my disk-size figures are just estimates provided for your convenience.

I also formatted my hard disk using HFS+. This results in files taking up less space than if you format your disk using standard HFS. If your Mac came with Mac OS 9 preinstalled, chances are your hard disk is formatted using the more efficient HFS+ scheme; if your Mac is older, it probably uses standard HFS. To find out, select your hard disk icon and then choose File⇨Get Info or press ⌘+I. If the Format type is Mac OS Extended, your hard disk is using HFS+; if it's Mac OS Standard, it's using standard HFS.

To convert a hard disk from Mac OS Standard (that is, regular HFS) to the more efficient HFS+, you need to back up all your data (more than once if you're smart) and then reformat (erase) the disk using Special⇨Erase Disk and choosing HFS+ from the Format pop-up menu.

Several third-party utilities, such as Space Doctor from PowerOn Software and PlusMaker from Alsoft, can turn HFS disks into HFS+ disks without reformatting.

Why is HFS+ better? Many of the files that weigh 32K or less on my 4GB drive formatted as HFS+ weigh 64K or more on hard disks formatted using standard HFS due to that file allocation block thing you don't need to know about.

The same goes for my RAM measurements. Your mileage may vary slightly. I measured RAM usage with the wonderful Conflict Catcher 8. If you use other software to measure RAM usage, your numbers might be slightly higher or lower.

One final point: I performed all the testing for this chapter using a fresh, non-customized installation of Mac OS 9. If you have other files in your System Folder, they're either part of a custom installation that I cover in Appendix A or not part of the Mac OS.

In your System Folder, you'll see several folders with "(disabled)" after their names, such as Control Panels (disabled) and Extensions (disabled). Leave them alone. The Extensions Manager disables control panels and extensions by moving them into these folders. Remember, if the control panel or extension isn't in the Control Panels or Extensions folder at startup, it doesn't load.

Control Panels

If you don't understand the cryptic comments or side effects, try reading that control panel's entry in Chapter 14.

Appearance

Disk space: 621K

RAM used: 0K

Side effects if disabled or deleted: Loss of control of window color, theme, highlight colors, system font, collapsing windows, and so on.

Comments: I'd keep it, especially until you've played with it enough to know how you would like your Mac to look.

Apple Menu options

Disk space: 61K

RAM used: 38K

Side effects if disabled or deleted: Loss of Apple menu submenus and recent item tracking.

Comments: I'd keep it. I love submenus and recent item tracking. Unless I was terribly RAM-constrained (using a 32MB Mac, for example), I would never even consider disabling it, much less deleting it.

AppleTalk

Disk space: 207K

RAM used: 0K

Side effects if disabled or deleted: Possible loss of printing and network services (shared disks, e-mail, and so forth).

Comments: If you're on a network, you definitely need it. If you have a printer connected, you definitely need it. Because it uses no RAM, I'd say leave it alone unless you're horribly short of disk space, in which case you may trash it. (But trust me, you'll probably want it back soon for one reason or another.)

ColorSync

Disk space: 107K

RAM used: 0K

Side effects if disabled or deleted: Loss of capability to use ColorSync.

Comments: Get rid of it unless you use ColorSync on all your monitors, printers, and scanners. And note that its related extension, ColorSync extension, is a RAM hog, using almost half a meg of memory.

Control Strip

Disk space: 32K

RAM used: 0K

Side effects if disabled or deleted: Loss of use of Control Strip and all its modules.

Comments: If you like and use Control Strip, keep it; if you hate Control Strip and never want to see it again, trash it and its close relative, the Control Strip Extension.

To save another 600-plus kilobytes of disk space, also trash the Control Strip Modules folder in the System Folder while you're trashing the Control Strip control panel.

Date & Time

Disk space: 141K

RAM used: 0K

Side effects if disabled or deleted: Loss of capability to set Macintosh internal clock. Loss of menu bar clock.

Comments: Keep it.

DialAssist

Disk space: 33K

RAM used: 0K

Side effects if disabled or deleted: Loss of dialing assistance for Apple Remote Access.

Comments: Keep it if you use ARA; otherwise, feel free to dump it.

Remote Access is not just for connecting to remote Macs. You'll use it to connect to dial-up Internet accounts using PPP. If you have a PowerBook and connect to the Internet from places other than your home, keep DialAssist around to help you with those long long-distance codes.

Energy Saver

Disk space: 203K

RAM used: 25K

Side effects if disabled or deleted: No automatic screen dimming and sleep (on Energy Star–compliant models only).

Comments: If it works with your Mac and monitor and you like it, keep it. If not, trash it. But I warn you: Trashing it is not ecologically correct.

Back again with a special admonition for PowerBook users. Energy Saver contains options for controlling your PowerBook's sleeping behavior. You wanna keep your battery running, don't you? Hold on to Energy Saver.

Extensions Manager

Disk space: 170K

RAM used: 0K

Side effects if disabled or deleted: Loss of capability to enable and disable individual control panels and extensions.

Comments: You need it. Keep it unless you opt for the superior commercial program Conflict Catcher (which I love). See also the EM Extension section.

File Exchange

Disk space: 595K

Ram used: 128K

Side effects if disabled or deleted: Loss of capability to use PC-formatted disks and file-translation capabilities for documents created by applications that don't reside on your hard disk.

Comments: It's a keeper.

File Sharing

Disk space: 517K

RAM used: 1K

Side effects if disabled or deleted: Loss of capability to turn file sharing (and Program Linking) on or off.

Comments: You need it only if you use file sharing. If you never use file sharing, make sure file sharing is turned off before you delete it.

General Controls

Disk space: 41K

RAM used: 5K

Side effects if disabled or deleted: Too numerous to mention.

Comments: Keep it. If 41K of hard disk space or 5K of RAM makes a difference to you, you've got bigger problems, and disabling or trashing the General Controls control panel isn't going to help you.

You can get along without General Controls, but you won't be able to change any of its settings without first putting it back in the Control Panels folder and restarting your Mac.

Internet

Disk space: 304K

RAM used: 0K

Side effects if disabled or deleted: Too numerous to mention.

Comments: Keep it unless you never use the Internet, in which case feel free to trash it or turn it off.

Keyboard

Disk space: 71K

RAM used: 0K

Side effects if disabled or deleted: Loss of capability to specify key repeat speed and rate or choose foreign-language keyboard layouts.

Comments: Keep it.

Keychain Access

Disk space: 808K

RAM used: 0K

Side effects if disabled or deleted: Loss of access to keychain items.

Comments: Chances are you won't use the keychain unless you have encryption keys to lots of secure servers and sites. If you do, keep it; otherwise, let it go and save almost a meg of space.

Launcher

Disk space: 60K

RAM used: 0K

Side effects if disabled or deleted: Loss of Launcher window.

Comments: You can hear what I think about Launcher in Chapter 8, if you don't know already. I trashed mine.

Location Manager

Disk space: 370K

RAM used: 0K

Side effects if disabled or deleted: Loss of Location Manager; primarily useful on a PowerBook.

Comments: Delete it unless you use a PowerBook or unless you want to create custom location setups for your desktop computer.

Memory

Disk space: 82K

RAM used: 0K

Side effects if disabled or deleted: Too numerous (and awful) to mention. (See Chapter 11 for details.)

Comments: Do not delete!

Modem

Disk space: 135K

RAM used: 0K

Side effects if disabled or deleted: Possible loss or disruption of modem services.

Comments: If you use a modem, keep it.

Monitors

Disk space: 131K

RAM used: 0K

Side effects if disabled or deleted: Loss of capability to switch monitor color depths and resolutions. Loss of additional capabilities if you have more than one monitor or a multisync monitor.

Comments: Keep it.

Mouse

Disk space: 65K

RAM used: 0K

Side effects if disabled or deleted: Loss of capability to change mouse tracking or double-click speed.

Comments: Keep it.

Multiple Users

Disk space: 828K

RAM used: 0K

Side effects if disabled or deleted: Loss of capability to create multiple user profiles for your Mac.

Comments: Unless you share your Mac and need to restrict certain applications, devices, or network activities, delete it to save more than 800K on disk.

Numbers

Disk space: 16K

RAM used: 0K

Side effects if disabled or deleted: Loss of capability to change thousands of separators, decimal separators, and symbols for currency.

Comments: I've never used it.

QuickTime Settings

Disk space: 90K

RAM used: 0K

Side effects if disabled or deleted: Loss of AutoPlay features for CDs and CD-ROMs and some MIDI (Musical Instrument Digital Interface) configuration options.

Comments: Your call. If you need it, you probably know it. I'm keeping mine.

Remote Access

Disk space: 387K

RAM used: 0K

Side effects if disabled or deleted: Loss of capability to dial the Internet and access your Mac remotely.

Comments: Like the old doctor joke (Patient: "It hurts when I do that!" Doctor: "Don't do that!"), if you dial out to reach the Internet or want to make remote connections to this Mac, don't trash it. Conversely, if you never surf by phone or dial in to this computer, trash that puppy.

Software Update

Disk space: 222K

RAM used: 0K

Side effects if disabled or deleted: Loss of capability to obtain updates to system software online.

Comments: If you don't use the Internet or don't ever plan to download software updates from Apple, make it go away. If you think you might want to have your Mac check for new Mac OS stuff regularly and bring it right to your computer, keep it on hand.

Sound

Disk space: 67K

RAM used: 0K

Side effects if disabled or deleted: Loss of capability to change your beep sound and select a new sound input or output device.

Comments: I'd keep this one. You'll need it to adjust the volume of your Mac's sound and to change that alert sound that's driving you crazy.

Speech

Disk space: 94K

RAM used: 32K

Side effects if disabled or deleted: Loss of capability to use Talking Alerts and Text-to-Voice.

Comments: Your call. It does use a little RAM, and its 9MB Voices folder, which you can find in the Extensions folder, takes up a bit of disk space. I think the voices are cute and I'm keeping them.

Startup Disk

Disk space: 38K

RAM used: 0K

Side effects if disabled or deleted: Loss of capability to choose a startup disk if more than one disk with a System Folder is connected at startup.

Comments: You may need it someday, especially if you're going to add an additional storage device — external hard disk, SyQuest, Zip, Jaz, magneto-optical disk drive, or whatever. I say keep it.

TCP/IP

Disk space: 284K

RAM used: 0K

Side effects if disabled or deleted: Loss of capability to connect to Internet.

Comments: If you use the Internet, keep it; if you don't, you don't need it.

If you're on a network but don't use the Internet, check with your network administrator before trashing this (or any other) piece of System software.

Text

Disk space: 15K

RAM used: 0K

Side effects if disabled or deleted: Loss of capability to choose Text Behaviors.

Comments: If you run only the American version of Mac OS 9, you'll probably never need it.

Web Sharing

Disk space: 586K

RAM used: 0K

Side effects if disabled or deleted: Loss of capability to use your Mac as a personal Web server.

Comments: If your Mac isn't connected to the Internet full-time, you can't use Web Sharing, so you may as well delete it.

Extensions

Four main types of extensions are among the approximately 113 items in your Extensions folder:

- ✔ System extensions
- ✔ Chooser extensions
- ✔ Libraries
- ✔ Apple Guide documents

Apple Guide documents and libraries use no RAM, nor do most Chooser extensions. System extensions, on the other hand, almost always grab a bit of RAM at startup. There are also a few other types of files in the Extensions folder; I talk about them after I finish with the big four.

To see these items by type, open the Extensions folder and then choose View⇨ As List; then choose View⇨Sort List⇨by Kind. If the View by Kind option isn't available, choose View⇨View Options and check Kind under the Show Column heading.

System extensions

System extensions are the most important extensions. They do the most work (meaning they add useful features to the Mac OS), but they can also save you lots of precious RAM if you disable or delete them (if, of course, you don't need them).

EM Extension

Disk space: 5K

RAM used: 0K

Side effects if disabled or deleted: Loss of use of Extensions Manager control panel.

Comments: Keep it.

Why is EM Extension first in an alphabetical list? Because Apple ships it with a space before the E so that it's first in alphabetical lists. Extensions load alphabetically, and because this is the extension that gives Extensions Manager its powers, it must load before the other extensions to turn them on or off.

Hold down the spacebar just after you power up your Mac to use Extensions Manager before other extensions begin to load.

Apple CD/DVD Driver

Disk space: 109K

RAM used: 51K

Side effects if disabled or deleted: Loss of capability to use CD-ROM or DVD disks.

Comments: Because you almost certainly have a CD-ROM drive, you need it.

Apple Enet

Disk space: 487K

RAM used: 0K

Side effects if disabled or deleted: Loss of use of Ethernet.

Comments: If you use Ethernet, keep it; if not, disable it.

Apple Guide

Disk space: 826K

RAM used: 117K

Side effects if disabled or deleted: Loss of Apple Guide (interactive help).

Comments: Tough call. It uses a great deal of disk space (if you count all its Guide files) and a significant amount of RAM, but I think it's worth keeping. Delete or disable it only if you absolutely must.

Apple Monitor Plugins

Disk space: 684K

RAM used: 4K

Side effects if disabled or deleted: Loss of support for Apple Studio Displays, AppleVision (AV) monitors and ColorSync.

Comments: If you don't use one of these monitors or the ColorSync display calibration system (I've already suggested you delete *that*), it's okay to get rid of this one, too.

Apple Photo Access

Disk space: 158K

RAM used: 0K

Side effects if disabled or deleted: Loss of capability to open PhotoCD files.

Comments: PhotoCD is the Kodak format for high-resolution image storage. PhotoCD files mostly come on CD-ROM disks. If you're likely to encounter PhotoCD files, keep it. If you don't have a CD-ROM drive, you definitely don't need it.

Apple QD3D HW Driver and Apple QD3D HW Plugin

Disk space: 15K and 42K

RAM used: 0K

Side effects if disabled or deleted: Loss of access to QuickDraw 3D–capable hardware. That means you won't be able to play Nanosaur or other 3D games on your iMac or iBook.

Comments: If you use QuickDraw 3D–capable hardware, keep it. If not, delete it.

AppleScript

Disk space: 856MB

RAM used: 0K

Side effects if disabled or deleted: Loss of use of AppleScript scripts and the Script Editor program.

Comments: If you read Chapter 15, you know whether you want to keep AppleScript. (I would.)

Application Switcher

Disk space: 85K

RAM used: 0K

Side effects if disabled or deleted: Can't tear off the application menu in the upper-right corner of the menu bar.

Comments: Keep it unless you never want to tear off the application menu.

ATI Driver Update, ATI Graphics Accelerator, ATI Video Accelerator

Disk space: 522K, 181K, and 36K, respectively

RAM used: 0K

Side effects if disabled or deleted: Loss of use of ATI-accelerated video, found in most newer Macs.

Comments: If you don't have ATI video, trash all three. If you have a newer Mac, such as a G3, PowerBook G3, iBook, or iMac, leave 'em alone.

Mac OS installs a graphics accelerator file that matches your Mac. It may be one of these ATI drivers or, as in older Power Macs, Built-InGraphicsAccelerator.

Audio CD Access

Disk space: 13K

RAM used: 0K

Side effects if disabled or deleted: Loss of capability to play audio CDs (that is, your David Garza and Elvis Costello CDs, or at least my David Garza and Elvis CDs).

Comments: If you don't have a CD-ROM drive, you don't need it. If you have a CD-ROM drive, you should probably keep it around, just in case.

Color Picker

Disk space: 487K

RAM used: 26K

Side effects if disabled or deleted: Loss of the Apple Color Picker.

Comments: This whole shebang refers to which Color Picker you see in programs that use a color picker to choose among colors (most graphics programs).

The new Color Picker is, in my humble opinion, prettier than the old one and probably easier to use. Trashing this extension usually has little consequence, but if you use color graphics programs of any sort, you may want to keep it around.

ColorSync Extension

Disk space: 816MB

RAM used: 495K

Side effects if disabled or deleted: Loss of use of ColorSync (Apple's color matching system for monitors, printing devices, and scanners).

Comments: You probably don't need it unless you scan or print color images. And it uses a lot of RAM and disk space for something most people have no need for.

If you delete the ColorSync extension, it's also safe to delete the Default Calibrator in the Extensions folder (239K) and the ColorSync control panel.

Contextual Menu Extension

Disk space: 74K

RAM used: 210K

Side effects if disabled or deleted: Loss of support for contextual menus in applications.

Comments: Keep it. Contextual menus are a cool new feature and are available in some applications. I'd keep it.

Control Strip Extension

Disk space: 76K

RAM used: 125K

Side effects if disabled or deleted: Loss of access to the Control Strip.

Comments: Keep it if you use the Control Strip. Otherwise, delete it.

Desktop Printer Spooler

Disk space: 68K

RAM used: 0K

Side effects if disabled or deleted: Loss of desktop printer support.

Comments: Lets you drag-and-drop documents onto desktop printer icons and change printers without opening the Chooser. Keep it.

FBC Indexing Scheduler

Disk space: 23K

RAM used: 0K

Side effects if disabled or deleted: Loss of capability to schedule indexing in the Find utility.

Comments: Keep it.

File Sharing extension

Disk space: 194K

RAM used: 4K

Side effects if disabled or deleted: Loss of file-sharing capability.

Comments: If you don't use file sharing, you can safely delete it.

Folder Actions

Disk space: 26K

RAM used: 0K

Side effects if disabled or deleted: Loss of capability to run AppleScripts attached to folders.

Comments: It's small and uses no RAM. I'd keep it even if you don't think you need it.

FontSync Extension

Disk space: 112K

RAM used: 0K

Side effects if disabled or deleted: Loss of font synchronization of fonts between computers.

Comments: It's small and may be useful if you exchange documents with others.

Foreign File Access

Disk space: 39K

RAM used: 135K

Side effects if disabled or deleted: Loss of capability to mount some CD-ROM disks.

Comments: If you have a CD-ROM drive, you need it; if you don't, you don't.

High Sierra File Access

Disk space: 19K

RAM used: 0K

Side effects if disabled or deleted: Loss of capability to mount some CD-ROM disks.

Comments: If you have a CD-ROM drive, you need it; if you don't, you don't.

Indeo Video and Intel Raw Video

Disk space: 253K and 13K, respectively

RAM used: 0K

Side effects if disabled or deleted: Loss of capability to view some types of video in your browser.

Comments: If you use the Internet, keep both.

Internet Config extension

Disk space: 113K

RAM used: 0K

Side effects if disabled or deleted: Internet configuration options won't be shared among applications.

Comments: Your browser and other Internet programs may not work properly without it. If you use the Internet, keep it.

Iomega Driver

Disk space: 82K

RAM used: 62K

Side effects if disabled or deleted: Loss of capability to mount Iomega Zip or Jaz disks automatically when inserted.

Comments: If you have an Iomega storage device — a Zip or Jaz drive — keep it. Otherwise you can safely trash it.

ISO 9660 File Access

Disk space: 20K

RAM used: 0K

Side effects if disabled or deleted: Loss of capability to mount some CD-ROM disks.

Comments: If you have a CD-ROM drive, you need it; if you don't, you don't. (I'm sorry if I sound like a broken record, but that's my advice.)

LocalTalkPCI

Disk space: 56K

RAM used: 0K

Side effects if disabled or deleted: Slower file transfers on LocalTalk.

Comments: If you use a LocalTalk network — AppleTalk or Ethernet — keep it.

Location Manager Extension

Disk space: 74K

RAM used: 0K

Side effects if disabled or deleted: Loss of capability to define Location Manager sets.

Comments: If you use the Location Manager, keep it around. If not, drop it.

MacinTalk 3 and MacinTalk Pro

Disk space: 351K and 790K, respectively

RAM used: 0K

Side effects if disabled or deleted: Loss of speech capabilities; see Speech control panel.

Comments: If you want your Mac to talk to you, keep them; if not, don't. Don't forget to also trash the Voices folder (see next section), Speech control panel (previous section), and Speech Manager extension if you decide to trash these two.

Multi-User Startup

Disk space: 162K

RAM used: 0K

Side effects if disabled or deleted: Loss of support for Multiple Users.

Comments: If you plan to share your Mac and create user profiles for each other person who will use it, you need this extension. If you don't share, you can delete it.

Printer Share

Disk space: 79K

RAM used: 12K

Side effects if disabled or deleted: Loss of capability to share certain devices, such as plotters, that could not be shared previously. Also, loss of the capability to password-protect color printers that use expensive printing materials.

Comments: If you're on a network, ask your network administrator before deleting or disabling.

QuickDraw 3D

Disk space: 1.3MB

RAM used: 0K

Side effects if disabled or deleted: Loss of use of QuickDraw 3D.

Comments: Keep it unless you're horribly pressed for disk space. If that's the case, you can also delete QuickDraw 3D IR, QuickDraw 3D RAVE, and QuickDraw 3D Viewer.

QuickTime, QuickTime FireWire DV Enabler, QuickTime MPEG Extension, QuickTime Musical Instruments, and QuickTime PowerPlug

Disk space: 984K, 17K, 270K, 2.1MB, and 1.6MB, respectively

RAM used: Approximately 1.3MB for all five pieces.

Side effects if disabled or deleted: Loss of capability to play QuickTime movies or use QuickTime applications.

Comments: I leave mine enabled all the time, but I probably have more stuff that requires QuickTime than you do. If you use QuickTime, even occasionally, leave these items alone.

QuickTime VR

Disk space: 552K

RAM used: 8K

Side effects if disabled or deleted: Loss of support for QuickTime VR.

Comments: QuickTime VR is a cool 3-D format used on some Web sites and games. Delete it if you don't go to multimedia sites and if you're sure that you don't have any games that need it.

Remote Only

Disk space: 4K

RAM used: 0K

Side effects if disabled or deleted: Can't access Mac from remote computer(s).

Comments: Keep it if you use Remote Access; dump it if you don't.

Shared Library Manager and Shared Library Manager PPC

Disk space: 165K and 207K, respectively

RAM used: 0K

Side effects if disabled or deleted: Many programs and utilities cease to function.

Comments: You need these. Don't delete them.

Software Update Scheduler

Disk space: 280K

RAM used: 0K

Side effects if disabled or deleted: Loss of support for scheduled online software updates.

Comments: You can delete this if you never plan to download a Mac OS update. Keep it if you have an Internet account.

Sound Manager

Disk space: 410K

RAM used: 29K

Side effects if disabled or deleted: Sounds may not work properly.

Comments: Keep it.

Speech Manager

Disk space: 30K

RAM used: 7K

Side effects if disabled or deleted: No speech. See also MacinTalk extensions, Speech Control Panel, and Voices in this chapter.

Comments: Keep it if you want your Mac to speak.

System Monitor Plugins

Disk space: 178K

RAM used: 0K

Side effects if disabled or deleted: The Monitors control panel quits working.

Comments: Don't delete it. Keep it.

Time Synchronizer

Disk space: 47K

RAM used: 0K

Side effects if disabled or deleted: Loss of capability to automatically update your computer's clock for daylight saving time and to synchronize your clock with a network time server.

Comments: I'd keep it. It's not essential and nothing bad happens without it, but I'm keeping mine anyway.

UDF Volume Access

Disk space: 363K

RAM used: 11K

Side effects if disabled or deleted: You won't be able to read UDF-formatted volumes, which include DVD disks.

Comments: If you don't have a DVD drive, you can trash it.

Video Startup
Disk space: 69K

RAM used: 26K

Side effects if disabled or deleted: Loss of use of Apple Video Player application.

Comments: If you use Apple Video Player, keep it. If you use QuickTime, keep it. Otherwise, you can trash it if you like.

Web Sharing Extension
Disk space: 369K

RAM used: 0K

Side effects if disabled or deleted: Loss of capability to use your Mac as a Web server.

Comments: Dump it unless you use your Mac as a Web server, which is unlikely.

Chooser extensions

Chooser extensions are extensions that appear in the Chooser desk accessory when you open it. AppleShare is one of them; all the others are printer drivers, the software that your Mac requires to talk to a printer.

AppleShare
Disk space: 624K

RAM used: 195K

Side effects if disabled or deleted: Loss of use of file sharing.

Comments: If you use file sharing, you need it; if you don't, you don't.

Printer drivers

The Installer puts several printer drivers into your Extensions folder for you: Color SW 1500, Color SW 2500, Color SW Pro, CSW 6000 Series, ImageWriter, LaserWriter 300/LS, and LaserWriter 8.

Disk space: Between 45K and 1.5MB each

RAM used: 0K

Side effects if disabled or deleted: None, as long as you leave the driver for your printer(s) — that is, the printer(s) that you use — in the Extensions folder.

Comments: You need only the driver or drivers that match the printer(s) you use. If you never use a color printer, for example, get rid of every Chooser extension with the word *color* in its name. If you never use an ImageWriter, get rid of all the ImageWriter Chooser extensions. And so on.

It's a good idea to keep LaserWriter 8 if you have any type of laser printer. LaserWriter 8 works with most laser printers and will usually serve in a pinch if the driver for your printer won't work (i.e. becomes obsolete or corrupted).

Apple Guide documents

The Extensions folder may contain as many as ten Apple Guide documents.

Disk space: 32K to 400K

RAM used: 0K

Side effects if disabled or deleted: Loss of use of Apple Guide interactive help.

Comments: If you don't use Apple Guide, you can safely delete all Guide files. But I'd leave them alone. You never know when you'll need help, and if you delete these files, help won't be available when you need it.

Other items in the Extensions folder

At least one of the following is not even an extension, and the rest you should probably leave alone.

Desktop PrintMonitor

Disk space: 77K

RAM used: 0K

Side effects if disabled or deleted: Loss of capability to print in background.

Comments: Keep it.

Desktop PrintMonitor is not an extension, although it lives in the Extensions folder. It is an application. Thus, it uses RAM only when background printing is taking place.

If you have problems with background printing, try increasing Desktop PrintMonitor's preferred memory size (in its Get Info window).

OpenTransport ASLM Modules, OpenTptModem, OpenTpt Remote Access, and OpenTpt Serial Arbitrator

Disk space: about 1.7MB altogether

RAM used: 0K

Side effects if disabled or deleted: Loss of capability to use Internet and networking features.

Comments: Leave these alone if you use a network or the Internet. Even if you don't, you might need them someday. Disable them in Extensions Manager if you must, but leave them on your hard disk if you can.

Anything with the word Lib or Library in its name

The extensions in this category include any item that is of the Library kind. If you sort your Extensions folder by kind when you're in List view, you can see all the various libraries.

Disk space: Varies

RAM used: under 100K total

Side effects if disabled or deleted: Lots of stuff will stop working.

Comments: Don't trash or disable any Lib or Library files. If you're horribly short of disk space, you're better off trashing a game you never play or some documents you may never need again.

GameSprockets files

Apple's Game Sprockets interface allows developers of game devices such as joysticks and peddles to write drivers that make these devices work with the Mac. Files with the word *sprocket* in their name make game sprockets work.

Disk space: 21K to 500K

RAM used: 0K

Side effects if disabled or deleted: Loss of support for some games and game devices.

Comments: Delete these files if you need the disk space and you don't play games on your Mac.

OpenGL files

OpenGL is a graphics standard used by big-time multimedia applications. As we go to press, not very many Mac applications support OpenGL, and those that do are high-end multimedia tools or recent vintage games.

Disk space: 13K to 5MB

RAM used: 0K

Side effects if disabled or deleted: Loss of support for OpenGL applications.

Comments: You can save a nice chunk of disk space if you delete all OpenGL files but you won't be able to play Quake 3: Arena.

Folders in the Extensions folder

Several folders are in the System Folder; you may or may not need them or their contents.

ActiveX Controls

This folder contains 128K of files your browser may need someday. Trash it at your own risk if you use the Internet.

Find

Stores searches and indexes. If you want Find to work properly, leave it alone.

Global Guide Files

This folder contains additional Apple Guide files for Monitors, Sound, and Color. Feel free to trash any that you don't need.

Location Manager Modules

This folder contains 224K of modules for the Location Manager, used with PowerBooks to customize network and Internet connections. Trash them if you don't have a PowerBook.

Macromedia

This 4MB folder contains files that support Macromedia's Shockwave Internet viewer. If you use the Internet, keep it around.

Modem Scripts

This folder contains almost 2MB of modem stuff, most of which you don't need. You can trash all the scripts except the one whose name matches your modem if you need the disk space.

MRJ Libraries

This folder contains over 12MB of Java-related stuff. You'll need it if you use MRJ (Macintosh Runtime for Java) to view Java-enabled Internet sites. If you don't use the Internet, you can trash it.

Multiprocessing

You don't need this folder or its contents unless your Mac has multiple processors (few do, at least so far).

Printer Descriptions

This folder in your Extensions folder contains printer description files for 30 Apple printers. They require from 21K to 144K of disk space and use no RAM. You can delete all but the one (or ones) that match your printer (or printers).

QuickTime Extensions

Here you'll find modules that add features to QuickTime 4. The folder is big, but you'll be glad you kept the 5MB of stuff if you view movies, Web sites, or streaming video.

The difference between applications and desk accessories

I promised in Chapter 6 to explain the difference between an application and a desk accessory (DA) here in Chapter 14. Being a man of my word, here goes.

Desk accessories are a throwback to System 4 and earlier, when there was no multitasking and no way to run more than one program at a time. Desk accessories were miniprograms that could be used even while other programs were open.

These days, now that opening multiple programs is the norm, desk accessories are the same as other programs — with three little differences:

- In list view, under the Kind category, desk accessories are listed as desk accessories (duh), not applications.

- You can't change a desk accessory's minimum or preferred memory requirements.

- Every desk accessory uses 20K of RAM (in About This Computer).

For all intents and purposes, a desk accessory is the same as an application program.

Voices

This whopping 9MB folder contains the voices used by Speech and MacinTalk. If you don't need the voices, you don't need the folder. And if you only use a few voices, delete the ones that you don't use.

The Rest of the Stuff in Your System Folder

The installer installed more than just control panels and extensions. Here's the rest of what it installed.

Appearance (folder)

Contains stuff associated with the Appearance control panel. If you want to use themes or sounds, leave it alone.

Apple Menu Items (folder)

The Apple Menu Items folder, which I cover extensively in Chapter 6, contains some folders, some desk accessories, and some applications.

The items in your Apple Menu Items folder use RAM only after you open them. So don't get rid of them to save RAM. If you're really short on disk space, use the old "View as list, sort by size" trick to find out how much each Apple Menu Item uses.

Application Support (folder)

Some programs stash their "stuff" in this folder. I suggest you leave it alone; otherwise, some programs might quit working.

Clipboard

Disk space: Varies

RAM used: 0K

Side effects if disabled or deleted: Loss of Clipboard contents at the moment of deletion.

Comments: This file is like a chameleon's tail — it regenerates if it's damaged or destroyed. So don't bother deleting it; it'll just grow back. Besides, why would you want to?

ColorSync Profiles (folder)

Disk space: 2.6MB, more or less

RAM used: 0K

Side effects if disabled or deleted: ColorSync won't work without it.

Comments: Don't delete it if you use ColorSync. Feel free to delete the entire folder if you don't use ColorSync.

Contextual Menu Items (folder)

Disk space: 112K, more or less

RAM used: 0K

Side effects if disabled or deleted: Contextual menus won't work.

Comments: Keep it. Contextual menus are a very good thing.

Control Strip Modules (folder)

Disk space: 640K, more or less

RAM used: 0K

Side effects if disabled or deleted: Loss of use of the module if it's not in this folder.

Comments: Don't delete it if you use Control Strip. Feel free to delete individual modules you don't use if you feel like it.

Favorites (folder)

Contains aliases of your favorite items created by choosing Add to Favorites from the contextual or File menu. Leave it be.

Finder

Disk space: 2.7MB

RAM used: Not applicable

Side effects if disabled or deleted: Loss of use of the Mac.

Comments: Don't even think about it. Your Mac won't boot without a Finder.

Fonts (folder)

Contains your fonts; leave it be.

Help (folder)

Contains files your Help system requires. Leave it alone.

Internet Search Sites (folder)

Contains information the Find utility needs to search the Internet. You can delete it if you never use the Internet. Otherwise, leave it be.

Language & Region Support

These little files support a whole bunch of languages that are not U.S. English. Delete it if you don't need them.

Launcher Items (folder)

Contains the items that show up in Launcher; you need it if you use Launcher. So if you use Launcher, leave this folder alone. If you don't, feel free to trash it.

Login and Panels

These files support Multiple Users. Delete them if you don't plan to create user profiles so that others can share your Mac. If you do want to use Multiple Users, don't touch 'em.

MacTCP DNR

Contains information used by TCP/IP. You need it if you use the Internet. If you're not planning to log on, you can delete it.

Preferences (folder)

The Preferences folder is where all programs, extensions, control panels, and desk accessories store their preferences files. These files store information that the program (or extension, control panel, or desk accessory) needs to remember between uses.

Most preferences files regenerate themselves when deleted, so trashing them is usually a waste of time.

When you get rid of a program, an extension, a control panel, or a desk accessory, there's a good chance that it has left behind a preferences file in the Preferences folder. It's not a bad idea to go into your Preferences folder every so often and trash any files that appear to belong to software no longer on your hard disk.

For example, if you decide that you never want to use the Launcher control panel again, you can delete the Launcher Preferences file. Although Launcher Preferences only uses a few K of disk space, after a while your Preferences folder may become quite crowded with preferences files that belong to software you don't even have on your hard disk any more.

Ack! I just looked at the Preferences folder on my main Mac and discovered more than 200 preferences files, at least half from programs that I no longer have or use.

I'll be right back — I'm going to practice what I preach and clean up my Preferences folder by trashing unneeded and unwanted prefs files.

I'm back. While I was doing my spring cleaning, I remembered another good tip having to do with preferences files: Trashing a program's preferences file can sometimes correct problems with the program itself. If you have a program, extension, control panel, or desk accessory that's acting strangely in any way — crashing, freezing, quitting unexpectedly — look in the Preferences folder and see whether it has a preferences file. If it does, try deleting it. Then restart your Mac. This tip doesn't always work, but it's worth a try if a program that used to work starts acting funky.

By the way, some programs store all your customized settings (key combinations, macros, window positions, serial number, and so on) in their preferences files. If you delete these files, you may have to reset some of your customized settings in these programs or reenter your serial number. In most cases, that's no big deal. But in the case of, say, my Microsoft Word preferences, I would have to spend about three hours recustomizing all my menus and keyboard shortcuts. Not fun. In fact, I keep a backup copy of my Word prefs on a floppy just in case the file gets corrupted or somebody comes along and changes things when I'm not around.

Print Monitor Documents (folder)

Print Monitor Documents will just come back if you delete it and do any background printing. So just leave it.

ROM files

Many newer-model Macs have a Mac OS ROM file in their System Folder. Like the System and Finder, this file is supremely important and should never be removed from the System Folder.

Scrapbook file

Disk space: Varies

RAM used: 0K

Side effects if disabled or deleted: Loss of contents of Scrapbook.

Comments: If you don't use Scrapbook, you can delete it. But if you have anything you care about in the Scrapbook, you'll lose it when you trash this file.

Scripting Additions (folder)

Contains files used by AppleScript. If you don't intend to use AppleScript, it's safe to trash this folder.

Scripts (folder)

Contains files used by AppleScript. If you don't intend to use AppleScript, it's safe to trash this folder.

Shutdown Items (folder)

You put aliases of items you want to execute when you shut down your Mac in here. Leave it.

Startup Items (folder)

You put aliases of items you want to execute when you start up your Mac in here. Leave it.

System

Disk space: 12.9MB

RAM used: Not applicable

Side effects if disabled or deleted: Loss of use of the Mac.

Comments: Don't even think about it. Your Mac won't boot if this file isn't in the System Folder.

System Resources

Disk space: 1000K

RAM used: Not applicable

Side effects if disabled or deleted: Loss of use of the Mac.

Comments: Don't even think about it. Your Mac won't boot if this file isn't in the System Folder along with the System and Finder files.

Text Encodings (folder)

Required for foreign language versions of Mac OS. If you use only one language, you can delete the other items in this folder if you like. I strongly suggest that you don't delete Unicode Encodings and Western Language Encodings, though. Your Mac might not work properly without them.

Chapter 17

Internet-Working

• •

In This Chapter

▶ Getting an overview of the Internet

▶ Pre-surfing with the Internet Setup Assistant

▶ Surfing with Internet Explorer

▶ Searching with Sherlock 2

▶ E-mailing with Outlook Express

▶ Finding out about the Internet-related control panels

• •

*T*he Internet, sometimes referred to as the Information Superhighway, is a giant worldwide network of computers. With an Internet connection, you can view text and graphics on your computer, even if the text and graphics are sitting on a computer in Tokyo. The Internet enables you to send and retrieve messages and computer files to and from almost anywhere in the world — in milliseconds. Simply put, the Internet connects your Mac to a wealth of information residing on computers around the world. Lucky for you, Mac OS 9 has the best and most comprehensive Internet tools ever shipped with Mac OS.

I admit right now that this chapter covers only the barest minimum of stuff you need to know to connect to the Internet. There's so much more to say that you could write a book about it, and in fact, Charlie Seiter has. So if you're really interested in knowing more about Macs and the Internet, look for the 3rd edition of *The Internet For Macs For Dummies* by Charles Seiter (published by IDG Books Worldwide, Inc.) at fine bookstores everywhere.

A Brief Internet Overview

The Internet, which is really nothing more than a giant conglomeration of connected computers, offers many types of services. This chapter covers the top two: the Web and electronic mail.

Other services offered on the Internet include live online chatting, bulletin board discussions called newsgroups, FTP (file transfer protocol), and video conferencing. After you have your connection set up (something I cover in a moment), I urge you to check out these nifty features. Unfortunately, while this is way-interesting stuff, it's also beyond the purview of this book, so that's all I'm going to say about them.

The most interesting part of the Internet, at least in my humble opinion, is the Web, the part of the Internet that lets you surf to Web sites and view them on your computer with software called a *browser*.

Mac OS 9 offers built-in Internet connectivity right out of the box. Although most previous versions provided some of the plumbing, in the form of MacTCP, it was still up to you to assemble appropriate programs — browsers, PPP client (you don't need to know what that means yet, but you will in a moment), FTP client, e-mail program, and so on — on your own. Mac OS 9 comes with its own built-in PPP client (for making modem connections to the Internet) plus Microsoft Internet Explorer and Netscape Communicator (browsers that enable you to browse the Web, download remote files via FTP, and more), and Microsoft Outlook Express (for e-mail and news reading).

Because Mac users like things to be easy, Mac OS 9 includes a cool piece of software called Internet Setup Assistant to help you get and configure an account with an Internet service provider. After your Internet connection is up and running, you can use one of the included Web browsers to cruise the Internet.

But before I can talk about browsers and e-mail software, I must first help you configure your Internet connection. When you're finished, you can play with Internet Explorer and Outlook Express to your heart's content.

Getting Set Up for Surfing

If you're a typical home user, you need three things to surf the Internet:

- ✔ A modem (or other connection to the Internet such as ISDN, ADSL, cable, or satellite)
- ✔ An account with an ISP (Internet service provider) or America Online
- ✔ Mac OS 9 default installation

If you use your Mac in an office setting or have a fast Internet connection through ISDN, ADSL, cable modem, or another scheme, you might use something other than a regular modem. Your network administrator (the person you run to at work when something goes wrong with your computer) or ISP will have to help you set up your Mac if you use one of these schemes instead of a modem because setting up those other configurations is, once again, beyond the purview of this book.

It starts with the modem

A *modem* is a small, inexpensive device that turns data (that is, computer files) into sounds and then squirts them across phone lines. At the other end, another modem receives these sounds and turns them back into data (that is, your files).

If you're going to buy a modem, you should know the following:

✔ Make sure the modem runs at 56 Kbps (or higher), or you'll be unhappy with the speed at which you surf. Most modems today run at 56 Kbps.

✔ Make sure the modem includes a Mac cable. WinDoze computers require a different type of modem cable, so be sure to ask whether your modem comes with an appropriate Mac cable. (This, of course, applies only to external modems.)

Now plug a phone line into the modem and plug the modem cable into the modem port on the back of your Mac. The modem port is the one with the little phone icon next to it. Finally, plug the modem into an AC power source.

If your Mac came with an internal modem (iMacs, PowerBooks, and some PowerMac G3s do), all you need to do is plug your phone cable into the modem jack on the Mac.

Your Internet service provider and you

Now that you have a modem, you need to select a company to provide you with access to the Internet. It's kind of like choosing a long-distance company — prices and services offered vary, often from minute to minute. After you do that, you can launch and use Internet Explorer, Netscape Communicator, or Outlook Express.

If you have already used your Mac with an ISP under a previous version of Mac OS, you may not have to do anything at all. Chances are, everything is already configured. To find out, launch Internet Explorer (look in the Internet folder that was installed with Mac OS 9) or your favorite browser. If the browser connects to the Internet when you launch it, you're golden. If not, follow the instructions in the upcoming section, "Using Internet Setup Assistant if you already have an ISP."

Finding an ISP

Here's a chicken-and-egg situation for you. The good news is that I found three great Web sites to help you choose an ISP:

✔ http://www.barkers.org/online/

✔ http://webpedia.ispcheck.com/

✔ http://thelist.internet.com/

The bad news is that you'll need a Web connection to view them, and if you don't have an ISP yet, you don't have a Web connection. With any luck, you can use a friend's computer or one at a public library; just make sure that it's connected to the Internet.

If you are an America Online subscriber, you don't need to do anything more than install the AOL software and log on to AOL. You can ignore the rest of this chapter except for the parts about surfing with Internet Explorer and the control panel section at the end. You don't need Outlook Express if you get your mail through AOL.

The going rate for unlimited access to the Internet, using a modem, is $19.95 per month. If your service provider asks for considerably more than that, find out why. If you have a cable modem, DSL, or other high-speed connection, you'll probably pay at least twice that much.

Anyway, first select a provider. Several national online services that you've probably heard of provide Internet access. They include CompuServe, America Online, and Prodigy. There are also pure Internet service companies such as Earthlink, Netcom, AT&T, and perhaps even your cable or local phone company, so shop around for the deal that works best for you.

Mac OS 9's Internet Setup Assistant lets you start an account with Earthlink, a decent national ISP. The advantage of this method, if you're looking for a new ISP account, is that the Internet Setup Assistant configures your whole setup automatically. The drawback is that you can't choose an ISP; your only choice using this option is Earthlink. But, from what I've heard, Earthlink is not bad as ISPs go.

Using Internet Setup Assistant to sign up with Earthlink

After you've installed Mac OS 9, you can find the Internet Setup Assistant in the Internet folder on your hard disk. Or you can choose it from the Internet Access submenu in your Apple Menu. The Internet Setup Assistant will take you through the process of setting up an account with Earthlink. You can also use it to configure or modify an existing account. We'll talk about that a bit later. For now, let's concentrate on setting up your new account with Earthlink.

The Internet Setup Assistant consists of a series of screens. You answer questions about yourself and your modem and then sign up with Apple's preferred ISP, Earthlink.

Of course, you don't have to use Earthlink. But Apple and Earthlink are probably offering some incentive for you to do just that. For example, when I wrote this, they were offering a $25 discount (they waived the usual $25 setup fee), but that deal could change by the time you read this. In any event, I don't think Earthlink is a bad choice. Their prices are similar to other ISPs, and they do understand Macs, something that can't be said for all ISPs.

That said, just do it:

1. **Launch Internet Setup Assistant.**

   The first screen asks "Would you like to set up your computer to use the Internet?"

2. **Click the Yes button.**

   The second screen asks "Do you already have an Internet account?"

3. **Click the No button.**

   (If the answer is yes, skip ahead to the section called "Using Internet Setup Assistant if you already have an ISP.")

   After a few moments, the first actual Internet Setup Assistant dialog box appears, with more information about setting up your account.

4. **Read the Internet Setup Assistant information and then click the right arrow at the bottom of the screen to move to the next screen.**

   The Modem Settings dialog box appears, as shown in Figure 17-1.

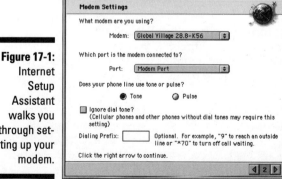

Figure 17-1: Internet Setup Assistant walks you through setting up your modem.

5. **From the upper pop-up menu, choose your modem. From the lower pop-up menu, choose the port that the modem is connected to — usually the Modem Port.**

6. **Click the option for tone or pulse dialing — usually Tone — and leave the Ignore Dial Tone check box unchecked.**

7. **Enter any dialing prefixes you need to make a toll-free phone call (such as 9, to get an outside line, or *70 to turn off Call Waiting).**

8. **When you've finished making your selections in the Modem Settings dialog box, click the right arrow at the bottom of the screen. Oh, and make sure your modem is connected and turned on.**

   Screen 3 appears, telling you about ISPs.

9. **Read Screen 3 and then click the right arrow at the bottom of the screen.**

   Screen 4 appears.

10. **Choose your country from the pop-up menu, type your area code and phone number prefix, and then click the Register button.**

    Your modem emits a shriek or two as it dials Apple's ISP referral server. After a few moments, Screen 5 appears.

11. **Read Screen 5 and then click the right arrow yet again.**

    Screen 6 appears.

12. **Click the Go Ahead button.**

Microsoft Internet Explorer launches and you can start the process of getting signed up for an Internet account with Apple's preferred service provider, Earthlink, by clicking the Begin Registration button on the Web page that Internet Explorer displays.

When you've entered all the information Earthlink asks for, including your credit card number, you're in business. You have an Internet account — and best of all, the software you need to use your account is all configured and ready to go. Congratulations. You can skip the next section and start surfing the Web.

If you decide you don't want to sign up with Earthlink, click the Cancel Registration button. After you choose another ISP, you can follow the instructions in the next section, "Using Internet Setup Assistant if you already have an ISP." But Earthlink is probably as good (or as bad) a choice as any ISP.

Using Internet Setup Assistant if you already have an ISP

If you opted not to sign up with Earthlink or you already have an ISP, you need to do some work before you can get out there and surf. (Funny, that's what my mom used to say to me.)

You need a bunch of information to configure your Internet connection; you should be able to get it all from your ISP:

- ✔ Your domain name server (DNS) addresses, or domain name, or both.

- ✔ Type of configuration. (I cover modem here, but you could be using Ethernet, Mac IP, or something else completely. If you are, see your network administrator or call your ISP for details.)

- ✔ Whether or not you need a PPP Connect Script.

- ✔ Whether or not you use a Proxy Server.

- ✔ Your IP address, subnet mask, and router address, and how the IP address is acquired (from a server or not).

- ✔ Your ISP's dial-up phone number.

- ✔ Your user name and password.

When you have assembled all these pieces, you're ready to do some configuring.

Actually, with Internet Setup Assistant, *configuring* is an awfully strong way to put it. Sure, you'll enter all the information you need to connect to the Internet, but you don't have to get lost in a maze of jargon and control panels to do it. Just open Internet Setup Assistant and follow the arrows. What could be simpler?

1. **Launch Internet Setup Assistant.**

   The first screen asks "Would you like to set up your computer to use the Internet?"

2. **Click the Yes button.**

   A second screen appears and asks "Do you already have an Internet account?"

3. **Click the Yes button.**

   (If the answer is no, go back to the preceding section and follow the directions there.)

   Screen 1 appears and reminds you of the info you'll need before you can configure your account. If something's missing, call your ISP before you go any further. Assuming you have everything you need, click the right arrow at the bottom of the window.

4. **Name your Internet account.**

   I called mine Bob's Account, as shown in Figure 17-2.

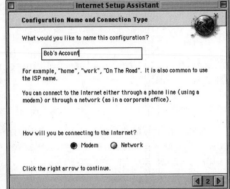

Figure 17-2:
Give your
Internet
account a
logical
name.

5. **Click the Modem option, and then click the right arrow at the bottom of the screen.**

   The Modem Settings dialog box — Screen 3 — appears.

6. **From the upper pop-up menu, choose your modem. From the lower pop-up menu, choose the port that the modem is connected to — usually the Modem Port. (Refer back to Figure 17-1.)**

7. **Click the option for tone or pulse dialing — usually Tone — and leave the Ignore Dial Tone check box unchecked.**

8. **Click the right arrow at the bottom of the screen. Oh, and make sure your modem is connected and turned on.**

   Screen 4 appears. Now you'll do some real configuring.

9. **Enter your ISP's phone number, your user name, and your password, just like I did in Figure 17-3, and then click the right arrow at the bottom of the screen.**

   Screen 5 appears and asks whether you need a PPP Connect Script. Only your ISP can tell you the answer to this question.

10. **So ask your ISP and then click the proper option — yes or no. Then move on by clicking the right arrow at the bottom of the screen.**

    Screen 6 appears. Everyone who connects to the Internet uses an IP address, a set of unique numbers that identifies your computer. Sometimes an ISP assigns you an IP address to use with your account. Most providers, though, assign you an IP address each time you connect. It really doesn't matter how you get an IP address, as long as you get one. The only time you have to worry about it is the first time you configure your account. That would be right now.

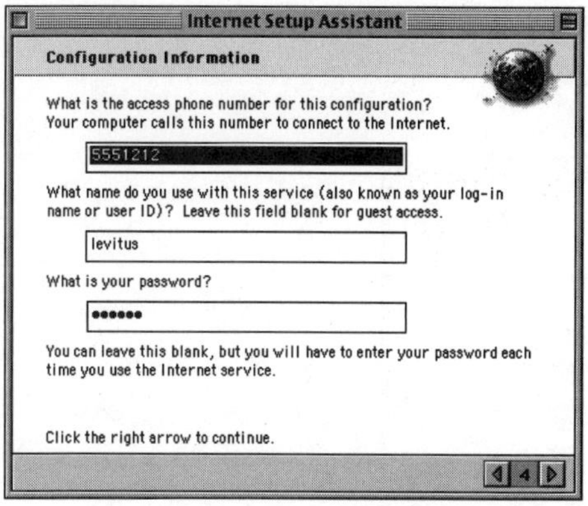

Figure 17-3:
Tell your
Mac where
to call and
who you
are.

11. **In Screen 6, if your ISP gave you an IP address, choose Yes. If not, leave No checked. Click the right arrow.**

    Screen 7 appears. Even if your ISP didn't give you an IP address of your own, you probably did get what's called a DNS address. Basically, that's the IP address of your ISP. Often, there are several. Look at Figure 17-4 to see how a DNS address (sometimes called a server address) should look. You'll also see a blank for a domain name. That's the equivalent of the DNS address in words. For my provider, it's outer.net.

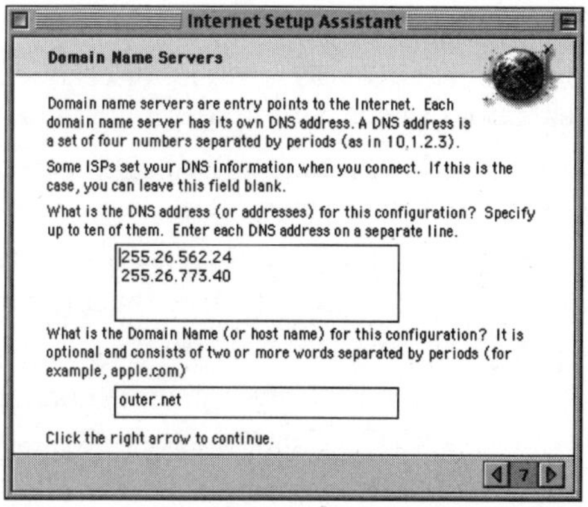

Figure 17-4:
This is
where you
enter your
ISP's DNS
address and
domain
name.

12. **Type the DNS address and domain name, and then click the right arrow to go to Screen 8.**

13. **Type your e-mail address and password, and then click the right arrow to go to Screen 9.**

    Your e-mail address is the address you give to people who want to send you e-mail and the address that appears at the top of messages you send.

14. **In Screen 9, enter the e-mail account and SMTP server address, as shown in Figure 17-5, and then click the right arrow.**

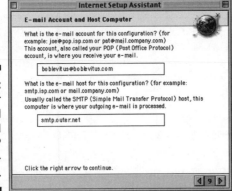

Figure 17-5:
Enter your
e-mail
account and
SMTP
server infor-
mation here.

Sometimes, the SMTP server address is the same as your e-mail address. Sometimes it's a little different. In this example, my e-mail address is boblevitus@boblevitus.com, but my SMTP server is smtp.outer.net. The SMTP server is the machine that processes mail for your ISP.

15. **In Screen 10, enter the name of your ISP's news server. Then click the right arrow to go to Screen 11.**

    A news server, which is also called an NNTP (Network News Transfer Protocol) server, makes it possible for you to read Usenet newsgroups.

16. **In Screen 11, tell Internet Setup if you use proxy servers and then click the right arrow.**

    Only your ISP or your network administrator can tell you the answer to this question. Often, if you're setting up an Internet account for home use, you don't have proxy servers to worry about.

    The final Internet Setup Assistant screen gives you the chance to review your work, enable your new configuration, and get online right away.

17. **If you would break like to review what you did, click Show Details.**

    If anything doesn't look right, click the left arrow to go back and correct it.

18. **When you're happy with your new configuration, click Go Ahead.**

    The Setup Assistant updates a few control panels while you wait.

That's it. You're good to go. Let's move on and meet your new Web browser, Microsoft Internet Explorer.

Surfing with Internet Explorer

Apple includes both Microsoft Internet Explorer and Netscape Communicator with Mac OS 9. The default browser — the one that launches when you work with Internet Assistant or click the Browse the Internet button, is Internet Explorer. Both browsers are pretty darn good, and I recommend that you try each one to decide which browser is best. If you're not sure which browser to use, try 'em both. You'll find Netscape Communicator in the Internet folder, right next to Internet Explorer.

You can launch Internet Explorer in a couple ways:

- ✓ Double-click the Internet Explorer icon in your Internet folder
- ✓ Double-click the Browse the Internet icon on your desktop

When you first launch Internet Explorer, you'll see that it has automatically connected you to the Internet and is displaying an Apple Web page designed especially for new Net surfers (see Figure 17-6).

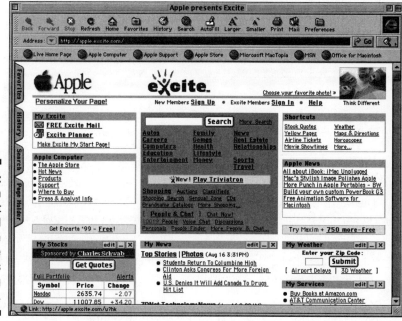

Figure 17-6:
Open Internet Explorer and you'll see a Web page that looks something like this.

If you click the <u>Personalize Your Page</u> link near the upper-left corner of the window, you can customize this startup page to display only stuff you like. Try it, you'll like it.

Your copy of IE comes with some pointers — known in Web parlance as *favorites,* or *bookmarks* — that will take you to other nifty Mac sites you'll want to check out.

Pull down the Favorites menu and take a look at the list your pals at Apple have put together. You'll find bookmarks to Apple sites (see Figure 17-7), hardware and software vendors, Mac publications, and more. Choosing any item from the Favorites menu takes you to that Web page almost immediately.

Figure 17-7:
Your copy of
Internet
Explorer
comes with
a set of
useful
bookmarks.

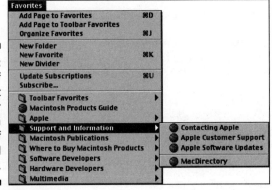

Be sure and explore all the included bookmarks when you have some time; they're all worth knowing more about.

There's a lot to IE that I don't have room to describe, but I'll hit the highlights from the top of the screen.

The buttons along the top of the window — Back, Forward, Stop, Refresh, Home, and so on — do pretty much what their names imply. Play with them a bit and you'll see what I mean.

Click the Search button to get to a search engine that can help you find Web pages on the Internet.

You don't have to launch IE to search the Internet. Just use the Finder's Find command — Sherlock 2 — and click the Search Internet tab.

The Address field is where you type Web addresses, or URLs, that you want to visit. Just type one in and press Return to surf to that site.

Web addresses almost always begin with `http://www`. But Internet Explorer does a cool trick: If you just type a name, you usually get to the appropriate Web site that way without typing http, //, or www. For example, if you type **Apple** in the Address field and then press Return, you go to `http://www.apple.com`. Or if you type **Microsoft**, you're taken to `http://www.microsoft.com`. Try it; it's pretty cool.

Below the Address field are some more buttons that take you directly to pages that may interest you, such as the Apple Web site, the Apple tech support Web site, and the Apple Store. Click one of them to be transported instantly to that page.

Finally, to manage your bookmarks, choose Favorites⇨Open Favorites (⌘+J) or click the Favorites button near the top of the window. To delete a bookmark, select it and then press Delete or Backspace.

Searching the Net with Sherlock 2

The new and improved Sherlock 2 lets you do more than search your own hard disk. You can scour general-purpose Internet search engines with the options under the Internet button or get more specific with one of the six other Internet buttons.

To use Sherlock 2, follow these steps:

1. **Choose Sherlock 2 from the Apple menu, double-click its icon on the desktop, or type ⌘+F in the Finder.**

2. **Choose one of the seven Internet buttons.**

   Labels appear under each label when you move your mouse over it.

3. **Type a word or a phrase you want to search for. If you're doing a people search, type the person's first and last name.**

4. **Choose one or more of the search engines listed by clicking their check boxes.**

5. **Press Enter or click the magnifying glass button.**

   Sherlock passes your request along to the search engines you've selected, and displays a list of search results in a new window.

6. **When you double-click a link (any item in the list at the bottom of the window), your browser launches and displays the page you selected.**

7. **Go back to Sherlock's results window to view more pages that match your query.**

TIP

You can add new search engines to Sherlock 2 by downloading new plug-in files from the Internet:

```
http://www.apple.com/sherlock/plugins.html
http://www.apple-donuts.com/sherlocksearch/index.html
```

Getting Your Mail with Outlook Express

You can use different applications to read Internet mail. Netscape Communicator, for example has a built-in mail reader. But the easiest and best mail reader around (that means, the best one on your hard disk right now) is probably Outlook Express. And you can't beat the price; it's free.

Remember the handy Browse the Internet icon that got Internet Explorer up and running? Well, you'll find another icon on your Mac OS 9 desktop. This one looks like a hand holding a letter and is called Mail. Double-click the Mail icon to send and receive mail.

Outlook Express is fast and easy to use. It lets you send and receive messages and create an address book that includes the addresses of your friends and family. Outlook Express's main window looks like Figure 17-8.

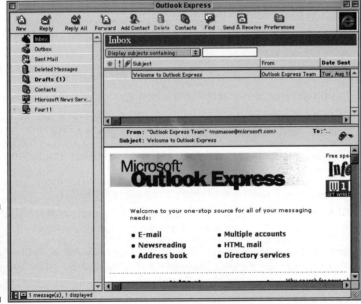

Figure 17-8:
The Outlook Express main window.

Here's how to create a message:

1. **Choose File⇨New⇨Mail Message (⌘+N).**

2. **Fill in the To field with someone's e-mail address.**

   Use my address, `levitus@outer.net`, if you don't know anyone else to send mail to.

3. **Press Tab three times and type a subject for this message.**

   After you've finished addressing a mail message, you can add the recipient to your Outlook Express address book. From then on, you'll be able to type the first few letters of the recipient's name, and Outlook Express will fill in the address for you. Neat, huh?

4. **Click in the main message portion of the window, as shown in Figure 17-9, and type your message.**

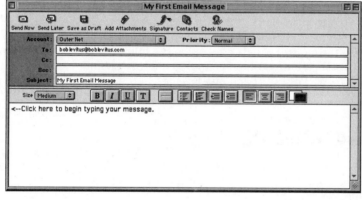

Figure 17-9: Using Outlook Express to compose a message.

5. **When the message says just what you want it to say, click Save as Draft to save it in the Drafts folder or click Send Now to send it immediately. (You can also click Send Later, which saves the message in the Outbox.)**

   If you save it to the Drafts folder (so you can write more later, perhaps), you can send it by opening the Drafts folder, double-clicking the message, and then clicking Send.

Now, I know what you're thinking: How do I check my mail? Easy. Just click the Send and Receive mail button at the top of the window. If you have mail in your Outbox and want to both send and receive mail, choose Tools⇨ Send and Receive⇨Send and Receive All, or use the shortcut ⌘+M.

You can configure Outlook Express to send and receive all mail every *x* minutes by choosing Edit⇨Preferences, and then clicking General in the list on the left side of the window.

I would love to tell you about reading newsgroups with Outlook Express, but I'm out of space. Blame my editor. She said we've already killed enough trees with this tome and that if I write one more page on this subject, she'll brain me. And I still have four control panels to cover! So if you want to know more about IE or OE, I urge you to explore their help systems (available in each program's Help menu).

Four Internet-Related Control Panels

You may be wondering what happened to all the information you provided to Internet Setup Assistant. The answer is that the Setup Assistant stashed it in the appropriate control panel.

If your Internet connection is working now, you have no need to even look at any of the control panels covered in the following sections. Still, in the interest of completeness (and because in another chapter I said I would cover them here), I discuss each one briefly.

Internet control panel

The Internet control panel (shown in Figure 17-10) stores many of the settings your computer needs to connect to the Internet. It remembers stuff like your name, e-mail address, company name, user name for mail, mail server name, and password (optional). If you ever need to change one of these items, the Internet control panel is the place to do it.

If you're familiar with the freeware program Internet Config, the Internet control panel does pretty much the same stuff. Choose Edit⇨User Mode and then click the Advanced button to reveal features such as firewalls, helper apps, and fonts.

If several people use your Mac, you can create settings for each one. Just choose File⇨New Set (⌘+N), name it something relevant, and fill out the information on all four tabs (Personal, E-Mail, Web, and News) for the other user or users. If the new set is similar to an existing set, you may find it easier to use the Duplicate Set command, which is File⇨Duplicate Set (⌘+D). This command creates a set with all the settings of the original set; you can then modify only the things you want to change instead of starting from scratch.

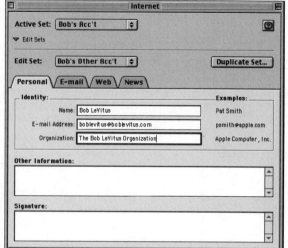

Figure 17-10:
The Internet control panel stores most of the information your Mac needs to use the Internet.

In the upper-right corner of the Internet control panel, you'll see a question mark in a circle. Click it and you'll get a ton of excellent help and information about this control panel.

If you want to use Netscape Communicator to surf the Web, or a program other than Outlook Express to read your mail, you can choose that program in the Internet control panel. Choose a new default e-mail application (under the E-mail tab) or a new default browser (under the Web tab).

TCP/IP control panel

The TCP/IP control panel stores settings your computer needs to make a connection to your ISP, including your IP address, subnet mask, router address, domain name, and name server address. If you ever need to change any of these settings, this is the place to go.

To create a set of TCP/IP settings, choose File⇨Configurations (⌘+K), choose the set most like the set you want to create, and then click the Duplicate button. Make the appropriate changes and close the TCP/IP control panel. You'll be asked whether you want to save your changes. Click OK.

Remote Access control panel

You encounter the Remote Access control panel also in Chapter 10, when I talk about connecting to other Macs remotely. If you use a modem to connect to the Internet and aren't an AOL user, you'll also use Remote Access to dial your ISP.

If you have multiple Internet accounts, you can use Remote Access to create a dial-up connection for each. Just like TCP/IP, you select and configure each new account by duplicating an existing set of options. For Remote Access (see Figure 17-11), you enter your Internet user name, password, and phone number.

Figure 17-11:
You use
Remote
Access to
dial
your ISP.

Modem control panel

The Modem control panel stores settings about (what else?) your modem. It's here that you choose the brand and model of modem you're using, whether sound should be on or off, whether to use tone or pulse dialing, and whether to ignore the dial tone.

To create a set of modem settings, choose File⇨Configurations (⌘+K), choose the set most like the set you want to create, and then click the Duplicate button. Make the appropriate changes, and then close the Modem control panel. You'll be asked whether you want to save your changes. Click OK.

The control panels I describe in this section each include a help button (look for the question mark) that will take you to Mac OS Help. You'll find more specific info about setting up and working with these control panels there.

Chapter 18

What to Do When Good System Software Goes Bad

I said Chapter 16 was "easily the most useful chapter in the book." It is. Unless you wake up one morning to find your Macintosh sick or dying. Then (and only then) this chapter is more useful because it's the one that's going to save your bacon.

As a bleeding-edge Mac enthusiast with almost twelve years of Mac under my belt, I've had more than my share of Mac troubles. Over those years, I've developed an arsenal of tips and tricks that I believe can resolve more than 90 percent of Macintosh problems without a trip to the repair shop.

Disclaimer: Of course, if your hardware is dead, neither you nor I can do anything about it. But if your hardware is okay, you have a 90-percent chance that something (or a combination of things) in this chapter will get your machine up and running.

Dem Ol' Sad Mac Chimes of Doom Blues

One thing we all dread is seeing the Sad Mac icon (shown in Figure 18-1) and hearing that arpeggio in G minor, better known as the Chimes of Doom, or the sound of breaking glass, or any of the other horrible sounds Macs make when they're dying.

Figure 18-1:
Something
is very
wrong.

The Sad Mac usually indicates that something very bad has happened to your Mac, often that some hardware component has bitten the dust. But Sad Macs are rather uncommon — many users go years without seeing one. If you have one, don't despair. Yet. There is something you can try before you diagnose your Mac as terminal — something that just might bring it back to life. Try this:

1. **Shut down your Mac.**

2. **If your Mac came with a Disk Tools floppy disk, insert it. Otherwise, if your Mac has an internal CD-ROM drive and came with a bootable CD-ROM System Software disk, insert that or the Mac OS 9 CD instead.**

3. **Restart your Mac.**

4. **If you are using a CD, hold down the C key on your keyboard during startup.**

   Some Macs require AppleTalk to be on for a CD-ROM boot to work. Go figure.

If you see the Mac OS startup screen when you boot from your Disk Tools or CD-ROM, there's hope for your Mac. The fact that you can boot from another disk indicates that there's a problem with your hard disk or your System Folder. Whatever it is, it will more than likely respond to one of the techniques discussed throughout the rest of this chapter, so read on.

If the forthcoming techniques don't correct the problem, or you still see the Sad Mac icon when you start up with Disk Tools or CD, your Mac is toasted and needs to go in for repairs (usually to an Apple dealer).

Before you drag it down to the shop, you might try 1-800-SOS-APPL. They may well suggest something else you can try.

If you get the Sad Mac immediately after installing RAM (which is the time you'll most commonly see it), double-check that the RAM is properly seated in its sockets.

Flashing Question Mark/Flashing Folder Problems

Go through the steps in this section in sequence. If one doesn't work, move on to the next.

Now would be a good time to reread the "Question Mark and the Mysterians" section in Chapter 1, which explains the flashing question mark and why Disk Tools or a bootable CD-ROM are the ultimate startup disks. Both are things you need to know before you continue.

The bootable Mac OS CD-ROM is soooo important, it's a good idea to have more than one copy around. That way, if one gets misplaced, damaged, eaten by the dog, scuffed, scratched, or otherwise rendered useless, you won't be out of luck. An older version of Mac OS and the CD that came with your computer are examples of "extra" bootable CDs you may have hanging around. The Mac OS 9 CD is bootable as well.

I keep the Mac OS 9 CD in my middle desk drawer and several other bootable CDs on the bookshelf.

If you have a removable media drive such as an Orb or a Jaz or a SyQuest, it's a good idea to create a bootable cartridge (by installing Mac OS 9; see Appendix A) and stash it someplace safe, just in case.

If you don't have a bootable CD-ROM, preferably a Mac OS 9 Install CD-ROM, you can't do the rest of the stuff in this chapter. So if you don't have one handy, go find it now.

Start with something easy: Rebuild the desktop

Before attempting more drastic measures, try rebuilding the desktop.

Actually, rebuilding the desktop should go under the heading of preventive maintenance. Apple recommends rebuilding the desktop once a month, and so do I.

Another good time to rebuild the desktop is if you notice icons disappearing, changing, or being replaced by generic icons (see Figure 18-2). This problem is usually a result of a desktop that needs rebuilding.

Figure 18-2:
Generic
icons.

The desktop you're rebuilding is an invisible database that keeps track of every file on your hard disk, manages what icon goes with which file, and manages which program launches when you open a document.

More strictly speaking, the desktop is a pair of invisible files called Desktop DB and Desktop DF. They're stored at the root level, but you can see them only with special software designed to work with invisible files. Leave them alone.

Another good time to rebuild the desktop is if you start getting "An application can't be found for this document" errors when you know that you have the application or have assigned a substitute using File Exchange.

Anyway, to rebuild the desktop, hold down the ⌘ and Option keys during startup until you see a dialog box asking whether you're sure you want to rebuild the desktop. Click OK, and you see a progress window as the desktop is rebuilt. In a moment or two, it disappears and you're off and running.

If you have more than one hard disk or hard disk partition, a dialog box appears for each disk that mounts on the desktop at startup. Click OK for every disk.

Just remember to rebuild your desktop monthly to keep your Mac in tip-top shape. And rebuild it again if you see the flashing question mark.

You're going to attempt to boot from your hard disk now, so remove the Disk Tools disk or bootable CD from the drive and restart.

If you still see the flashing question mark, it's time to . . .

Send for the ambulance: Run Disk First Aid

The next step in the program is to run the Disk First Aid application.

The desktop isn't the only place where hard disks store information about themselves. B-trees, extent files, catalog files, and other creatively named invisible files are involved in managing the data on your disks. Disk First Aid is a program that checks all those files and repairs the damaged ones.

You'll find the Disk First Aid program in the Utilities folder installed with OS 9.

The version of Disk First Aid in Mac OS 8.6 was the first ever to be able to verify and repair the startup disk. Before this you had to boot from another disk or CD to repair your startup disk. Yuck.

Here's how to make Disk First Aid do its thing:

1. **Launch the Disk First Aid application.**

2. **Click the icon for your hard disk at the top of the Disk First Aid window.**

   See Figure 18-3.

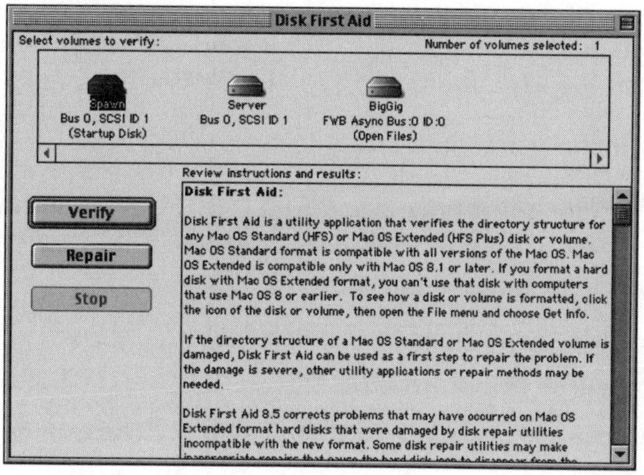

Figure 18-3:
Click your
hard disk's
icon and
then click
Repair. Disk
First Aid
does
the rest.

[Figure: Disk First Aid window showing three volumes to verify — Shawn (Bus 0, SCSI ID 1, Startup Disk), Server (Bus 0, SCSI ID 1), and BigGig (FWB Async Bus :0 ID:0, Open Files) — with Verify, Repair, and Stop buttons and a results text area describing Disk First Aid.]

3. **Click the Repair button.**

   Your Mac whirs and hums for a few minutes, and the results window tells you what's going on. Ultimately, Disk First Aid tells you (you hope) that the disk appears to be okay. If so, go back to work.

If Disk First Aid finds damage that it can't fix, a commercial disk-recovery tool such as Norton Utilities for the Macintosh or TechTool Pro may be able to repair the damage. And even if Disk First Aid gave you a clean bill of health, you may want to run one of the commercial utilities anyway, just to have a second opinion.

If the software can't repair the damage, you have to initialize your disk. But that's okay, right? You have that backup software and you use it.

If everything checks out with Disk First Aid, try to boot from your hard disk again. If you still get the flashing question mark, try . . .

Installing new hard disk drivers

This section applies to Apple-brand hard disks only. If you have a third-party hard disk, the procedure is different. That means if you have a Mac clone or you bought your hard disk from anyone but Apple, read your manual and do what it says. You may not want (or even be able) to use Apple's Drive Setup application. Sorry.

What you're going to attempt next is to install (update) your hard disk drivers.

Drivers are invisible bits of code that tell your hard disk how to communicate with a Mac. They occasionally become damaged and need replacing. When performed properly, the technique is harmless and can make the flashing question mark disappear. Mac OS 9 installs new drivers automatically (on Apple-brand hard disks) when you first install it.

Here's how you install a new hard disk driver:

1. **Restart your Mac using your Mac OS 9 CD-ROM as the startup disc (remember to hold down the C key at startup).**

2. **Launch the Drive Setup application.**

   The application should be in the Utilities folder.

3. **Click the name of your hard disk.**

4. **Choose Functions⇨Update Driver, as shown in Figure 18-4.**

   You should see a message telling you that the new driver won't be available until you restart your computer.

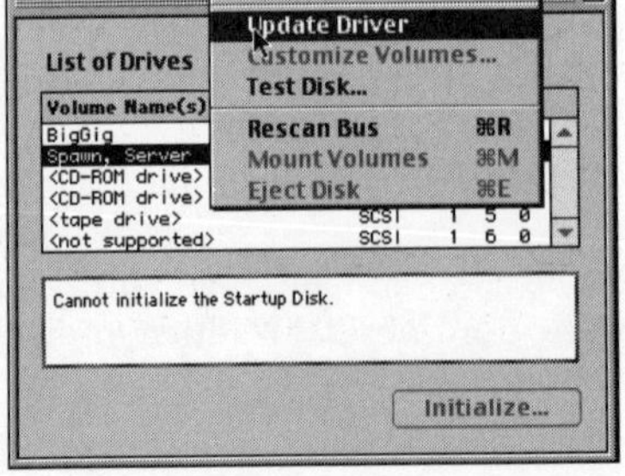

Figure 18-4:
Choose this
to update
(install new)
hard disk
drivers.

Do not click Initialize or choose Functions⇨Initialization Options! If you initialize your hard disk, it will be erased completely and irrevocably. You get a warning or two first, but if you're not paying attention, a few false clicks (or presses of the Return or Enter key) and you're hard disk is blank. So update, don't initialize, okay?

If that solution doesn't get you up and running, and you're still seeing that danged flashing question mark when you try to boot from your hard disk, don't despair. You can still try a few things, such as . . .

The latest dance craze: Zapping the PRAM

Sometimes your parameter RAM (PRAM) becomes scrambled and needs to be reset. PRAM is a small piece of memory that's not erased or forgotten when you shut down. It keeps track of things such as printer selection in the Chooser, sound level, and monitor settings.

Try zapping your PRAM if your Monitors control panel or your Chooser seem to forget their settings when you shut down or restart.

Restart your Mac and hold down ⌘+Option+P+R (that's four keys — good luck; it's okay to use your nose) until your Mac restarts itself. It's kind of like a hiccup. You see the smiling Mac or flashing question mark for a second, and then that icon disappears and your Mac restarts.

Zapping the PRAM returns some control panels to their default settings (but, interestingly, not the date or time), so you may have to do some tweaking after zapping the PRAM.

SCSI voodoo

This section is for folks whose Mac includes a SCSI port and external SCSI devices. If you have an iMac or another Mac with USB, rather than SCSI, ports, you can skip this part of the chapter.

Don't know whether you have SCSI? Look on the back of your Mac for a long connector with a diamond-shaped icon above it. If, instead, you have one or more small connectors to an external drive, you have USB. If you have USB, you're probably a happy, well-adjusted human being with no problems. If you have SCSI, read on.

It is said that connecting more than one SCSI device — an external hard disk, a SyQuest, Zip, or Jaz drive, an optical disk, a scanner, and so on — requires the luck of the gods.

The first bugaboo is SCSI termination. According to Apple, the first and last device on a SCSI chain must have a terminator. No devices in between should have termination. Internal hard drives are always terminated. And the total length of a SCSI chain can be no more than 22 feet.

But sometimes you can't get your SCSI chain to work by following the rules. Sometimes it requires terminating a drive in the middle of the chain as well as the first and last drives. Other times, a chain won't work if the last device is terminated. The physical order of devices matters. And, of course, there are those SCSI ID numbers.

So if you're seeing a flashing question mark and any external devices are attached, shut down your Mac and unplug them. After they're all disconnected, try restarting your Mac and booting from the Mac OS 9 CD.

Never plug or unplug SCSI devices with the power on. Turn both your Mac and the device off before you attempt to connect or disconnect any cables.

If your Mac starts up when no SCSI devices are connected, you have a problem on the SCSI chain: a termination problem, a bad cable, or a SCSI ID conflict.

I'll be back: The terminator

A terminator is a plug that fits into the empty cable connector of the last device on your chain. Many newer external hard disks have termination built in. Consult your hard disk manual to see whether your device has built-in termination.

Some terminators are pass-through connectors, which can have a cable connected to them. Others block off that connector completely; these are known as block terminators.

If you see the flashing question mark and your last device isn't terminated, terminate it. If it is terminated, unterminate it. If you have more than one device and your terminator is a pass-through terminator, connect it to a device in the middle of the chain (instead of the end) and try to start your Mac.

If you have two terminators and two or more devices, try two terminators, one in the middle and one at the end. This trick isn't recommended, but sometimes that's what it takes to make it work.

If all this terminator juggling isn't working for you, try changing the physical order of the devices. If right now your Mac is connected to the hard disk, which is connected to the Zip drive, then try connecting the Zip drive to the Mac and the hard disk to the Zip drive.

I add and subtract SCSI devices more often in a year than most people do in two lifetimes. I'm always firing up some new storage device that someone wants me to check out. And I've had good luck since switching to a drive with Digital Active Termination.

Digital Active Termination senses how much termination your SCSI chain requires and then supplies it automatically. It's almost a miracle, and it's included on almost all storage devices from APS Technologies. Just put any device with Digital Active Termination at the end of your chain, and you are virtually guaranteed perfect termination, regardless of the number of devices in the chain or the physical order of the devices.

Cables: Cheap is bad

When troubleshooting SCSI problems, you should check your SCSI cables. If you can borrow others, try that option. Cheap cables, usually ones that are thin and flexible, are more prone to failure than heavy, shielded cables. Again, APS has excellent thick cables at fair prices.

Gotta have some ID: Unique SCSI ID numbers required

If you have multiple SCSI devices, don't forget that each must have a unique SCSI ID between 0 and 6. Your internal hard disk has ID 0, so external devices can have numbers from 1 to 6. Internal CD-ROM drives are frequently assigned the ID number 3.

You usually select the ID number using a wheel or button on the back of the device. Just make sure that each drive in the chain has a unique number, and you'll be all set.

Try again to restart from your usual startup disk. If nothing so far has cured the flashing question mark, you have to suspect damage to the System software on your hard disk. So now you're going to try to replace your old System software with fresh, new System software.

Reinstalling the System software

The reason that the procedure to reinstall the System software is last in this section is that it takes the longest. The procedure is detailed at great length in Appendix A, affectionately known as "Anyone Can Install Mac OS 9."

Read it and follow the instructions.

If nothing has worked so far

If none of my suggestions have worked — if you've rebuilt the desktop, run Disk First Aid, installed new hard disk drivers, zapped your PRAM, disconnected all SCSI devices, and reinstalled your System software — and you're still seeing the flashing question mark, you have big trouble.

You may have any one of the following problems:

- ✔ Your hard disk is dead and so is your floppy drive.
- ✔ Your hard disk is dead but your floppy drive is okay.
- ✔ You have some other type of hardware failure.
- ✔ All your startup disks — your Disk Tools and Install Disk 1 floppies and your System software CDs — are defective (unlikely).

The bottom line: If you're still seeing the flashing question mark after trying all the stuff in the previous pages, you almost certainly need to have your Mac serviced by a qualified technician.

If You Crash at Startup

Startup crashes are another bad thing that can happen to your Mac. These crashes are more of a hassle to solve than flashing question mark problems but are rarely fatal.

A *crash* is defined as a System Error dialog box, a frozen cursor, a frozen screen, or any other disabling event. *Startup* is defined as any time between flicking the power key or switch (or restarting) and having full use of the Finder desktop.

A startup crash may happen to you someday. If it does, here's what to do.

Restart without extensions and control panels

The first thing you need to do is establish whether an extension or control panel is causing the crash by starting up with all of them disabled.

If your Mac is already on, choose Special⇨Restart, holding down the Shift key until you see Extensions Off in the Welcome to Mac OS window. After you see Extensions Off, release the Shift key.

If your Mac is off, power it up and hold down the Shift key until you see Extensions Off in the Welcome to Mac OS window. Then release the Shift key.

If your Mac starts up successfully when you hold down the Shift key but crashes or freezes when you don't, you can deduce that one (or more) of your extensions or control panels is responsible for the crash. Read the section "Resolving extension and control panel conflicts," which is up next.

If your Mac still crashes when you hold down the Shift key, you can deduce that something is wrong with your System or Finder. Read the section "How to perform a clean System reinstallation," later in this chapter.

Resolving extension and control panel conflicts

If you're reading this section, you have an extension or a control panel that's causing your Mac to crash at startup. The trick now is to isolate which one (or, occasionally, more than one) is causing your troubles. Chances are, it's a third-party extension or control panel, but you can't rule out Apple extensions and control panels either. They, too, can conflict with other extensions or control panels or become corrupted and not function properly.

Because you know that your Mac will start up with the Shift key down, you can use Extensions Manager to track down the rogue extension or control panel file.

The first step is to establish whether any Apple Mac OS 9 extensions or control panels are causing problems:

1. **Launch the Extensions Manager control panel.**

2. **From the pop-up menu, choose Mac OS 9.0 All (see Figure 18-5), and then click the Restart button.**

   - **Situation 1:** You can now boot successfully, which means that the culprit must be one of your third-party extensions or control panels.

   - **Situation 2:** You still crash at startup, which means that the culprit must be one of the Mac OS extensions or control panels.

In Situation 1, repeat these steps until your Mac crashes again:

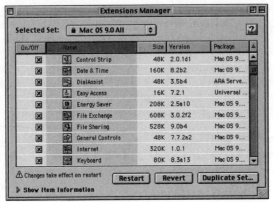

Figure 18-5:
Load only
the
standard
issue
Mac OS
extensions
and control
panels.

1. **Power up or restart your Mac, and then press and hold the spacebar until the Extensions Manager window appears.**

2. **Add half your extensions or control panels to the enabled list by clicking them so that a check mark appears.**

3. **Click the Continue button to begin the startup process.**

If you start up successfully, you know that one of the extensions or control panels you just added is not the culprit. Repeat these three steps, enabling half of the disabled items each time you restart, until your Mac crashes. When you do, one of the items in the last group of extensions or control panels you enabled is the culprit.

See the section called "Dealing with recalcitrant extensions and control panels" for possible solutions.

In Situation 2, repeat these steps until your Mac stops crashing:

1. **Power up or restart your Mac, and then press and hold the spacebar until the Extensions Manager window appears.**

2. **Disable half of the currently enabled extensions or control panels by clicking them so that their check mark disappears.**

3. **Click the Continue button to begin the startup process.**

Repeat these three steps, disabling half of the currently enabled items each time you restart, until your Mac stops crashing. When you do, one of the items in the last group of extensions or control panels you disabled was the culprit.

See the next section, "Dealing with recalcitrant extensions and control panels," for some things you can try.

Sometimes you can tell which extension or control panel is causing your crash by looking carefully at the little icons that appear at the bottom of your screen during startup. Each icon you see represents a control panel or an extension loading into memory. If you can determine which icon was the last to appear before the crash, you can try disabling it before going through the iterative and frustrating process of determining the culprit as described in this section. You may get lucky and save yourself hours of boring detective work.

Casady & Greene's Conflict Catcher automates this entire "turn stuff on/turn stuff off" dance and makes it almost painless to track down the recalcitrant extension or control panel that's causing your woes.

Dealing with recalcitrant extensions and control panels

In the preceding section, you determined which particular extension or control panel was giving you fits. In this section, I have a couple of suggestions — replace and reorder — that may let you use the offending item anyway.

How to replace a recalcitrant file

To replace a misbehaving extension or control panel, follow these steps:

1. **Delete the guilty control panel or extension from your hard disk by dragging it to the Trash.**

2. **Open the Preferences folder in your System Folder, and delete any preferences file with the same name as the guilty file.**

3. **Replace the guilty file with a fresh copy from a master disk.**

    If it's an Apple extension or control panel, use the Mac OS installers as described in Appendix A. If it's a third-party product, follow the installation instructions in its manual.

4. **Restart and see whether the problem recurs.**

If the problem hasn't gone away, you may still be able to use the recalcitrant extension or control panel by diddling with the loading order of extensions and control panels at startup. Read further.

How to reorder a recalcitrant file

In some cases, extensions and control panels crash only if they load before or after another extension. Ergo, by diddling with the loading order, you can force one file to load before another.

How do you diddle the loading order, you ask? When extensions and control panels load at startup, they load in alphabetical order by folder. To wit:

1. The Extensions folder's contents, in alphabetical order

2. The Control Panels folder's contents, in alphabetical order

3. Control panels or extensions loose in your System Folder (that is, not in the Extensions or Control Panels folders), in alphabetical order

So, if you have a recalcitrant extension or control panel, try forcing it to load either first or last. This trick works more often than not.

To force an offending control panel or extension (Snapz Pro in the example shown in Figure 18-6) to load first, precede its name by several spaces and move it into the Extensions folder if it's a control panel. It will then load before any other extensions or control panels.

Figure 18-6:
The first item to load will be the control panel renamed Snapz Pro.

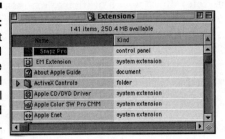

By putting the Snapz Pro control panel in the Extensions folder (so that it loads before items in the Control Panels folder or System Folder) and preceding its name with several spaces, I ensured that Snapz Pro would be the first control panel to load.

Going the other way, to force an extension or control panel to load last, precede its name with several • symbols (Option+8) and move it out of the Extensions folder and into the System Folder itself.

More sophisticated startup managers, such as Casady & Greene's Conflict Catcher 8, let you change the loading order of extensions and control panels by dragging them around, avoiding the inconvenience of renaming or moving them manually. It also performs the conflict resolution three-step boogie automatically. I wish Extensions Manager had these capabilities. If you find yourself resolving many conflicts with extensions or control panels, Conflict Catcher 8 is a good investment.

If you're still reading and your problem hasn't been resolved, you can try one last thing: namely, a clean System software installation.

How to perform a clean System reinstallation

A System reinstallation is a drastic final step. If nothing so far has corrected your startup problems, a clean System reinstallation, also known as a clean install, very well may. I saved this solution for last because it's the biggest hassle, and you don't want to go through the trouble if something easier can correct the problem. So if you're doing a clean install, it's more or less your last hope.

Don't worry. This solution corrects all but the most horrifying and malignant of problems. So let's get to it.

The Mac OS installer contains a barely hidden feature that lets you perform a clean install automatically, with no muss or fuss. Here's how:

1. **Start up or restart your Mac with the Mac OS 9 CD in your CD-ROM drive.**

   Remember, you have to hold the C key to boot from the CD.

2. **Launch the Install Mac OS 9 program.**

3. **Click Continue in the first screen you see.**

   The Select Destination screen appears.

4. **If you have more than one hard disk, choose the appropriate one.**

5. **Click the Options button.**

6. **Click the check box for Perform Clean Installation (see Figure 18-7), and then click OK.**

   When the Install Mac OS program is finished, you have a brand-spanking-new System Folder on your hard disk. Your old System Folder has been renamed Previous System Folder. Nothing has been removed from it.

Figure 18-7:
The clean installation option appears.

☑ **Perform Clean Installation**

Installs a completely new System Folder that does not include your third-party extensions, control panels, or fonts. System software and application preferences are reset to their default settings.

[Cancel] [**OK**]

Clean versus regular installation

To understand why you need to do a clean install, or even what a clean install is, you have to understand a little about how the Install Mac OS program works and what resources are.

Resources are the building blocks from which all programs, control panels, extensions, and so on are built. The Install Mac OS program is, technically, a resource installer. It installs the resources that become programs, control panels, extensions, and so on.

And the Install Mac OS program is very smart about which resources it installs. It looks at your hard disk; then, if it sees a System Folder containing System and Finder, it installs only the resources it thinks you need. So, for example, if the Install Mac OS program sees a System and a Finder, it looks to see whether they contain the proper resources. If they do, Install Mac OS doesn't install anything, even if the resources are damaged.

Therein lies the rub. The Install Mac OS program can sometimes outsmart itself. If the reason your Mac is crashing is that a resource inside the System, the Finder, a control panel, or an extension has become damaged or corrupted, the Install Mac OS program may not replace the defective resource if you perform a Regular Install.

A clean install, on the other hand, ensures that every single file and every single resource is replaced with a brand-spanking-new one. In fact, a clean install gives you a brand new System Folder.

The folder called Previous System Folder contains all your old third-party extensions, control panels, and fonts. Because it's possible, even likely, that one of these items contributed to your problem, I recommend that you reinstall them one item at a time. In other words, move one extension or control panel from Previous System Folder into the new System Folder's icon. Then restart and work for a while to see whether any problems occur before reinstalling another extension or control panel.

It's a good idea to trash the System and Finder in the Previous System Folder as soon as possible after performing the clean install. It's simply a bad idea to have two System Folders on one hard disk, and as long as Previous System Folder has a System and a Finder in it, your Mac could confuse Previous System Folder with the real System Folder, and that confusion could cause you major heartache. So delete the old System and Finder files, the ones in the Previous System Folder, now. Just in case. Thanks.

Don't forget that the System Folder is smart. If you drag a control panel or extension onto its icon (but not into its open window), it puts the file in the proper folder for you.

Part IV
The Part of Tens

The 5th Wave   By Rich Tennant

In this part . . .

We're in the home stretch now. Just three more chapters.

These last three are a little different — they're kind of like long top-ten lists. I'd like you to believe that it's because I'm a big fan of Dave Letterman, but the truth is, IDG Books has always put a "Part of Tens" in books with ...*For Dummies* in their titles, and this book continues the tradition. Because IDG pays me, I'm doing these chapters their way. (Actually, it's kind of fun.)

First, I briefly describe ten (actually, 11) pieces of Mac OS 9 that you might someday need (and that haven't been discussed much previously). I tell you what they do and why you might need them. A few might actually be useful to you someday.

I then move on to a subject near and dear to my heart: Ten awesome things for your Mac that are worth spending money on.

But wait, there's one more. How would you like the addresses of ten thoroughly cool Web sites that will help you use and enjoy your Mac more? You want 'em? You got 'em.

Chapter 19

At Least Ten Pieces of Mac OS 9 That You Might Someday Need

· ·

· ·

*W*hen you run the Mac OS 9 installer, you can choose to install or not install a bunch of things.

If you just perform a standard installation, the Install Mac OS 9 program automatically installs Internet Access, Apple Remote Access, Personal Web Sharing, Text-to-Speech, Mac OS Runtime for Java, and ColorSync, plus the core components of Mac OS 9. (You can choose a custom installation and elect not to install one or more of these components. Custom installations are covered in Appendix A.)

In addition to having pieces installed automatically, you can choose a custom installation and also install English Speech Recognition, Language Kits, Network Assistant Client, CloseView, and Easy Access.

In this chapter, I tell you what each of these pieces of Mac OS does and whether or not it makes sense for you to install it. Unfortunately, due to space limitations, I can't really explain how to use each of these potentially useful goodies. Instead, I briefly describe each one and then provide some insights on whether you need it or not.

Almost everything mentioned in this chapter includes Mac OS Help, Balloon Help, or both. Use them to discover more about how these goodies work.

Internet Access

The Internet Access installation consists of a set of tools for accessing the Internet. Included in this set are several extensions, control panels, and utilities required to access the Internet, plus Microsoft Internet Explorer, Microsoft Outlook Express, and Netscape Communicator. An installation of all the pieces in the Internet Access software package uses about 64MB of hard disk space.

Internet Access is installed automatically unless you choose a custom install (see Appendix A).

Bob sez: If you use the Internet, of course you need this stuff. But if you don't use your Mac to connect to the Internet and don't expect to, you can save almost 64 megs of disk space by choosing not to install it. But (and this is getting to be a big *but*), many programs today provide their documentation in HTML format. To read that documentation, you need a browser — Microsoft Internet Explorer or Netscape Communicator. I'd install at least one browser on my hard disk even if I weren't planning on using the Internet.

Apple Remote Access

The Apple Remote Access installation consists of the tools you need to connect to a remote Mac OS computer by modem (direct) or through the Internet using PPP and a modem. The installation includes the Apple Remote Access software, Apple Remote Access Modem Scripts, and X.25 Modem scripts. An installation of all the pieces in the Apple Remote Access package uses about 2.5MB of hard disk space.

Apple Remote Access is installed automatically unless you choose a custom install (see Appendix A).

Bob sez: If you intend to use your Mac to connect to other Macs or to the Internet by modem, by all means install it. If you don't, don't.

Personal Web Sharing

The Personal Web Sharing installation consists of software that allows others to share documents on your computer through the Web. The installation includes the Personal Web Sharing control panel and Control Strip module, plus documentation. An installation of all the pieces in the Personal Web Sharing package uses about 1MB of hard disk space.

Personal Web Sharing is installed automatically unless you choose a custom install (see Appendix A).

Bob sez: If you want to make files on your Mac available to others through the Web, by all means install it. If you don't, don't.

Personal Web Sharing works only while your Mac is connected to the Internet. In other words, if you use a modem, this stuff won't be a lot of use to you unless you keep your modem connected to the Internet 24 hours a day.

Text-to-Speech

The Text-to-Speech installation consists of software — extensions and voice files — you need to have your computer read text and alert messages aloud. A complete installation includes the actual Text-to-Speech software, a set of high-quality voices, MacinTalk3 and MacinTalk Pro, plus Speech Manager. An installation of all the pieces uses about 21MB of disk space.

Text-to-Speech is installed automatically unless you choose a custom install (see Appendix A).

Bob sez: Text-to-Speech is kind of cool, but I don't use it all that often. The talking alerts are fun, but again, I don't use them much. And this stuff does use a little bit of RAM. If you're tight on disk space or memory, you can probably do without it.

Mac OS Runtime for Java

Mac OS Runtime for Java (MRJ) is Apple's version of Java. Java is a programming language (or a platform, depending on who you ask) that's most frequently used in Web pages you view on the Internet. Stand-alone Java programs, mostly called *applets,* are beginning to become available as well.

MRJ lets you run programs written in Java on your Mac with the included Applet Runner program, with most popular Web browsers, or with any other Java-enabled Mac OS application.

A complete installation of Mac OS Runtime for Java includes the MRJ software, the Apple Applet Runner and demonstration applets, and two extensions necessary for reading foreign language text and using MRJ with older Macs.

Mac OS Runtime for Java is installed automatically unless you choose a custom install (see Appendix A).

Bob sez: If you use the Internet (and who doesn't these days), use stand-alone Java applets, or use a Java-enabled Mac OS program, this is the implementation of Java you want. It's better and faster than any before it. It will cost you about 12MB of disk space.

ColorSync

The ColorSync installation consists of software that helps ensure color accuracy when scanning, printing, and working with color images. A complete installation includes the ColorSync software, ColorSync profiles for a variety of monitors, scanners, and printers, and Photoshop plug-ins that let you use ColorSync from Adobe Photoshop. An installation of all the pieces of ColorSync uses about 6MB of disk space.

ColorSync is installed automatically unless you choose a custom install (see Appendix A).

Bob sez: If you're not a graphics artist working with color files and calibrating monitors and printers to achieve accurate color matching, you don't need it.

English Speech Recognition

English Speech Recognition allows your Mac to recognize and respond to human speech, so you can say stuff like "Get my mail" to your Mac and have it actually get your mail. A complete installation consists of the English Speech Recognition software and uses about 2.5MB of disk space.

English Speech Recognition is not installed unless you explicitly choose to install it using a custom install (see Appendix A).

Bob sez: It's clever and kind of fun, but it uses a bit of RAM and a few megs of hard disk space and requires a microphone. And I've never been able to get it to work well enough to continue using it beyond a few days. Still, it's kind of neat (and it's a freebie), so you may want to install it and check it out just for kicks.

Language Kits

Language Kits enable you to use languages other than United States English with Mac OS. You can install one or several language kits, which vary widely in disk space requirements. Languages such as Japanese and the two Chinese options take up 10MB to 30MB of disk space, whereas Arabic and Hebrew use less than 1MB each.

Language Kits are not installed unless you explicitly choose to install them using a custom install (see Appendix A).

Bob sez: If you use your Mac for only English language stuff, you don't need them. If you need one of the foreign languages just mentioned, install the one you need.

Network Assistant Client

If your Mac is on a network, your network administrator may use Network Assistant software to manage the network — to keep track of computers, the versions of Mac OS they use, their status on the network, and so on. Chances are that your administrator will install Network Assistant for you if you need it, or ask you to do it.

Network Assistant is not installed unless you explicitly choose to install it (see Appendix A).

Bob sez: If you manage a network of Macs or are part of one, install this software, which will be used by the Network Assistant application to keep track of your computer. If no one in your office uses Network Assistant or if you have a single Mac, don't bother.

Two More Things You Should Know About

A few items are usually not installed when you choose the Easy Install option in the Mac OS 9 Installer program. I talk about them in Appendix A.

Two other items that are installed only with a custom installation (see Appendix A) are well worth knowing about. They're the Universal Access control panels: Easy Access and CloseView.

Easy Access

Easy Access, which is shown in Figure 19-1 is a control panel designed primarily for people with impaired mobility. That doesn't mean it might not come in handy for anyone.

Figure 19-1:
The Easy Access control panel may come in handy for any user.

Easy Access lets you do three things:

- ✔ Use the numeric keypad on your keyboard (instead of the mouse) to control the cursor on the screen
- ✔ Type keyboard shortcuts without having to press both keys at the same time
- ✔ Type very slowly

Mouse Keys

When you turn on Mouse Keys, the numeric keypad replaces the mouse in controlling the cursor. The 5 key is the mouse button; the 0 key is the click and hold button. The rest of the numbers control the cursor direction, as shown in Figure 19-2.

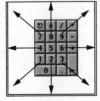

Figure 19-2:
The numeric keypad controls the cursor.

The keyboard shortcut ⌘+Shift+Clear toggles Mouse Keys on and off. If you have the audio feedback option checked, you'll hear a whoop when Mouse Keys is turned on and another when it's turned off.

The Mouse Keys options control the delay before movement occurs (after you press the key) and the speed at which the cursor travels across the screen.

Slow Keys

Slow Keys delays the Mac's recognition of keystrokes. In other words, if the acceptance delay is set to Long, you would have to hold down a key for almost two seconds for it to be recognized. This feature is designed to filter out inadvertent and accidental keypresses.

Sticky Keys

Sticky Keys lets you type keyboard shortcuts one key at a time. In other words, to open an icon, you would ordinarily press the Command and O keys simultaneously. Sticky Keys makes it possible to press the Command key first and then the O key after it.

The keyboard shortcut for turning Sticky Keys on and off is to press the Shift key five times in rapid succession. To lock the modifier key down, press it twice in rapid succession.

When you press the modifier key, you see a little icon in the upper-right corner of your menu bar that gives you visual feedback on the state of Sticky Keys.

Bob sez: Easy Access can come in handy. For example, in programs that don't have a nudge command for moving objects one pixel at a time using the arrow keys, Mouse Keys makes a decent substitute. It may be worth keeping around for this feature alone. You can always turn it off using Extensions Manager.

CloseView

CloseView blows up your screen. No, it doesn't make it explode; it enlarges the image, and you can do it with keyboard shortcuts.

The CloseView control panel appears in Figure 19-3. The black frame around it is the area that will be displayed when you turn magnification on. CloseView also lets you reverse your screen's video, so that text appears white on a black background. You can use this feature with or without screen magnification. That's useful for users with visual impairments who want a high-contrast display.

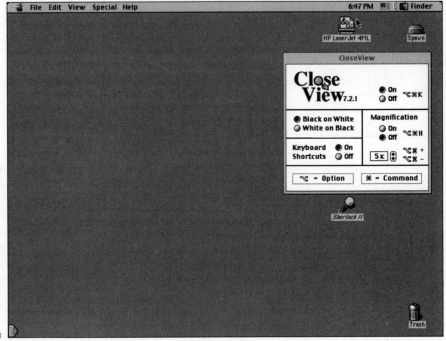

Figure 19-3:
If I turn on magnifica-tion now, the area in the frame will be mag-nified, and fill the screen.

CloseView uses a lot of memory — from a few hundred K to more than a thou-sand K, depending on the resolution and the number of colors you're using. If you can afford the RAM, it's a useful little doohickey to have around. It can give you a zoom feature in programs that don't allow zooming. On the other hand, hundreds of K is a lot of RAM to waste if you don't use CloseView often.

Bob sez: Install it but turn it off using Extensions Manager. If you need it, enable it in Extensions Manager and restart.

Chapter 20

Ten Ways to Make Your Mac Better by Throwing Money at It

· ·

In This Chapter

▶ Stuff I think you ought to buy

· ·

This is one of my favorite chapters. As you've probably figured out by now, I love souping up my Mac. I live to find ways of working smarter, saving time, and saving hand motion. And I revel in tweaking my Mac and Mac OS 9. So it gives me great pleasure to share this chapter, my personal top ten (actually, eleven, but don't tell my editor) things you can buy for your Mac to tweak it and make it faster, easier to use, and (I hope) more fun.

The items listed in this chapter are things I have, use every day, love dearly, and would buy again:

✔ **RAM:** It's worth every penny. If you have anything less than 64MB in your Mac, you'll like it a lot better if you upgrade to 64MB or more. If you like to do a few things at once, 64 or more megs of RAM will make you a happier camper. (For what it's worth, RAM has never been cheaper than it is today.)

✔ **Backup software:** The only two kinds of Macintosh users are those who have lost data and those who are going to. If your work means anything to you, get something that helps automate the task of backing up your files. Retrospect or Retrospect Express, both from Dantz Development, are the names to trust. And please, please read Appendix B.

✔ **A great monitor:** You'll spend less time scrolling and rearranging windows. You'll spend more of your time getting actual work done, which is a good thing, right? If you still have a tiny monitor, get a bigger one. I use a multisync Sony 20sfII and love it to death. For what it's worth, I also love my 15-inch Apple flat-panel Studio Display a lot.

- **Modem:** Your capacity to communicate will increase tenfold. Join an online service, surf the Internet, e-mail your friends, and much, much more. Get a modem that can do 56 Kbps. A 14.4 Kbps modem doesn't cut it anymore; nor does a 28.8. If you're a real Internet hound, check out ISDN, ADSL, or cable modems for even faster Net access.

- **Games:** I just love MYTH II from Bungie Software. It may just be the best game ever invented. I still like all the episodes of You Don't Know Jack. The recently released Sim City 3000 and Quake III Arena are cool, too. My point: Gaming on the Mac has never been better.

- **CD-ROMs:** Some great games, references, and educational titles are out there. You'll love 'em, and so will your kids.

- **Some big honking speakers with a subwoofer:** Turn your boring Mac into a multimedia entertainment and education center. If you don't have great external speakers, you absolutely need them if you want the full CD-ROM or game experience on your Mac. Crank it up!

- **Action Files:** This utility puts the Mac OS 9 Open and Save dialog boxes on steroids. Basically, it adds a menu bar that lets you get info, duplicate, create an alias, label, move to trash, and rename files and folders. Plus it has menus and keyboard shortcuts for easy, fast access to frequently used files and folders. Download a demo from www.actionutilities.com/. Use it for a week, and you'll wonder how you lived without it.

- **QuicKeys or OneClick:** These utilities create macros called shortcuts that can perform a task or a series of tasks (a sequence) with a single command — a keystroke or mouse click. They're like AppleScript, only better. Download a QuicKeys demo from www.cesoft.com. A demo wasn't available for OneClick when I wrote this, but you may want to check www.westcodesoft.com and see whether perhaps one is there now.

- **A PowerBook or an iBook:** Because one Mac is never enough.

- **A new desktop CPU:** If you have any money left, consider upgrading to a newer, faster Mac. They've never been faster, cheaper, or better equipped.

So there you have it: Eleven awesome ways to spend a big chunk of change. So ladies and gentlemen, start your checkbooks. Go forth, throw money at your Mac, and most of all, have fun.

Chapter 21

Ten Great Web Sites for Mac Enthusiasts

In This Chapter

▶ Some Mac Web sites you ought to know about

▶ Some more Mac Web sites you ought to know about

A s much as I would love to think that this book will tell you everything you need to know about using your Mac, I know better. You have a lot more to discover about using your Mac, and new tools and products come out almost daily.

The best way to gather more information than you could ever possibly soak up about all things Macintosh is to hop onto the Web. There, you'll find news, free and shareware software to download, troubleshooting sites, and lots of places to shop. So make sure you've read Chapter 17 and are set up for the Internet, because this chapter is all about finding cool stuff on the Web that will help you use your Mac better while having lots of fun.

The sites in this chapter are the best, most chock-full o' stuff places on the Web for Mac users. By the time you finish checking out these ten Web sites, you'll know so much about your Mac that you'll feel like your brain is in danger of exploding. On the other hand, you may just be a whole lot smarter. Happy surfing!

MacFixit

```
http://www.macfixit.com
```

Mac writer and consultant Ted Landau has put together an awesome troubleshooting site that will help you solve common problems and keep up on compatibility issues with new system software and third-party products. The site is searchable, too.

MacinTouch

http://www.macintouch.com

For the latest in Mac news, updated every single day, check out MacinTouch. Authored by longtime *MacWeek* columnist Ric Ford and his staff of news hounds, this site will keep you on the bleeding-edge of Mac news, including software updates, virus alerts, and Apple happenings.

Info-Mac HyperArchives

http://hyperarchive.lcs.mit.edu/HyperArchive.html

Looking for free or shareware stuff? Try Info-Mac HyperArchives. It's not the most glamorous site in the world, but you can search for software by keyword.

Apple Tech Info Library

http://til.info.apple.com

Do you have a technical question about Mac OS or an Apple product? March your question right over to the Tech Info Library, Apple's searchable archives of tech notes, software update information, and documentation. The library is especially useful if you need info about your old Mac. Apple has archived all its info here; just type the keyword you're interested in, and choose from a list of helpful documents. The site even has tools that can help narrow your search.

RAMSeeker

http://www.macseek.com/

One of the best ways to make your Mac better is to buy more RAM. As cheap as RAM is, the price you pay can vary quite a lot. The best way I know to get the lowdown on RAM prices is RAMSeeker, which organizes memory prices by Mac type.

MacCentral

http://www.maccentral.com

Here's another great source of up-to-the-minute Macintosh news, along with a whole bunch of cool columns and troubleshooting information. I could be biased, because I'm a columnist for *MacCentral,* but I don't think so. It's a great site, with lots of useful info.

Outpost.com

http://www.outpost.com

This site is all about buying stuff. You'll find lots of Mac products, including Apple CPUs and accessories. Their prices are very good, and they offer free shipping.

EveryMac

http://www.everymac.com

The author of this site claims that it is "the complete guide of every Macintosh, Mac Compatible, and upgrade card in the world." You can't argue with that.

Inside Mac games

http://www.imgmagazine.com

The best of the Mac gaming sites, at least in my humble opinion.

DealMac

http://www.deal-mac.com

Shopping for Mac stuff? Go to DealMac first to find out about sale prices, rebates, and other bargain opportunities.

Part V
Appendixes

The 5th Wave   By Rich Tennant

ORIGINAL VAN-GOGH-OF-THE-MONTH CLUB

"SINCE WE BEGAN ON-LINE SHOPPING, I JUST DON'T KNOW WHERE THE MONEY'S GOING."

In this part . . .

I saved some important topics for last because, as an intelligent Mac user, you already know much of what I cover in these appendixes.

First, I cover installing Mac OS 9. The whole process has become quite easy with this version of the System software. You may wonder why I bothered to write about it.

Second, I deal with the whole process of backing up. You know that your files are important, and I'm sure that you already know how to copy files from your hard disk to a floppy or some other form of media. But just in case you don't, read this appendix.

Appendix A

Anyone Can Install Mac OS 9

● ●

*T*he Mac OS 9 CD-ROM can install more than just System software. So in the first section, I discuss the plain vanilla installation that happens if you just keep clicking OK and Continue and Agree.

After that, I explain how to install each item that requires a separate installation.

Finally, several other optional pieces of System software — such as Easy Access and CloseView (see Chapter 19) — require a separate custom installation process in the main Mac OS installer program. I cover them in the final section.

If the reason you're installing (actually reinstalling) Mac OS 9 is that your Mac is acting up, you may need to perform a clean install. See the "If You Crash at Startup" section in Chapter 18.

The procedure for installing Mac OS 9 is the same regardless of whether you're upgrading from an earlier version of System software or installing Mac OS 9 on an empty hard disk.

Ready? Take a deep breath.

Installing Mac OS 9

Before we get ready to install, here are a few bits of information you'll need.

Hard disk drivers are bits of computer code installed by the software that formatted your hard disk. They manage how the disk talks to the Mac. Old disk drivers may be incompatible with new system software, so it's always a good idea to check with the manufacturer before installing a new version of Mac OS if you have a non-Apple hard disk. The drivers of Apple hard disks are updated automatically as part of the installation process.

If you have a non-Apple hard disk, you should contact its manufacturer before installing Mac OS 9. This could be important. You need to know whether you need to update your hard disk drivers. Although you may be able to install Mac OS 9 without updating your hard disk drivers, it's a bad idea. Your Mac may not boot after the installation if your current hard disk drivers are incompatible with Mac OS 9.

To install Mac OS 9, follow these steps:

1. **Shut down your Macintosh if it's turned on.**

2. **Insert the Mac OS 9 CD-ROM disc and turn on your Mac.**

   If you're starting from a CD, hold down the C key on your keyboard.

   Your Mac starts up.

3. **Launch the Install Mac OS 9 program.**

   You see a comforting welcome screen like the one in Figure A-1. (Are you beginning to detect a pattern? Macs are warmer and fuzzier than other personal computers.)

Figure A-1: The opening screen of the Install Mac OS 9 program.

4. **Click the Continue button.**

   The Select Destination dialog box appears.

5. **From the pop-up Destination Disk menu, choose a disk to install Mac OS 9 onto.**

   If you have only one hard disk, the nice installer program automatically selects it for you.

6. **Click the Select button.**

7. **Now read some important information about this software.**

   Print it and read it. Really. It's important, and I'm not going to repeat it all here.

8. **Click the Continue button.**

   The License Agreement window appears.

9. **Read the License Agreement if you like, and then click the Continue button.**

10. **You may have to click an Agree button now.**

    I had to with some versions of the installer and didn't have to with others. Eventually the Install Software screen appears, as shown in Figure A-2. This is where you choose what software you want to install.

Figure A-2:
The Install
Software
dialog box,
ready to
rock.

11. **Do one of the following:**

    a. For a normal (easy) install, just click Start.

    Internet Access, Apple Remote Access, Personal Web Sharing, Text-to-Speech, Mac OS Runtime for Java, and ColorSync are installed along with the basic system software.

    b. If you want to add or delete components now, click the Customize button and manually select the components you want installed. Then click Start.

    Refer to Chapter 19 to find out what they are and what they do.

The installer checks your destination disk with Disk First Aid to make sure it's in tip-top shape. It then updates your hard disk drivers automatically if you have an Apple hard disk.

After whirring and clicking for a while, your Mac politely informs you that the installation was successful. Quit, restart your Mac, and away you go.

If you have more than one hard disk or a hard disk that wasn't made by Apple, you may see a warning that the installer is not going to try to update these disks. That's okay; it's what you want.

That's it. Your hard disk now has Mac OS 9 installed. Piece of cake. The waiting is the hardest part. Onward!

Custom Installs

To install or remove Internet Access, Apple Remote Access, Personal Web Sharing, Text-to-Speech, Mac OS Runtime for Java, ColorSync, English Speech Recognition, Language Kits, or Network Assistant Client, click the Customize button on the Install Software screen, and then check or uncheck their names before clicking the Start button.

Don't forget that Internet Access, Apple Remote Access, Personal Web Sharing, Text-to-Speech, Mac OS Runtime for Java, and ColorSync were probably installed when you first installed Mac OS 9. Unless you manually deselected them when you first installed Mac OS 9, they're already installed. The instructions that follow show you how to install them if you haven't already.

Follow the instructions in the first section of this chapter right up to the part where you click the Start button. Then, instead of clicking the Start button, click the Customize button. The Custom Installation and Removal dialog box appears. Click next to the names of the options you want to install, and choose Custom Installation from the Installation mode pop-up menu.

You can quickly check an item's installation status (as shown in Figure A-3); it changes depending on whether or not its box is checked.

Figure A-3:
All checked items will be installed when I click Start.

In this example, the Mac OS 9, Internet Access, Apple Remote Access, Mac OS Runtime for Java, and ColorSync installers will run in sequence when I click Start.

The Install Mac OS 9 program is nothing more than a little launcher program that launches the installer for each piece of System software. Don't believe me? Look in the folder called Software Installers. Each custom installation option has its own personal installer program. If you want to save time, you can launch these installers separately and avoid dealing with the Install Mac OS 9 program completely.

Optional Mac OS Items

Some Mac OS components — including useful ones such as Easy Access and CloseView — require a separate installation using the Custom Install feature.

To install optional components, follow the directions in the first section of this appendix right up to the part where you click the Start button. Instead of clicking the Start button, click the Customize button. Now deselect everything but Mac OS 9.

Now choose Customized Installation from the Installation mode pop-up menu. A new dialog box appears where you can select individual Mac OS 9 features to install (see Figure A-4). You can find Easy Access and CloseView in the Universal Access folder.

Figure A-4:
The Select
Mac OS 9
Features to
Install
dialog box,
ready to
rock.

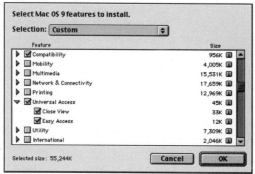

When you've selected the items you want to install, click OK and then click the Start button or press Return.

After some whirring and clicking, you're told that the installation was successful. Click the Quit button.

Appendix B

Back Up Now or Regret It Later

- -

Although Macs are generally reliable beasts, someday your hard disk will die. I promise. They all do. And if you haven't backed up your hard disk, there's a good chance that you'll never see your files again. And if you do see them again, it will only be after paying Scott at the DriveSavers data recovery service a king's ransom, with no guarantee of success. DriveSavers is the premier recoverer of lost data on hard disks. They do good work and can often recover stuff nobody else could. (Ask the Simpsons' producers about the "almost-lost" episodes.) They charge accordingly.

I'm going to give you DriveSavers' phone number. It's 415-883-4232. Now pray you never need it. Back up often, and you won't. If, somehow, none of this sinks in, tell Scott I said Hi.

In other words, you absolutely, positively, without question MUST BACK UP. Just as you've adopted the Shut Down command and made it a habit, you must remember to back up your hard disk and back it up often.

How often is often? That depends on you. How much work can you afford to lose? If the answer is that losing everything you did yesterday would put you out of business, you need to back up daily or possibly twice a day. If you would only lose a few unimportant letters, you can back up less frequently.

Backing Up Is (Not) Hard to Do

You can back up your hard disk in lots of ways. Some are better than others.

The manual, "brute force" method

Drag your files a few at a time to floppy or other removable disks.

Yuk. If it sounds pretty awful, trust me, it is. It takes forever; you can't really tell if you've copied every file; and there's no way to copy only the files that have been modified since your last backup. Almost nobody sticks with this method for long.

Commercial backup software

You must buy backup software if you don't already have some. There's nothing else in this book that I insist that you buy.

For some unfathomable reason, Apple has almost never seen fit to provide backup software with new Macs or include it with System software releases. I know some Performas had a crummy backup program, but Apple has left millions of Mac owners clueless.

Mac owners get nothing more than a brief passage regarding backing up in the Macintosh *User's Guide.* Information on backing up ought to be in big red letters, in the first chapter, and include a warning from the Surgeon General or something. And it wouldn't kill them to provide a backup utility either. Sheesh, even DOS has a backup command, albeit a lousy one. C'mon, Apple, give Mac owners a fair shake. At least include the lame Apple Backup program some Performa owners got.

Fortunately, plenty of very good backup programs are available for well under $150, including the excellent Retrospect (around $150) and Retrospect Express (around $50) from Dantz Development. If you want the best, most flexible, most powerful, top-of-the-line backup software, spend a little more and pop for Retrospect.

Backup software automates the task of backing up. The backup software remembers what is on each backup disk and backs up only files that have been modified since the last backup. Your first backup with commercial software should take anywhere from an hour to many hours and use a couple of hundred 1.4MB floppy disks (Zip, Jaz, CD-R, CD-RW, Orb, or magneto-optical disks, or any kind of tape backup are better). Subsequent backups, called incremental backups in backup-software parlance, should take only a few minutes.

Be sure to label the disks that you use for your backups because, during incremental backups, the backup software is going to ask you to "Please insert backup disk 7." If you haven't labeled your media clearly, you have a problem.

Why You Need Two Sets of Backup Disks

You're a good soldier. You back up regularly. You think you're immune.

Now picture this: One day you take a floppy disk to QuicKopyLazerPrintz to print your resume on their laser printer. You make a few changes while at QuicKopyLazerPrintz and take the floppy home and stick it into your Mac.

Virus trivia

A computer virus, in case you missed it in *Time* or *Newsweek,* is a nasty little piece of computer code that replicates and spreads from disk to disk. Most viruses cause your Mac to misbehave; some viruses can destroy files or erase disks with no warning.

If you use disks that have been inserted in other computers, you need some form of virus-detection software. If you download and use files from Web and FTP sites on the Internet, you need some form of virus detection as well.

Don't worry too much if you download files from commercial online services such as America Online or CompuServe. They are very conscientious about viral infections. Do worry about that Web site called Pirate's Den that an unsavory friend told you about.

On the commercial front, Virex and Norton Anti-Virus (formerly Symantec Anti-Virus) each have their fans. I'm using Virex right now, but I've used NAV for years and have never had a virus while using either program.

The big advantage of buying a commercial antivirus program is that the publisher will contact you each time a virus is discovered and provide you with a software update to protect you against the new strain. Or, for a fee, the publisher can send you a new version of the software every time a new virus is found.

Many shareware and freeware antivirus solutions are available, but none that I know of are as trustworthy as Virex or Norton.

If you use only commercial software and don't download files from Web sites with strange names, you have a very low risk of infection. On the other hand, if you swap disks with friends regularly, shuttle disks back and forth to other Macs, use your disks at service bureaus or copy shops, or download files from various and sundry places on the Internet, you are at risk.

If you're at risk, do yourself a favor and buy a commercial antivirus program.

Unbeknownst to you, the floppy became infected with a computer virus at QuicKopyLazerPrintz. (I discuss viruses in the nearby "Virus trivia" sidebar.) When you insert the disk into your Mac, the infection spreads to your hard disk like wildfire.

Then you back up. Your backup software, believing that all the infected files have been recently modified (well, they have been — they were infected with a virus!), proceeds to back them up. You notice that the backup takes a little longer than usual, but otherwise, things seem to be okay.

A few days later, your Mac starts acting strangely. You borrow a copy of that excellent virus-detection software, Virex or Norton Anti-Virus (formerly Symantec Anti-Virus), and discover that your hard disk is infected. "Aha," you exclaim. "I've been a good little Mac user, backing up regularly. I'll just restore everything from my backup disks."

Not so fast, bucko. The files on your backup disks are also infected.

This scenario demonstrates why you need multiple backups. If you have several sets of backup disks, chances are pretty good that one of the sets is clean.

I keep three backup sets. I use one set on even-numbered days, one on odd-numbered days, and I update the third set once a week and store it in my bank's vault. This scheme ensures that no matter what happens, even if my office burns, floods, is destroyed by a tornado or a hurricane, or is robbed, I won't lose more than a few days' worth of work. I can live with that.

Appendix C

What Mac OS 9.1 Brings to the Party

● ●

*J*ust before the dawning of the year 2001, Apple released the latest in its series of regular Mac OS update releases, Mac OS 9.1. If you use Mac OS 9 (and I'm betting you do — you're reading this book...), you'd be wise to consider the upgrade to OS 9.1. It fixes lots of little bug-like things ("issues") you may have experienced in OS 9.0-whatever (9.0, 9.0.1, 9.0.4, and so on). It replaces many System Folder components with new, better, sometimes faster versions. And it adds a cool new Finder feature that I tell you about in this appendix.

So what are you waiting for? Visit Apple's Web site (www.apple.com) and get your copy of Mac OS 9.1 today. (Upgrade pricing and details haven't been set at press time, or I'd tell you what the deal is.) I'll wait. When you get back, I'll give you a quick rundown of what's new and improved in OS 9.1.

To find out what version of Mac OS you're currently using, read the tip on page 16 of Chapter 1.

Installing OS 9.1 is exactly the same as installing OS 9.0. See Appendix A for instructions.

What's New and Improved in OS 9.1?

What's new and improved in OS 9.1? Almost everything. Really. From Aliases to Virtual Memory, almost every piece of OS 9 has been overhauled, improved, de-bugged, made faster (in a few cases) and, at least in theory, more reliable.

Interestingly, only a few things have changed in OS 9.1 that OS 9.0 users will notice, as most of the improvements went on under the hood, so to speak. Still, a few things *do* look different, so let's take a peek...

Macs now sport a "Window" menu!

That's right. The most noticeable change between OS 9 and OS 9.1 is the addition of the Window menu to the Finder, as shown in Figure C-1.

Bill Gates must be cackling in his castle. A "Window" menu on every Mac! Who'd have thunk?

Okay. Now for the bad news: It only works for Finder windows, not for windows in applications. So you can't choose Letter to Pop from the Window menu in the Finder. Unfortunately. Still, it's a pretty nice improvement.

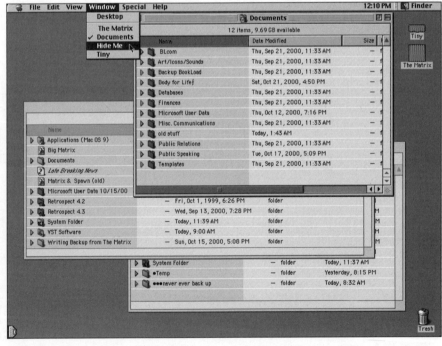

Figure C-1:
The Finder's new Window menu allows you to bring any Finder window, even one hidden behind others, to the front.

There is good news. This new-fangled Window menu *does* come with some very useful keyboard shortcuts. When selecting an item from the Window menu, hold down:

- ⌘ to close that window.
- ⌘+Shift to both close and put away that pop-up window.
- ⌘+Option to expand that window and close all other windows.
- Control to expand that window and minimize all other windows. (This one is my favorite!)
- Control-Option to make that window active and expand all other open windows behind it.

And speaking of Finder menus, two old favorite menu items get new keyboard shortcuts in 9.1:

- Empty Trash is ⌘+Shift+Delete. Yea!
- View Options is ⌘+J.

Control panel makeovers

A handful of control panels have received makeovers in version 9.1 and one new one — USB Printer Sharing — has been added. Here's the rundown:

Energy Saver

The Energy Saver control panel gets a new tab called Notification, which provides some new options for automated shutdowns. (See Figure C-2.)

Figure C-2: The Notification tab gives you some new options before an automatic shutdown.

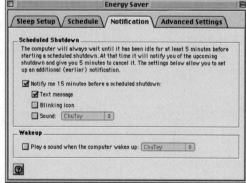

General Controls

The General Controls control panel gets a minor facelift, but all of its six functions remain. (See Figure C-3.)

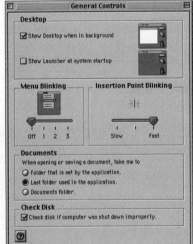

Figure C-3:
The General
Controls
control
panel gets a
minor
facelift.

Notice in Figure C-3 that the Menu Blinking and Insertion Point Blinking controls are now sliders. In Mac OS version 9, they were radio buttons. And if you don't believe me, take a gander at Figure 14-15 on page 252.

One other thing about General Controls is that it now works with Multiple Users. So your settings are *your* settings, even if you share a Mac with someone else and use Multiple Users.

Mouse

The Mouse control panel gets a very minor facelift, with new mouse pictures. (See Figure C-4.) The hockey-puck mouse is gone and is replaced by pictures of the sleek Pro mouse. (See Figure 14-19 on page 258 for comparison.)

Figure C-4:
The new
Mouse con-
trol panel
has new
mouse
graphics.
Wow.

Sound

The Sound control panel gets a new look and feel (as shown in Figure C-5) plus a new tab called Speakers. I think you'll find it prettier than the old control panel (refer to Figure 14-22 on page 264).

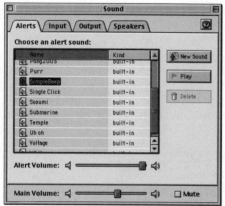

Figure C-5:
The new Sound control panel has a more Mac-like look and feel, but works the same as before.

The Speakers tab automatically identifies certain types of speaker systems and provides additional features such as left and right volume controls and a speaker test, as shown in Figure C-6.

What kind of speakers? Best I can tell, it recognizes speakers connected through USB, like my Harmon-Kardon SoundSticks shown in Figure C-6.

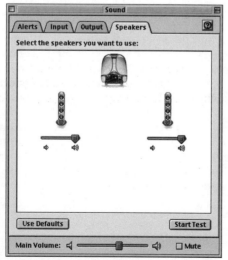

Figure C-6:
The new Speakers tab provides additional features for certain types of speakers.

Startup Disk

The new Startup Disk control panel lets you choose a disk *and a System Folder*, as shown in Figure C-7. In the figure, I have two bootable volumes (hard disks or disk partitions are called *volumes*) to choose from: Tiny, which has OS 9.1 on it, and The Matrix, which has OS 9.0.4 on it.

A Restart button is also new to this control panel — what a handy touch.

This feature was added for better compatibility with Mac OS X. In the past, the rule was: 1 System Folder per volume, period. The jury is still out on how safe it is to keep multiple OS 8 or 9 System Folders on a single volume (for example, a disk partition, removable disk such as Jaz or Orb, or a hard disk) using this control panel. I wouldn't advise it. If you want to use two System Folders, use two volumes (partitions) or two different hard drives.

Figure C-7:
The new
Startup Disk
control
panel lets
you choose
a disk and a
System
Folder.

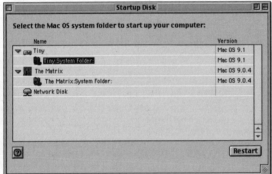

USB Printer Sharing

Hey! USB Printer Sharing is a brand-new control panel that lets you share USB printers on your network (see Figure C-8). If your computer is connected to a TCP/IP network, you can let other Macintoshes on the network print to a USB printer connected to your computer, or you can print on a USB printer connected to another Mac on your network.

To use this feature, open the USB Printer Sharing control panel (Apple Menu➪ Control Panels➪USB Printer Sharing) and then click the Start button to turn on USB Printer Sharing. Click the My Printers tab and choose the USB printer that you want to share with your network-mates. Click the Network Printers tab to see what printers are available to you on the network. That's it — it's that simple.

Figure C-8:
The USB
Printer
Sharing
control
panel is
brand-new.

To find out more about the USB Printer Sharing control panel, choose
Help⇨Mac Help or use the shortcut ⌘+ ? and then search for *share printer*.

Two more little changes...

Before I end this appendix, I need to mention two more changes:

Network Browser

The Network Browser isn't a control panel (it's in your Apple menu...), so it
didn't fit in the previous section. But it has one cool new feature I need to
mention, so here it is in a word: Connect to iDisk. Okay. I know that's three
words. But that's the new feature, as shown in Figure C-9.

Figure C-9:
Network
Browser's
new
Connect to
iDisk com-
mand.

If you've created a remote iDisk using Apple's iTools (available at the Apple
Web site, www.apple.com), you can now open it directly from the Network
Browser application.

I still like the old way of opening an iDisk. First, mount your iDisk on the desktop. Now make an alias of it. Leave the alias on the desktop. Next time you need the iDisk, double-click the alias. The password window will appear almost instantly.

The final difference...

One last difference you may notice when you first visit your OS 9.1 Finder is that the Internet, Apple Extras, and Utilities folders, which used to be installed on your hard disk at root level, are now installed inside the renamed *Applications (Mac OS 9)* folder. You'll now find Netscape Communicator and Internet Explorer in this folder as well. Having one folder for all the applications makes sense to me.

Note that you won't see this effect if you upgrade from an earlier version of OS 9; you'll only see it happen if you perform a clean install or install on a disk without a System Folder.

And that's it. That's everything I can find that is noticeably different from OS 9. So go on now. Get out of here!

P.S. If you discover something new or interesting in OS 9.1 that I *didn't* mention in this appendix, send e-mail to boblevitus@boblevitus.com. If it's interesting enough, I'll try to get it into the next edition of this book. Thanks!

Index

• *B* •

• *C* •

• Y •

• Z •

Notes